AF573724

MARGARET

A Love Story

THE AUTHOR

Simon Regan spent several years on the "Royal Beat", Fleet Street's term for the Palace specialists . . . gaining a unique insight into the private lives of the Royal Family.

He then became a freelance reporter in the trouble spots of the world, but returned home to concentrate on writing books. He has since written a very successful biography of his former boss, publishing magnate Rupert Murdoch; and a book based on Prince Charles's sense of humour entitled *The Clown Prince*.

He lives with his family in a cottage in the Dorset Purbecks, and his interests include backgammon and the breeding of otters.

MARGARET

A Love Story

Simon Regan

EVEREST BOOKS LIMITED
4 Valentine Place London SE1

Published in Great Britain by Everest Books Ltd, 1977

ISBN 0905018 605

Printed in Great Britain by The Anchor Press Ltd
and bound by Wm Brendon & Son Ltd
both of Tiptree, Essex

To
George and Bett Thomas,
friends and royalists.

Preface

There is a black sheep in every family. Nearly always it is the person with the most personality and character, the person no one can keep down, and often the person most loved by those who know him.

In his day Edward VII took on the black mantle because he fell in love with a woman the establishment would not accept as Queen. In the seventies the title has been inherited by HRH Princess Margaret. The girl we hated to love but could not help it.

Across the almost half-century of her tempestuous, stormy and often controversial life, an awful lot of speculative rubbish has gone the rounds. She has always put up with it all and gone on doing her job.

Those close to her were unable or unwilling to defend her because protocol forbade them. Those not so close to her have helped fan the flames, volubly, often ignorantly and sometimes even libellously.

On the other hand there is nothing quite so frightful as reading fifty years of royal gush, as I have had to do while compiling this biography. Acres of newsprint are filled with ridiculous platitudes about how "human" Margaret is. Of course she is!

After studying both sides, wading through literally millions of words of collected memories, statements and other paraphernalia, and talking frankly to scores of people, I have made my own assessment of Margaret. Not the Royal Margaret we all know from our newspapers, but Margaret the woman. This is a true account of that assessment. It may well offend those people who have been fed a continued diet of gushing rubbish; it may well be scoffed at by those who read only the more salacious of continental magazines. This is not a book for either type.

This is a book about a woman who loved three men and how fate took a hand each time until she was finally alone with little but her memories.

SR Corfe Castle, January 1977

The Characters

PRINCESS MARGARET ROSE WINDSOR: Younger sister to the British Queen, who started life at Glamis Castle, Scotland in 1930. Profession: Being a Royal. Marital status: Separated.

GROUP CAPTAIN PETER WOOLDRIDGE TOWNSEND: Started life in Rangoon, Burma, in 1914. Profession: Former fighter pilot and RAF Officer; Royal Equerry; diplomat; now retired. Marital status: Divorced. Remarried.

THE EARL OF SNOWDON: Started life in London in 1930. Profession: (As Antony Armstrong-Jones) photographer and designer. Marital status: Separated.

RODERICK PATRICK LLEWELLYN: Started life in Berkshire, England, in 1946. Profession: Playboy with minor business interests in Bath, England. Marital status: Bachelor.

The Plot

The Queen of England's younger sister is born fourth in succession to the throne in Scotland in 1930. Some years later she has a crush on, and falls in love with, a dashing war-hero called Peter Townsend. He is just sixteen years her senior and an equerry in the palace. Because of the affair, Townsend divorces his wife and plans to marry the Princess with whom he has fallen deeply in love. The romantic couple decide to wait until she is twenty-five. But protocol is against them and Townsend is banished from the land. After terrible remorse, the Princess flings herself into the gay life of London, finally meeting an attractive young photographer who is her own age. They have clandestine nights together in a small terraced house in London's dockland. They fall in love and marry to the absolute enthralment of the nation. For fifteen years they have a stormy on-off love affair, until, lonely and frustrated, the still gay Princess turns to a young London playboy called Roddy Llewellyn, for romance and comfort. They holiday together in mysterious places and she visits her lover at a small Wiltshire commune where she sleeps on a mattress on the floor. Roddy is just sixteen years her junior. Once again protocol demands her love affair must be stopped, and they finally separate. The Princess throws herself back into her official duties. The three men in her life all hide themselves from the glaring eyes of the world. The story covers nearly half a century.

BOOK ONE
TOWNSEND

Chapter One

An autumn sky draped itself across St. James's Park as Peter Townsend's Renault came to a halt on the gravelled drive of Clarence House. As always he was dressed immaculately. He walked the twenty or so yards up to the front door of the seventeenth century palace and knocked briskly on the dark oak. It was October 15th 1955, a day Princess Margaret would never forget. Townsend, after his long exile in Brussels, had been invited by the Queen Mother. He had spent a sleepless night carefully weighing up his position. But as dawn creaked across Eton Square where he was staying, he had firmly made up his mind. That afternoon, he would have to tell Princess Margaret that it was all over. He did not relish the interview, partly because he was genuinely sorry that the affair had to end, but mainly because he knew he would have to face Margaret's wrath; a wrath that had withered many lesser men; a fury which Margaret could turn on in an instant and which seemed to be fed from the burning bowels of hell itself.

As Margaret waited she had no idea at all that her romantic world was about to be completely shattered. She had even had some sketches made of a possible wedding dress. She was still convinced they would marry early in the next year.

The butler dutifully welcomed Townsend and led him across the deep green pile carpet through a small reception room to the heavily-gilded drawing room where Margaret and her mother were waiting. He bowed gently to each of them (however intimate they had become in private, Townsend still referred to her as Princess Margaret whenever anyone else was present). The Queen Mother sat on a comfy chair by the fire and Margaret and Townsend sat on the sister couch opposite. A few minutes after his arrival the butler brought in a tray of tea, toast and crumpets. The Queen Mother poured as

Margaret chatted busily, oblivious to Townsend's mood of despair. But the Queen Mother, a remarkably observant woman, caught the listless, depressed tone of his voice and after a respectable time she withdrew gracefully from the room.

It was then that Townsend knew he must drop the bombshell. He did not immediately tell her the marriage was off, but speaking in a quiet voice, he made it plain he had grave doubts about the affair and that he thought they should reconsider the whole situation. God knows, he had listed the hundred and one things against the marriage night after lonely night in his mind. Now they came tumbling out point by point as Margaret listened to the dreadful words. In the past, as each objection had been made to her by others, she had managed to brush them aside, one by one, in her usual style of brash determination. She was always able to ignore the niggling points and get on with the big job. Now, shocked and crestfallen, she heard them all together for the first time, and the speaker was her lover.

As Townsend coolly weighed up the situation as he saw it, Margaret at first listened in shocked silence. Then she became very agitated and started answering Townsend point for point. She became so distressed that the Queen Mother eventually came back into the room and joined the discussion. Margaret said that their love for each other was more important than any other consideration. Peter said he did not feel their love could stand up to the pressures fate had put upon it. The Queen Mother agreed.

Townsend left a distraught and crying Margaret at Clarence House just after eight p.m. Neither of them slept a wink that night.

In the twenty days between this unfortunate and tragic meeting and the time when Margaret made the announcement on November 1st, the couple met nearly every day to try and thrash out a solution. Over these emotion-packed days and nights, in which both of them tossed and turned until dawn brought a blessed sleep, Margaret began to realise the inevitability of a breakup. She kept up a barrage of telephone calls to Peter, some of them so hysterical that he had to put the phone down. She declared her undying love for him and begged him to reconsider. The Queen Mother could do nothing to quell Margaret's rampant fury. She could only use the very words Margaret refused to listen to: "It's probably all for the best."

After seven days of torment, argument, crying and pleading, Margaret reluctantly started to accept that Peter Townsend was not going to marry her. She had moods of terrible depression spiced with fury and anger. She blamed herself, and blamed all the people who had actively worked against their love, and more than anything else she blamed the fate which had brought Townsend into her life, nurtured their love, and then cruelly prised them apart.

To the very end, until Townsend had actually been away for a year, she did not give up hope that they would eventually marry. Between October 20th and November 1st, she pleaded with Townsend that they should not make the absolute final decision until they had been parted for two years. She told him if she could not marry him, she would not marry anyone else. She threatened to go into a convent. She argued volubly and forcefully about the wording of the inevitable announcement. She would not allow a single word to go out which showed they had broken up for personal reasons; the situation would be blamed on the technical factors which had driven them apart.

Margaret had never needed her friends like she needed them during this period, and they went out of their way to help her. She and Townsend spent a lot of time in each other's company at one friend's home or another. All the time she was looking for ways in which he would capitulate.

There is no doubt Peter Townsend was terribly upset by the whole breakdown. But he was determined to end the liaison and hide himself away from the avalanche of publicity the announcement would bring. Margaret wrung from him a promise that, before he exiled himself into the most primitive areas of the world, they would spend a whole weekend alone together. In this he conceded defeat, against his better judgement.

Margaret had faced every adversary in her total determination to marry the man she loved. Every adversary that is, except Townsend himself. When he backed down, her entire world was shattered. She grasped on to every last minute she could have with him. As he penned his resignation to the Air Ministry, went to Harrods to buy tropical clothes, had his green Renault fully overhauled, and studied maps of the world, Margaret demanded more and more of his time.

The circumstances surrounding the Townsend Affair had lasted thirteen years – only three years less than the difference in their ages, and exactly half of Margaret's life. It had gone through many periods. She had grown from precocious puberty into the glorious fullness of womanhood. He had succumbed to the freshness and vitality of a vivacious girl who had insisted on loving him. He had loved her against a background of fear, secrecy and awesome emotional turmoil. He had suffered the bitterness of divorce and the traumas of a love he knew he should not have. Both of them had felt that uncontrollable urge found only in love which is forbidden. They had succumbed to it for a while with a gay abandon, hoping only that when the time came, some gift from heaven would make it all officially possible. His ambition had been rampant; now he was finished. His dedication and determination were formidable; now he was beaten. His passion was unquestioned; now he would hunger in a world of loneliness and remorse.

In simple terms a man had met a woman under circumstances neither of them could control. They had felt a strong mental and physical attraction for each other which, because of their very positions in life, they had to spend long periods denying. Townsend's first feelings of guilt were gradually eroded by her sheer determination to love him.

But eventually, and not for the first time in his life, he found himself in a position from which he had to take evasive action in order to survive.

Over these final saddening days they discussed the affair morning, noon and night. When they were separated they thought of nothing else. It was thirteen years since he had first met her, but the real dramas in their relationship had leaped across the geography of their lives in quick, short, emotion-packed spurts.

From the very moment when Margaret, youthful, petulant and exuberant, had decided to fall in love with someone, it was clear she was the architect of the love affair she imposed upon her choice. She had planned it as a meticulous entrepreneur. She was articulate, ambitious and stubborn with her romantic ambitions. She wanted to build a monument of love, friendliness, reliability, and even sensuality, in the middle of a barren waste of a desert called loneliness. Townsend was it, and Townsend had slowly succumbed to her adoration and had finally become the wholehearted recipient of her love.

If Margaret was the architect of the romance, Townsend was the designer of its downfall. Locked deep inside he had always known his role of monument would never last. Now he reverted quickly to the age-old Townsend. He had finally grasped the fundamentals of the problem, made a difficult decision, and was now determined to follow that decision through to the very bitter end.

Now that he had managed to stop the dreadful torture of internal worry, and replace it with the unhappy certainty of the liaison's end, he immediately became the cool and calculating fighter-pilot who had added thirteen images of Messerschmitts to the fuselage of his Spitfire.

Once the decision had been made he was forever powerful, sometimes vindictive, occasionally charming in his arrogance and always nerveless and to the point. As they went through these traumatic eighteen days he managed to switch off his emotions, almost to the point of callousness. He became again the same Townsend who had ordered his bodily functions not to operate as he swerved to avoid the penetrating gunfire of a dozen swooping enemies. His escape from the situation was classic. It was intelligent, nerveless, utterly selfish and quite unique in its determination.

Seven days before the official communique hit the headlines the Queen advised Margaret that she should inform the Archbishop of Canterbury, Dr. Michael Fisher. She drove to Lambeth Palace the following morning and immediately sparked off the ironic rumour that she had gone to tell him she was going to get married. She found him in his library surrounded by reference books marked in certain places. He clearly thought the same. Margaret said simply but tearfully: "My Lord Archbishop, you may put your books away."

That night she joined the Queen in a party entertaining the visiting President of Portugal. They sat in the Royal Box at Covent Garden and saw *The Bartered Bride*. She watched it with a film of tears continually in her eyes. The words had a dreadful significance for the Princess. As she sat in the merciful darkness Margaret watched as the two lovers in the opera clung to each other steadfastly promising they will never be parted. The heroine came to the front of the stage and the house rang with her promise: "I have a lover, I will not forsake him. I will NOT change my mind."

Margaret would never see *The Bartered Bride* again.

On Friday, three days before the announcement was made, Margaret and Peter Townsend spent the promised weekend with their old friends Lord and Lady Rupert Nevill. It was arranged that Margaret would stay at their Sussex farmhouse, while Peter Townsend stayed in nearby Eridge Castle, home of the Marquis of Abergavenny, in Tunbridge Wells. That evening Townsend drove to Uckfield House and joined his Princess for the last time. They ate a quiet dinner by candlelight and sat and talked until two a.m. Townsend did not go back to the Marquis's castle until Monday night.

On Saturday morning the couple got down to the dreaded drafting of the final communique. After lunch the Queen's Secretary, Captain Oliver Dawnay, arrived at Uckfield to try and persuade Margaret not to issue the statement. He found her adamant and he took it with him. He returned the following day to beg her to change certain words. She was firm in her refusal.

That day the Marquis also visited them to find out if he could help. It was significant that the Marchioness of Abergavenny was the Queen's principal Lady of the Bedchamber.

Sunday night was the last night they would ever spend together. It was a quiet, gentle evening as they sat in front of the fire holding hands. There was really no more to be said. The traumas had ended and had been replaced only by a sickening sadness. There were no more recriminations, merely a hopeless acceptance that the romance was over. Early on

Monday morning the Princess sped back to Clarence House. Townsend waited until the reporters had left Uckfield House and drove himself over to Tunbridge Wells. That afternoon a spokesman at Buckingham Palace issued the following statement:

> I would like it to be known that I have decided not to marry Group Captain Townsend. I have been aware that, subject to my renouncing my rights of succession, it might have been possible for me to contract a civil marriage. But mindful of the Church's teaching that Christian marriage is indissoluble, and conscious of my duty to the Commonwealth, I have resolved to put these considerations before any others. I have reached this decision entirely alone and in doing so I have been strengthened by the unfailing support and devotion of Group Captain Townsend. I am deeply grateful for the concern of all those who have constantly prayed for my happiness.
>
> (signed)
>
> Princess Margaret

The next day curious sightseers stood in the rain watching Peter Townsend supervise the loading of his Renault on to an air freighter at Lydd Airport. He did not wave goodbye. At a little after noon, the plane took off for Brussels. The onlookers could still see it as it soared slowly over the English Channel. Peter Townsend looked down at the cliffs of Dover through the tiny porthole. He would not see them again for two years.

Chapter Two

The unique set of fateful events which had preceded these eighteen traumatic days were locked deep in the small idiosyncrasies and large coincidences of history. Somewhere, deep down in that unaccountable world where fate rides high, a train of events was set in motion which would eventually lead to the sad moments of this autumnal day some generations later.

With any member of the Royal family it is possible to trace the significant trends of their genealogical structure, indeed it is a matter of public record. But no one could recall the small quirks and innuendos of history which inexorably drew these two people together from the obscurity of the past into the huge significance of the present.

The beginnings are locked down somewhere in the abyss of time – the end is somewhere out in the mysterious fathoms of the future. The present merely locks and interweaves the two together. Just over 100 years ago – a mere pittance of time – an obscure Scottish country parson fathered a daughter. At around the same time, a military gentleman of some social standing passed the brandy around the Mess to celebrate the birth of his son.

Both events, at the height of Victorian Britain, caused immense joy to the two families involved. But neither were recorded beyond the Parish records. Neither birth had any significance to the outside world. As the parson prayed for the health of his offspring, and the military gentleman drank brandy for much the same reason, neither of them could imagine the series of events they had just put into motion.

The baby boy would eventually sire Peter Wooldridge Townsend, destined to carve his name in social history. The parson's daughter would become maternal grandmother to

Margaret Rose Windsor; Princess, romantic, and eventual recipient of a triple personal tragedy.

The parson's daughter grew up and married the Earl of Strathmore and Kinghorne. He was honest, but poor. The family seat was Glamis Castle in Scotland and he had ten children. The ninth was Lady Elizabeth Bowes-Lyons who married the Duke of York. It then only needed an abdication to make the parson's great-grandchild the Queen of England.

Lady Elizabeth, the present Queen Mother, was a frequent visitor to the Royal households. Her father, despite his relative poverty, was highly respected by the Royal family. Elizabeth and some of her other nine brothers and sisters were often brought to Balmoral to act as companions to the children of George V. Elizabeth first met Albert, as the Duke of York was then called, at such a children's party when she was just five years old. He was ten; a quiet, sensitive infant much bullied by his father. The childhood friendship blossomed into teenage love. Elizabeth was given a "sensible" upbringing in the country. She was trained to be a housewife rather than a Queen. She learned how to cook, sew, knit and run a home. Her mother showed her how to keep household accounts and lay a table. She rode an old "granny's" bike down to the local shops and she was unpretentious, lovely, exquisitely well-mannered and softly genteel.

Albert was incredibly shy and rather feeble. He was a sickly youth who suffered from a speech impediment when he was not with his close friends or family. His father George was a robust, rugged man who detested what he thought was his son's weakness. His very birth caused George great anguish. Albert was born on December 14th 1895 – it just happened to be the thirty-fourth anniversary of the death of Queen Victoria's beloved husband Prince Albert. She was not amused. She wrote to her son saying she thought the birth was most inappropriate and a "personal affront" to her memories. Incredibly, George wrote back apologising for his second son's untimely arrival and said the whole affair was deeply regrettable.

George V, it seems, never did get around to forgiving his son for the untimely arrival. He bullied him unmercifully during his entire youth. His discipline was always harsh and rigid and the King never tried to hide his overbearing impatience with his son's poor health.

As the Duke of York, Albert eventually lived in a gaunt forty-five-roomed house at 145 Piccadilly. After at least three unsuccessful attempts, he finally persuaded Lady Elizabeth to marry him and she became the mistress of 145. He looked forward to an obscure, quiet life with his new wife. He desperately wanted a family and was absolutely determined to behave towards his children in exactly the opposite way to his overbearing father.

Elizabeth was born on April 21st 1926. She was third in line to the throne after her uncle and her father. But few people thought she would ever reach it. For the first ten years of her life Elizabeth enjoyed a blissful family atmosphere in Piccadilly. Her Uncle David, the Prince of Wales, was young and healthy. He could marry and have children of his own. Alternatively her own parents could have a son. It seemed most unlikely that Elizabeth would be anything more than a Duke's daughter living in some comfort in a fashionable town house.

This, then, was the situation when Elizabeth, Duchess of York, gave birth to a second daughter at her parents' home in Scotland. The Scots, in particular, were deliriously joyful over the birth. Margaret was the first child in direct line to the throne to be born in Scotland for more than 300 years.

A sixteen-year-old Peter Townsend was on holiday from school when, on August 21st 1930, he learnt, along with the rest of the world, that Queen Mary had a new grand-daughter.

The four-year-old future Queen Elizabeth was taken in to see the new arrival early the next day. Despite the fact that the night of Margaret's birth was one of the most stormy for almost a century, villagers in the tiny village of Glamis stood a silent vigil outside the castle walls. The birth itself occurred as thunder and lightning flashed across the gaunt grey turrets of the castle and rain smashed against the bedroom windows.

In the nearby county town of Forfar the news of the oncoming birth swept down the little grey high street and people literally flocked the eight miles to Glamis by foot and pony and trap to salute the new arrival. There was a crowd of several hundred waiting silently in the stormy night as the Home Secretary,

John Clynes, drew up at the castle gates at exactly nine p.m. They stood patiently as the lodge keeper ran to open the gates so the black saloon Rolls-Royce could pull up at the steps of the castle itself. Clynes had been on holiday at Airlee Castle nearby and was one of the first in the country to hear the news. He had been told at eight o'clock that the birth was imminent. He had set off immediately along the dark country lanes in the blinding storm. He was met by the butler and shown into the central drawing room in the old part of the castle. There he was joined by John Boyd, the Ceremonial Secretary. They were offered a light supper and spent until 10.15 drinking port together.

At 10.16 on the dot Sir Henry Simpson, one of the Royal family's physicians, hurried into the drawing room and told the waiting men that a baby girl had been born and both mother and child were "very satisfactory". They toasted the birth. Then Sir Henry took them up the massive stone stairway to the master bedroom to see the child. They went into the tapestry room next door where they were met by the Duke of York, the Earl and Countess of Strathmore, and the Duchess's sister, the Lady Rose Leveson-Gower. The whole room was bursting with joviality. Brandy was being poured and Sir Henry was beaming with pride. Each of them were allowed into the room for a few moments to see the child. As Clynes smiled at the baby she let out a shrill shout followed by a lusty bellow. This brought a tear to the Duke's eye and each member of the party congratulated him again. It was the first time Margaret was the very centre of attention, but she would crave that kind of attention for the rest of her life.

It was constitutionally necessary to tell the Government of the birth of a child so close to the throne. It became the Home Secretary's job then, to inform the Prime Minister, Parliament, the Lord Mayor of London and, in those days, the Governor Generals of the Dominions. He sped through the night and arrived in Downing Street during the following morning where he put into motion the protocol needed for officially announcing a Royal birth.

The Duchess rested that night and the following morning a tribe of journalists from the Glasgow offices of the national papers came streaming to Glamis. Sir Henry and the other two physicians in attendance, Dr. Neon Reynolds and Dr. David Myles, issued a statement in which they said "the infant Princess is doing fine". All three men had spent some time carefully working the statement. "Doing fine" was considered to be a good old Scottish expression and one perfect for the occasion.

As the statement was read to the waiting reporters, the family nurse, Mrs. Knight, was awakening Elizabeth of York. She told the child that a big surprise awaited her downstairs and the four-year-old quickly washed and dressed. The nanny, Mrs. Beevors, insisted Elizabeth eat her breakfast before being shown into her mother's bedroom. As she crept in with Nurse Knight they found that Margaret, a very chubby-cheeked little baby, was still fast asleep. Elizabeth was allowed to just touch her sister's tiny hand before being ushered out of the room again.

Outside in the village of Glamis all hell had broken loose. The tiny village Post Office received 5,000 cables of congratulations in an hour. Thousands of people flooded into the area from all over Britain. Girls played bagpipes and crowds flocked to the top of nearby Hunter's Hill where they lit beacons. From the centre of the village they had to tramp more than a mile through ankle-deep mud and slush. On top of the hill a special giant beacon had been erected years before when the Duke and Duchess had married. Its light could be seen in six counties – and even by sailors far out at sea. As the bagpipes wailed and the dancing started, three schoolgirls lit the beacon again. The dancing went on until the Princess was three days old.

One person, with incredible foresight, had visualised the circumstances in which Elizabeth of York would become Queen Elizabeth II of England. Her grandmother, Queen Mary, worried constantly that her eldest son Edward had not yet married. Now that Elizabeth had had a second daughter instead of a son, she immediately felt the child should get special training in case of her eventually becoming Queen.

Queen Mary was sixty-three when Margaret was born. She decided, there and then, to take the four-year-old Elizabeth in hand for special tuition. The Duke felt she was going a bit too far too soon, but Mary, who was reputed to have incredible psychic powers, was adamant the training should start forthwith. Later, when Margaret was about five years old, she and her elder sister had to set aside one afternoon a week which was actually written into their curriculum as "educational visit with Queen Mary".

Mary tutored the two girls in just about everything – from how to wave at crowds to the workings of a pyramid. They were taken on their grandfather's Birthday Parade and shown how to stand to attention and told of the significance of the British flag. Mary sweated for hours over their curriculum each year. Arithmetic was almost out. They would not need much of that. But history was in. She wanted them to know all about their heritage. Poetry, Queen Mary insisted, was excellent for training the memory. To this day both women can recite whole reams of classical British poetry.

Both girls trotted after grandmother obediently as she whisked them around art galleries and museums. And she would not tolerate any slackness. Every now and then she would suddenly give them a spot test on what they had learnt the month before. If they had not paid attention, Grandma got exceedingly angry.

The Duke became rather distressed about what was going on. He was trying to bring his daughters up in a homely atmosphere. He loved having a close family and disliked the public side of his life. Queen Mary's attention to his children was not the only thing he had to put up with. The world had taken a keen interest in the two young Princesses from the minute they were born, and every last scrap of information about them was eaten up and devoured by a greedy press.

As toddlers, usually dressed in tweed skirts and woollen jerseys, they would play in the gardens at Piccadilly. Crowds would immediately gather around the railings and Margaret would quite unashamedly perform for them. She would do hand-stands, climb trees, or even, on occasions, pull faces at the laughing onlookers. She was a most precocious child and very much the apple of her father's eye. She charmed him outrageously and got away with behaviour which would have brought a scolding to Elizabeth. She was always determined not to be overshadowed by her older sister. She was drawn to the limelight and after finding it, she went to any lengths to stay in it.

In fact the only person who Margaret could not bend was the stately Queen Mary. Mary, with her ramrod back, her nineteenth century air, her classic toques and her long parasol, refused to let Margaret get away with anything.

She expected the girls to be perfectly behaved and polite at all times. They even had to call her Queen Mary and in public they had to curtsy to her.

Conversely, as sometimes happens when people become grandparents, George was a doting grandfather. He had brought up his own sons to call him "Sir" at all times. They had to send a page ahead of them if they wanted an interview and he had always bullied them unmercifully. At one stage his relationship with his own children had become so strained that they talked to each other through a third party. Yet this stern disciplinarian now unbent completely and even romped and wrestled with the Princesses. In turn the girls loved him, but still managed to hold him rather in awe.

The girls led a rather sheltered life, mainly within the walls of 145 Piccadilly. Only trips out with Queen Mary and the odd family visit to Balmoral or Windsor took them away from the cloistered corridors of the family home. A trip incognito with their nanny and a detective on a London underground railway was a highlight of their childhood. For them it was a journey almost out of this world.

Queen Mary regularly summoned them the one and a half miles across London to Buckingham Palace. There they would be given lessons in art, music and literature. She constantly told them of the importance of being born a Royal and gave them both a solid and constant grounding in religious instruction.

When their father once complained that he was very tired after a visit to a hospital the Duke was told by his mother that a Royal was *never* tired and that a Royal always loved hospitals.

It was the kind of guidance she constantly gave her grandchildren.

But no member of the Royal family was loved by the girls more than Uncle Edward who adored them and fussed over them whenever he saw them. He quite unashamedly spoiled them and they loved him for it. Edward had an effervescence and light-heartedness which even the burden of his Royal duties could not diminish. Despite the rigorous training from his father he could never quite conceal the wilfulness which was so endearing to those who knew him well.

As Margaret grew up, drama, excitement, showing off, and being the centre of attraction were the keynotes to her early years. She never tired of it and she was very good at it. Her mother tried to keep some kind of disciplining hand over her, but her father indulged her at all times.

She struck up a fairly sophisticated friendship with the great dramatist, Sir James Barrie, telling everyone he was her best friend. When Barrie was telling her about the play he was writing then, he said he would give her a penny for every performance in its first West End run. She eagerly awaited the first night of the play. It was called *The Boy David* and eventually ran for 170 performances. Margaret regularly checked to make sure it was still running and on the last night Barrie delivered 170 pennies to Glamis Castle. She counted every penny three times to make sure the payment was right.

Even at a very early age she delighted her father with her exhibitionism and precociousness. She was always quick and impatient, never wanting to waste a single second of her life. Before she could spell properly she was writing mini-pantomimes in which she tried to get everyone to act. She could not read music until she was about six, but by the time she was four she could play several tunes on the piano. As a child she roamed through Glamis Castle and was always finding little rooms, corners or turrets, or forgotten cellars, which all held new mysteries for the inquisitive child. One day she found a chest full of old clothes discarded by some ancestor. She spent the whole day dressing up and playing charades with anyone who she could find. That evening the Duke of York found her dressed up and when he remonstrated with her she told him she was a glamorous spy.

For her first fully fledged panto, with the two Princesses and other children taking part for the family and friends, she succeeded in persuading the others to do *Cinderella*. Typically, she chose the central character for herself and gave Elizabeth the role of ugly sister. Sister "Lillibet" had got used to this kind of behaviour. She was very much the elder sister, but affectionately allowed Margaret to have her own way most of the time. In public, however, Elizabeth tried to keep a restraining hand on her little sister's over-indulgences. She would constantly chide her for pointing at people who Margaret thought looked funny. She would make Margaret stop slouching when she was bored and always tried to restrain her more energetic activities, like sticking her tongue out or running when she should have been walking. It was significant that, when a chubby-cheeked chatterbox called Margaret Rose went to her first children's fancy dress party dressed as an angel, she remarked to the host that her mother had said she was really a holy terror in disguise.

She even managed to bring high drama to the customary girl's pastime of playing with dolls. She lined up the Royal toys and teddy bears in prams and anything else she could find on wheels and ran them down the hallway in chariot races. The Duke at last frowned on this game because he thought his enterprising daughter might learn the art of gambling at far too early an age.

Her whole childhood was spent much in the limelight and lap of her family. It was as happy a childhood as any pre-teen Royal could hope to have, but it was doomed to suffer radical and dramatic changes when she was only six years old.

So it was, that from the very earliest days, Margaret was the precocious scamp; the indulged show-off; the witty showman; and the attention-seeking theatrical, always trying to upstage her elder sister. Even in her infant years she showed a massive determination when she saw something she wanted. Her tantrums were furious and even an occasional smack would merely put grim defiance in her eyes. She was fiery, indulgent, even spoiled, and managed through a mixture of charm, chicanery, determination and guile, to get her own way nearly all the time. The only thing that ever held her back – the thing which was drummed into her despite her carefree abandon towards everything else – was the deep rooted awe and respect she held for the sovereignty, drilled into her unmercifully by her vigilant grandmother.

Chapter Three

As the nation heralded the New Year, 1936, London was carefree, almost abandoned, and the famous Chelsea Arts Ball had one of the greatest revelries ever recorded. A thousand balloons popped, there was so much champagne the young bloods of London were squirting bottles of it at each other as if they were water pistols. January began with a thousand blue-blooded hangovers. Despite Churchill's almost lone warnings against the upsurge of Nazism in Europe, things seemed to be very satisfactory. Britain still had an Empire; the Bank of England sat like a staunch lion above the world currencies; trade flowed through Threadneedle Street and the Cavalry still rode horses when they weren't attending the Hunt Balls.

Five-and-a-half-year-old Princess Margaret slept soundly in the Piccadilly Mansion, despite the chaos in the streets below as midnight struck out from Big Ben. There was nothing in her tiny, privileged world at that time which need give her sleepless nights and she was oblivious to the revelries. Her parents were seeing the New Year in at Buckingham Palace and soon after midnight they went on to the balcony on the second floor of the Palace and a few homeward stragglers waved and cheered at them.

Despite the false calm and the air of jovial tranquillity, 1936 would be a crucial and emotional year for Britain. Only a month later King George V died in his sleep and his son Edward became the new Monarch; after 325 days in power he abdicated, and the ten-year-old Elizabeth of York became, in one fell swoop, the heir to the English throne.

At the time all these events had little influence on Margaret. Despite the tremendous significance it would have on her in later life, her only reaction on hearing of the King's death was to say flippantly: "I'm sure God will find him very useful in

Heaven." But for the rest of the Royal family the year became one of severe trauma, soul-searching and misery as the following 325 days spelled out the disaster of abdication.

For several years Edward had been deeply in love with a glamorous American woman called Mrs. Wallis Simpson. As the Crown Prince he enjoyed some freedom, enough anyway to see his lover at least once a week without being detected.

The affair had been a considerable bone of contention between him and his father, in the end to the point that they would not speak to each other. Mary sternly disapproved and George was forced into a position where he kept the liaison as private and secret as possible. Now the situation had changed, as he knew it would, literally overnight. As the new Monarch he was virtually forbidden from seeing her in any capacity. Every single one of his days in power were full of torment and misery and finally, rather than give up his love, he decided on an unprecedented historical move: to give up the throne and all the trappings that went with it.

The whole affair was treated by some as the scandal of the century – in a century which had many scandals. By others it was mooted as one of history's greatest love stories. (Even a quarter of a century later, eight-week serials in the Sunday papers would tell the story to a fanatical public over and over again.)

When the King died, the scene at 145 Piccadilly was one of distress and confusion. Neither Edward nor his brother had any deep affection for their father but they had to console their mother Mary. And another thing was clearly upsetting the young Albert. He knew full well that his brother was most unhappy at the prospect of being King. He himself had no ambitions for the Crown. Yet on the days that followed the death of his father he became more and more aware of the fact that fate was drawing him closer and closer to the simple mahogany desk in Buckingham Palace which sovereigns had used for signing state papers since Victoria's day.

Margaret was young and didn't understand the implications. She knew only that instead of visiting Uncle Edward at Kensington Palace, the family now took her to see him in the gaunt, draughty corridors of Buckingham Palace. The Palace had never been a favourite residence of the Royal family. It is central and it can house the kind of massive public relations job like the quarterly tea party. But it is also inhospitable. George V himself tried to pull it down. Only a public outcry saved the building from the contractor's hammer. He felt Kensington Palace should be modernised as a practical new Royal London residence. But when the war came, Buck House, as it is called by members of the family, had become, almost like St. Paul's Cathedral, a symbol of resistance against enemy warplanes. No British monarch has contemplated pulling it down since.

When Edward took it over it was a sad, lonely place. He pined for the woman he loved, sitting alone in front of the fire most of the day wrestling with his emotions. He allowed her to the Palace as often as he dared, but each visit was a visit nearer the terrible date when he would have to make a decision. He took her occasionally to see friends or family. They went to tea with the Yorks about once a month. When Margaret enquired as to who she was, she was fobbed off with "a friend from America".

The King spent the year in complete gloom and despondency. He paced the floors of the Palace hating every moment of his brief kingship. He had terrible rows with Queen Mary, the only one who had guessed, years before, the events which were about to unfold. She now had to bow to his wishes, but she was never averse to giving him her opinion in the firmest possible way and that opinion did nothing to lighten the King's aching heart.

In early December 1936 he called a family conference at Windsor Castle. The Prime Minister, Stanley Baldwin, attended and so did some key members of the Privy Council – the Monarch's own council which is consulted on any and every matter concerning the constitution of the monarchy. At this historic meeting the King was a man alone. Each member of the Privy Council said the divorced Mrs. Simpson was completely unacceptable for marriage. His family showed themselves firmly against him. The Prime Minister gave the views of his government. They were no comfort to this man in his hour of desperate need. The King nodded gravely as each member made his views felt. At the end of about an hour he said, faltering with each word: "Then there is no alternative than abdication."

With one quiet sentence, the last hopes that they could persuade their Monarch to give up his marital ambitions were dashed. An immediate discussion arose as to whether the constitution even allowed him to throw in the towel when he felt like it. The King said there were only two alternatives, marriage or abdication. He would consider no others. The argument raged for two days and the country wilted under the sudden and unexpected turn of events.

As a sub-plot to the early life of Margaret, the King's abdication was second to none. It would ironically leave a terrible hangover dangling across the marital affairs of every Royal for the next three decades. Margaret would later bear the brunt of the hostile public opinion generated from the Wallis Simpson Affair. The King had been absolutely defiant in his steadfast wish to marry the twice-divorced woman. He had gadded about Europe with her while she was still married and foreign newspapers had gloried in the scandal. Baldwin had, along with everyone else but Winston Churchill, pleaded with the King to give her up. The British public had been denied any information until a bishop unwittingly let the cat out of the bag. During his Sunday sermon he berated the King for his "playboy activities". The press felt he was attacking Mrs. Simpson and told the story for the first time. For nine full days Edward had battled against all the odds, while Mrs. Simpson fled from London after Londoners had stoned her house.

Mrs. Simpson had no idea that the notion of her becoming Queen would receive such vitriol from the public and she physically wilted under the immediate storm the story brought. Before leaving London she lunched at Claridges with an old friend, Esmond Harmsworth, who suggested she could possibly marry the King in a deal which would mean her children had no rights of succession. She refused. And as the hornets' nest buzzed angrily around her she decided to flee.

Nine days later Edward abdicated and gave a last message to the nation from Windsor. He then set off in the battleship *Fury* to meet his lover in Cannes. The startled nation watched as the new King George was hurriedly installed. Christmas was coming and cockney children sang a new rhyme:

Hark the Herald Angels sing,
Mrs. Simpson's pinched our King.

As the new Royal family stood for the first time together on the balcony of Buckingham Palace, the multitudes below sang the National Anthem. Moments after the band had stopped playing and the crowds were roaring their approval, Margaret piped up to her father: "Papa – do you sing 'God save my gracious me'?"

George VI smiled wanly, but it was an empty smile. He knew that when his beloved Margaret grew up and understood the full calamity of the unfolding events, she would find no room for humour.

As a teenager Elizabeth was the opposite to her sister in most ways. She was thoroughly conscientious about her duty, whereas Margaret would do properly only the things she was keenly interested in.

Elizabeth was shy, reserved, compassionate and forgiving. She was a nervous girl and had to fight very hard to stop biting her nails. Her grandparents had told her from a very early age to never show her emotions in public. She had a great sense of warm humour when she could relax with the family, but in the open, her public engagements gave her extreme agony. Margaret on the other hand loved them. She was never shy or nervous in public. On the contrary, she was extrovert and warmed up greatly when people were watching her.

Elizabeth hated extravagance and was neat and tidy. Margaret was extravagant about everything, including her behaviour, and could never be bothered to tidy up after herself. They both had a witty humour and enjoyed a basic common sense. They have always shared a total respect for their position in history. But Margaret was never subjected to the constant grilling Elizabeth was given to prepare her in her role as the future Queen.

One of the last events before war broke out was significant concerning the relationship of the two sisters. Elizabeth had joined the Girl Guides and become highly successful in passing all her tests. In 1939 she was awarded her 100 yards swimming certificate. Everybody congratulated her for her efforts. Papa in particular made a fuss of it and Margaret became green with envy. She was then nine and could thrash about in the water in a semblance of swimming. She felt her sister was getting too much limelight for something she could do equally well herself.

Her answer was a typical one. In a tantrum the next day she picked up her sister's corgi dog, Dookie, and threw it into the lake at Buckingham Palace. Then, despite her neat and pretty party dress – they were entertaining several other children and youths at the time – she dived into the lake and fished the poor creature out. Margaret protested that she had saved the dog's life as a concerned Nanny hustled her into the Palace for a change of clothes. As a punishment she was not allowed to join the children again and had no idea of whether any of them had been as impressed as she had wanted.

Not until Elizabeth put the crown on her head at Westminster Abbey nearly fifteen years later would she manage to up-stage her younger sister.

As affairs of state quickly took up more and more of the King and Queen's time, the girls were left almost permanently to their own devices. The abdication had signalled the end of that family life their parents craved. The girls spent most of the time at Windsor Castle and saw their parents only briefly during the week, and sometimes for the weekends. Late in 1938 the King and Queen toured Canada and the United States and the girls were left, for the first time, completely in the hands of servants.

They were lonely days at Windsor and both of them missed their parents terribly. The feeling of family that both parents had been able to instil had a mental backlash when the family was parted. The King tried to be the kind of father who came home from the office to his wife and children every evening, the epitome of the family man. The Queen Mother, a typical parson's grand-daughter, was a homely woman who went to any and every length to try and shield her children from the fantastic drawbacks and privileges of their rank. Because of this the children missed their parents in the same way that any other loving child would be perturbed if his Mum and Dad were suddenly and continuously whisked off for three months at a time. But this tour was a prelude to a much longer parting.

In mid-1939 the Royal family were having their traditional month's holiday at Balmoral. Summer holidays at this neat, pretty and sizeable country mansion always had a special meaning and place in their hearts. The family took only a minimum of staff, enough for their personal needs and to oil the wheels if a real emergency called for the Sovereign suddenly to resume his duties as Head of State.

The summer holiday had become almost sacred with the family. Nothing was allowed to disturb this one tranquillity of domestic life. Parliament was in recess, though the despatch box still dominated the King's after-supper reading. Beyond this single duty the King belonged entirely to his family.

It was with great consternation then that during the summer holiday of 1939, the King, with a worried frown on his face, told his children after supper one evening he would have to break the vacation and hurry back to London. For the time being they would stay in Balmoral without him. He did not explain in detail the reasons for his hasty departure but the Queen knew full well, and Elizabeth could make a good guess.

The King rushed to Weymouth to review the Fleet.

He returned to Balmoral shortly after, a clearly worried man who could no longer spend the long summer evenings walking around the estate with his children or playing on the lawn with the family dogs. There was no time for the traditional morning canters across the downs. The King spent all day in his private drawing room, receiving messages, instructing aides and issuing orders. On the last day of the month he told the family he had to go back to London.

On the following day Germany invaded Poland and the Queen herself left to be by her husband's side. The children remained at Balmoral when, at eleven a.m. on September 3rd, war was declared. They joined the nation in listening to Neville Chamberlain's speech on the radio. The full horror and significance of their father's behaviour over the past month now became clear. An age of extreme austerity was upon them all and they would not be able to resume their family pastimes until it was all too late and they were both blossoming teenagers.

Chapter Four

As soon as Europe was plunged headlong into that five-year holocaust known as the Second World War, the King acted swiftly in two directions. First and foremost he raised the Royal Standard high over Buckingham Palace and told his nation it would stay flapping over the capital until the hostilities ceased. Where the Royal Standard is, the Sovereign is, and it was a clear indication to a heavily bombarded London that their Monarch wanted to share the oncoming hell with them. But amid tears and some consternation, the Princesses were sent to Windsor where they would sit out the loneliest of wars.

While Buckingham Palace was a natural (and became an habitual) target for enemy air raids, Windsor Castle was an impregnable fortress. An enemy commando squad could have captured Buck House, but it would have taken a division to take Windsor.

After a long cabinet meeting at Downing Street, Prime Minister Neville Chamberlain told the King they would all feel much happier if the Royal family got out of England altogether. At the very least, out of London. As the Nazi invasion began to seem inevitable, the cabinet implored him to take his Royal headquarters to Scotland, or even Canada. The Queen was brought into the meeting, but both of them held firm. Until they could hear the enemy guns on the outskirts of London itself, they said, they would remain in the capital.

The Queen told Chamberlain that they had discussed sending the girls on their own to Canada, but turned the notion down. Even with a war going on they would be able to spend some time together in a semblance of family life. From now on, they both considered, this would be of the utmost importance to the girls' upbringing. "The King will not leave London until the enemy is knocking on his door and it is my clear duty to stay beside him," she said. On taking his leave Chamberlain said: "I should have known better. It is this, of course, of which British Kings and Queens are made."

There was another aspect of the war the King found disquieting. He was in some physical danger while he remained in London. Although it was unthinkable that he should leave when the very capital was on fire nightly and the people looked to him for supreme leadership, he had to face the possibility that he could be killed.

When he had taken over from his brother as King he had been appalled to find how little he knew about the workings of the monarchy. He felt like a general who had to ask the lowliest Corporal how to fire a gun. He had no idea how he should deal with the Government or how the famous despatch boxes should be dealt with and he felt thoroughly vulnerable, ignorant and at first unable to govern. He had, of course, quickly learned the rudiments and was soon able to put this right. But he was determined Elizabeth should be fully trained for her own eventual take-over. This played a significant part in his refusal to let his daughters go abroad, despite the danger. He had stepped up her training ten-fold since she had become a teenager and she was brought into royal affairs at every possible moment.

His decision to make them stay was an important one for both girls. Elizabeth met Philip at Windsor during the war, and Margaret first felt the childish whims of love flutter through her heart when a certain Group Captain became a wartime equerry to her father.

The girls, of course, knew Windsor well and the family made sure there were plenty of other young people around to help entertain them. But there was no compensation for the constant happiness a proper family home life can bring. As for many people, the war years were lonely ones, difficult and strained for the family life for which the King yearned. He had to give up the best years of his children's life and he never forgave Hitler for it.

At the outbreak of war Elizabeth was thirteen, and Margaret nine. When pressure allowed them the King and Queen stayed at Windsor on Saturday nights and spent most of Sunday with their children. The Queen sometimes made mid-week visits and she kept in constant touch with the family by phone. It is exactly twenty-two miles between the gates of Buckingham Palace and Windsor Castle. As the King and Queen sped along, every one of them was a mile nearer happiness.

The children soon noticed their father was not the kindly old dad they had grown to love. He was careworn and haggard, his speech impediment had become a lot worse and he was physically buckling under the strain of leadership during such disturbing times. King George, also, genuinely *cared* about his subjects. As each bombing raid took its toll, as each casualty list appeared in *The Times* and as each tiny child was wrenched from the rubble, the King felt it very deeply. He felt like a father to the nation and he loaded their woes on his back. This caused acute depression which, in his later years, gave him a very short temper. He was indeed a different man on those Saturday nights at Windsor.

The Queen herself would arrive at the Castle limp with exhaustion. She had spent the week lying awake at night with the sirens wailing, the thunder of anti-aircraft and the strain of listening to her husband pace the floor of his own bedroom. Each barrage of bombs preceded what had now become a daily sight in London. Even though the King was struggling to fulfil a job for which he was unprepared, he went to the East End of London, the docks and South London each day to inspect the damage and try and encourage the populace to stand up to it. Each time he visited hospitals full of maimed, broken bodies he would come away and be physically sick with horror.

The Queen was always by his side and whatever slim vitality and strength she had left at the end of each day she used to bolster her husband. Neither of them had much left by Saturday night.

Meanwhile the King and Queen tried to do everything possible to help the children sit out the war without them. They were given extra lessons and nearly all their leisure time was carefully planned. They stepped up music and dancing lessons and spent a lot of time with the local Girl Guide unit. With them they went camping, did a lot of gardening and spent whole evenings knitting furiously for the Services.

Windsor was safer than London but every now and again enemy raiders flew over the castle, setting sirens wailing and the local anti-aircraft batteries into action. The handpicked Grenadier Guards were always on hand to protect their charges. Should the children be in the grounds of the castle, an armoured truck would whisk them to safety. Margaret caused consternation several times by always being the last one to clamber in. She had an insatiable desire to see the excitement. Once when a raid took place and Margaret dallied to watch, the poor soldier employed with the task of getting them into the truck got fed up with polite appeals. As the planes actually came into view he barked: "Your Royal Highness, if you don't bloody well hurry up, I'll throw you in." Elizabeth was said to have winked at him and remarked: "Good for you."

The only real compensation of the war years for Margaret was the fulfilment of her burning ambition to become much older than her years. During the war she aged from nine to fifteen. At nine she acted like a ten-year-old, but tried to emulate her sister's thirteen. At fifteen she had mastered the art and behaved like a twenty-year-old. This was an important aspect of her youth because at the war's end, in her mid-teens, she appeared to be a fully developed woman, mentally and physically.

Had the sisters remained in Buckingham Palace during their youth, they would have been far more cloistered. As it was, without direct parental control, and with everyone around them trying to make sure they stayed amused, they were exposed to many strange facets of our society. The circumstances of the war helped Margaret considerably in her wish to get through childhood as fast as possible.

There were regular visits from young people who had been screened as suitable company for the Royal pair. Obviously with Elizabeth being four years older, the company tended to be older and more experienced than Margaret's tender years. The Princess struck up gay friendships with the young Guards officers within the castle itself. The men were regularly entertained to tea; they would joke with the girls while doing their rounds and they were always first on the invitation list for any Windsor dance at which the Princesses would be present.

During the war Elizabeth became a self-possessed, rapidly maturing young woman who was intensely aware of her own destiny. Margaret, during this early period, had found her appetite for fun and gaiety almost unquenchable. Her attraction to and for the opposite sex became highly developed. Her constant desire to be the centre of attention was fed with limitless opportunities which would have been impossible in a peacetime Buck House.

In all of this, the many responsibilities Elizabeth faced actually helped Margaret to steal the limelight. Elizabeth tended to be quieter and more serious. She would converse deeply on all sorts of subjects with a young Guards officer while her sister danced away the night with as many different partners as she could fit in. In terms of her physical attraction and her gaining of wit, sophistication and aplomb, she went from an actual age of nine to a mental age of twenty, all within the confines of the castle walls during those terrible years.

The King was more than happy to see this situation develop. Elizabeth had become the young woman he knew would don his crown one day. He was proud of her self-possession and reliance. She complemented his sense of duty. Margaret on the other hand, was gay and cheerful and did much to liven up the weekends when they could get to Windsor.

The King was happy that, even without their constant guidance, the girls seemed to be living out the war years with as much humour as they could muster. It was a constant relief from the affairs of state and he urged them to try and enjoy themselves.

He encouraged it to such an extent that he would personally supervise weekly dinner parties at which eligible young officers would be invited. An equerry would arrange a list each week of the young men in England at that time who would be suitable for such an engagement. Many of them were from the Dominions. The King would select a dozen or so and the command would go out. The idea, which was the King's own, had a double advantage. It enlivened the lives of boys stationed far from home and flattered each of the regiments selected. And it provided lively young company for the Princesses.

There is no doubt that Elizabeth enjoyed these evenings immensely. But there is also no doubt Margaret revelled in them. Even at the age of twelve or thirteen she would gather four or five young men around her and immediately put them at their ease with pleasant chat and jokes. Elizabeth took a little longer to settle down in mixed company and would select her conversations one at a time. Margaret would flirt outrageously with the young men, though none were allowed the slightest liberty. (Even at this tender age she insisted they call her "Ma'am", something which has upset many a young man who thought he was close enough to her to become familiar.)

At one such party a young Guards officer requested the third dance and duly came to claim her arm. They got to the floor just as the music struck up. To his horror he realised it was the polka – the only dance he could not do. He was miserable but frank about his dilemma and was delighted to find Margaret could not do it either. She told him she did not intend to learn unless "they" forced her. "It really is the most frightful dance," she said.

Instead they sat it out and talked of several things. The officer never did find out that Margaret was a keen and perfect polka dancer. Even at twelve years old it was typical of her expert diplomacy with men.

And all the time her father beamed on indulgently. When he caught her drinking a rather large quantity of champagne when she was only just a teenager, the King went to take away the glass with a look of severe disapproval on his face. Margaret veered the glass out of his reach and told him, giggling, that if she wasn't allowed to finish it, she would never launch any of his ships. A defeated King allowed her to down the wine and always enjoyed telling friends about the incident later.

This love was a two-way traffic. Margaret adored her father. To this day tears come to her eyes when she hears the community song *The Chestnut Tree*. It was "Papa's song". He loved it. Whenever he visited his annual camp for schoolboys their rendering of it was a highlight of his visit. When there were enough people around him during family occasions, they invariably struck up the song with Margaret on the piano. Since her father's death it has been unwise to play the song in her presence. Always volatile – able to be gay one minute and sad the next – it will ruin her evening.

It seemed to some that at such a tender age, it was a little naughty of Margaret to throw herself so completely into the gay and tantalising life of mixed company. Others thought maybe it was just that; a little naughty, but nothing more. Princess Elizabeth was always around to give her sister a reproving glance if she thought she was getting a little too lively. (Throughout Elizabeth's life a single glance has often been more than enough to give anyone a long message.)

But certainly Margaret got a taste of how much fun a small party could be and after the war, as she gradually grew up, she became more and more eager to get out and about in the bright spots of London. More than this though, Princess Margaret excelled as a hostess. She really was excellent, and one of those people who loved being one. She had considerable wit, but more than this, she had a fantastic ability to draw things out of people. She had a genuine desire to know where they came from, what they were doing, how their own specific war was going on, and so on. People who talked to her, even as a young girl, were impressed with her knowledge of affairs and extremely flattered at her interest in them – two of the greatest merits a good hostess can have. She insisted they tell her of the nightlife of London and doted on any social scandals they could dig up. She was at once thrilling and thrilled and always trying to find the spicy sides of life.

It was Margaret, when she thought the conversation might lag, who rolled back the carpets, with the aid of a dozen willing hands, and ordered that the dancing should begin. On occasions they had the use of a small band, mostly off-duty musicians from the services; more often than not they played the giant family gramophone. Things stopped only for the nine o'clock news, which Elizabeth insisted on listening to, and this normally quietened the room considerably. But soon the party got back into full swing and Margaret swung well and truly with it.

Most of the officers had to be back at their camps by midnight. It was always Margaret who protested about the party breaking up. It was she who was the very last to leave, and although her lady-in-waiting would try and lure her into bed, she rarely got to her room before the early hours of the morning.

It was at one of these dance parties, much later in the war, that two young officers would attract a special interest for the royal pair.

One of them, an angular, handsome, well-presented sort of man, was Prince Philip, son of Prince Andrew of Greece who had been born into relative poverty on the tiny island of Corfu on June 10th 1921. The other was the young, dashing Marquis of Milford Haven, one of the most eligible young playboys of the war years. Both girls had known them as gangling children and more or less forgotten them. Now they had come back, handsome and dashing young men in uniform and both Princesses showed a remarkably keen interest.

Without parents knowing, this particular party stretched on for three separate nights – each lasting well into the early hours. To the royal staff at Windsor it was obvious from the very first time Philip and Elizabeth met, there was a strong attraction between them. They managed to turn a blind eye to the succession of late nights and Margaret, seeing the advantage of her sister's influence, did everything she could do to foster the relationship. With Philip visiting her sister in the castle, it meant more parties, more late nights and more and more dancing. With both of them enjoying it so much no one had the heart to make Margaret go to bed. She took a very special interest in the young Marquis and when the time came it was to him she turned when she wanted to get out into the bright spots of the London nightlife.

Life went on like this for most of the war. By 1944, Elizabeth, now aged eighteen, was getting too old for such things as the Girl Guides and she implored her father to let her do some really useful work. He was unhappy with the prospect but during that year allowed her to carry out eight public engagements for him. This did not satisfy the future Queen. She wanted to get stuck in. The Queen helped her persuade her father she should join the ATS. Margaret was fuming with jealousy. She was now, at fourteen, left much to her own devices at Windsor, while Elizabeth was allowed out into that big, bad, exciting world outside. She could not grow up fast enough and the Queen could see her point. Margaret was allowed more freedom. She went to visit friends. She was allowed to stay at Buckingham Palace for days at a time, and she was allowed to leave the Girl Guides. One of her last acts as a Guide was to take a test for her 'Hostess' badge. It seemed ludicrous to the young Princess, who was already such an adept hostess, to have to take such a test. Part of the exam was to write an imaginary letter replying to an invitation. She wrote a very funny letter to "Lady Godiver" and signed it "Yours affectionately, Diaphenia."

There were no existing records to show whether Princess Margaret ever got her Hostess badge, but the letter is still prized at the Windsor Guides' Association.

Chapter Five

At a handful of minutes after ten o'clock on a dull Tuesday morning, November 28th 1943, a tall, angular, somewhat dashing young man padded quickly across the plush carpeting in the corridors on the second floor of Buckingham Palace. He seemed lost in thought as he glided along with some dispatches under his arm. In the distance, across a wintry Trafalgar Square, where even the pigeons had guessed there was a war on, he could hear air-raid sirens wailing another warning to the five million or so inhabitants who through love, poverty or duty had decided to stay in bomb-scarred London. Group Captain Peter Townsend had been summoned to see the King for the second time that morning. It had so far been a busy day – even by his standards.

He paused for a second outside the heavy oak-panelled door of the King's private drawing room. Then he knocked discreetly and waited for the bark of entry, for he knew well enough the King was his usual testy self this morning. The door opened and a petite girl, already in the full throes of puberty and showing the blossom of teenage youth, swept gracefully out. Townsend bowed slightly as she passed, bidding her good morning and ending with the compulsory "Ma'am". The young Princess said: "My father says you may go straight in."

They then parted and Townsend, King George VI's favourite equerry, found a much different Sovereign than the one he had left less than an hour before. He was smiling, walking around the room and rubbing his hands together. Earlier they had talked of the oncoming meeting between Churchill, Stalin and Roosevelt in Teheran which was due to start in an hour's time. After three years of blitz and the harassment of ruling wartime Britain, the King was edgy, testy, complaining and extremely tired. Now, suddenly, he seemed full of beans. He warmed his hands by the fire and walked over to the window where he could see the last of the morning mist hovering over St. James's Park. "The girl's a tonic to me," he explained. "She's a holy terror sometimes but she cheers me up every time I see her."

Townsend handed the King the despatches which included the very latest report on the situation in Teheran. But the King put them down on the huge mahogany desk he always used during office hours and it was plain to Townsend he wanted to talk about other things. He even asked the equerry to pour a couple of small glasses of sherry, a rare occurrence so early in the morning. Townsend remembered the King had been out at six a.m. to inspect the latest bomb damage and to him the day was already five hours old.

The King talked for about twenty minutes, mainly of his family and the years together they were missing because of the war. He talked of their days in the Piccadilly mansion when they had been a "real" family, and Christmases at Windsor when he had romped with his daughters after the Royal feast. Townsend was the ideal listener. He had only been at the Palace for a few weeks but he had already implanted himself deeply into the King's affections.

England was plunged into a bitter winter. London was subject to fogs, incessant rain, and an occasional few hours of drizzly, dirty sleet. It would be another sixteen months of gruelling hardship before the enemy finally surrendered. It was a gloomy month for England and the highlight was the summit conference.

When the King was edgy he invariably sent for Townsend. When he was testy, Townsend was just about the only person in Buckingham Palace who did not try and keep out of his way. He had very quickly learned how to deal with the Monarch when he was troubled. And he was consequently much in demand in the private drawing room where the King paced up and down in front of the fire or sat for long hours at his desk deliberating on the delicate matters of state.

Peter Wooldridge Townsend was born in Rangoon, Burma,

on November 22nd 1914 just as the first world war was getting into full swing. His father was Lt. Col. E. C. Townsend, a regular army officer then serving in the Indian Civil Service. He had a fascination with aeroplanes from as far back as he could remember. Certainly his desire to go into the RAF was rampant when he was at Haileybury School. He left there to go to the Royal Air Force College at Cranwell and was finally commissioned in 1934. He had been marked down as a "brilliant" cadet and as a commissioned officer he looked forward to an equally forthcoming career. Within a mere eight years he had raced up the promotion ladder to the rank of Group Captain – an almost unprecedented rise.

On the day he was commissioned Margaret had settled down to a delightful existence at 145 Piccadilly. It would be like that for another two years. She would be only six years old when the events in her life would swing her suddenly closer to the throne.

Before the war, Peter Townsend had been thought of as rather snobby and aloof by the rest of the Air Force. He would go to his own rooms in the evening rather than join in the revelries found in every RAF Officers' Mess during the evenings. He was studious; did his job remarkably well; was generally fair with his men and had their respect. But he never went overboard in either seeking popularity, or deep friendships. He was an attractive man, but seemed strangely shy. He rarely got into conversations about the oncoming war, or the subject of courage, unless it was during business hours where he proved himself an excellent instructor. On those few conversations when he did talk to fellow officers in the Mess he made it known he thought the war would be hateful and ghastly. Everyone subconsciously knew this to be true, but it contrasted strangely with the mood of the day. Most of these boys were raring to go. There was a mood of blood-lust which Townsend abhorred. He was cool, efficient and dutiful, but one of the few officers of his day who was not looking forward to a war which would put these attributes fully to the test; a war which he knew would be long, bitter and very dangerous.

It would be stupid to suggest that Townsend was not as courageous as his fellow officers – when the time came he proved himself to be infinitely more so than most – but he was a realist about the war. In the beginning he had no illusions about glamour or heroics. And on occasions he became rather unpopular when he tried to diffuse some of the enthusiasm rampant in the Mess.

When the war came Townsend changed drastically with it. At the end of the Battle of Britain he had undergone a personality change so radical that few people recognised him as the Townsend of the halcyon pre-war days. He flung himself absolutely and completely into the mêlée with a dogged determination to come out of any fight the complete victor. He became hardened, almost cruel, in his attitude towards the enemy. On land, to everyone's surprise, he joined in the carefree activities of the Mess, and became quite a devoted buccaneer. Unlike the old days when he tended to frown on the boyish pranks and joviality of the Mess, he now engineered his own evenings of riotous behaviour and became very quickly the life and soul of his surroundings.

Townsend's war record was actually quite astounding. Many, if not most, officers who took part in that first penetrating piece of warfare, the Battle of Britain, got some kind of major decoration like a Distinguished Flying Cross (DFC), or at least the Distinguished Flying Medal (DFM). Many went on to get the more highly regarded service medal, the Distinguished Service Order (DSO). All of them meant service way beyond the call of normal duty and were usually given for both specific acts of terrific courage, or long service under extremely gruelling and exacting positions which needed a great deal of fortitude and leadership. Townsend qualified in both ways.

On April 30th 1940, Townsend was awarded his first medal, a DFC. It was because of his activities during the dog fights above the Scapa Flow. The citation read: "While on patrol over the North Sea, Fl. Lt. Townsend intercepted and attacked an enemy aircraft at dusk and, after a running fight, shot it down. This was his third success, and in each instance he displayed qualities of leadership and determination of the highest order, with little regard for his own safety."

A few months later, as the war raced across a lazy British

summer, he became a Squadron Leader. He was sad to be leaving 43 Squadron but happy to take up a new command of the now famous 85th. It was a Squadron that would have probably been blasé about anyone less than Townsend. Their successes had been phenomenal. Their losses incredible. Their *esprit de corps* was indefatigable and their reputation was impassable. Townsend immediately took them on to greater victories and within weeks he was sporting a bar to his DFC.

By now the exploits of this fighter pilot were getting the attention of the nation. The Battle of Britain had its own special kind of magic. And the leaders, the Government and the press, to say nothing of the newsreels – which were compulsive viewing to a news-hungry nation – were all concentrating the glare of their propaganda machines on the "few" who had defended the skies of Britain.

Townsend got his fair share of the acclaim and was not averse to it because he understood its propaganda importance. But by now he was living the role circumstances and the media had created for him. He became more and more cavalier and buccaneering. He even started unfastening the top button of his flying jacket, a prevalent habit of the fighter pilots and supposed to signify their superiority over the "bomber boys".

The fighter stations were lonely places, continually on edge. The men slept with their clothes on, mentally attuned to the sudden and penetrating blast of the klaxon. In May 1941 the powers that be in the Royal Air Force decided that Squadron Leader Peter Townsend had done his bit of active flying. He had defeated the odds and seen most of his contemporaries disappear – to the grave, to a prison camp, or to permanent hospitalisation. New pilots were just coming into their own in such numbers that the "old dogs" could take a breather. The RAF command did three things, they gave Townsend the coveted DSO, then they promoted him to Group Captain and put him behind a large mahogany desk where he co-ordinated the movements of the squadrons he had helped build and been such a part of.

He took it with good grace, but despite the fact that his injured foot twitched involuntarily under the table, he always felt a hard yearning every time he heard a fighter plane start up its engine.

Great fighter pilots are rarely in real life the bantering public-school boys you read about in the comic books. They are subtle, deadly, cool, tenacious, forceful men who invariably have a very mean streak. Townsend was no exception. As a Battle of Britain pilot he used any and all forms of wit and deceit to defeat his opponents. He came at them from nowhere, lulling them into false security and zooming up on them when they thought they were safe. His mind worked perfectly for a pilot. His senses were remarkably accurate and his timing was superb. His brain worked neither too fast nor too slow.

Other pilots were wary of him. Whether Townsend was in the pilot's seat or in the Mess, it was near-suicide to pick a fight with him. When fighting he had no pity for his opponent.

All this is what fighter pilots were made of, but once down from the cockpit, he could only leave his helmet behind. He couldn't drop his personality, and that was now of a very tough nature.

In the Mess he was popular but people made very sure they didn't cross him. He had an extremely forceful character and a tremendous strength of will. He showed compelling personal magnetism which fascinated others. He would quickly draw a crowd around him and people always got more from him than he got from them. He seemed completely unassailable.

Not many people, above or below him, tried to pick an argument with Peter Townsend. To cross him, and make an enemy of him, was considered a silly thing to do. This did not keep his enemies away completely. Some people found him pompous and overbearing and tried to take him down a peg. They rarely succeeded.

However, with those who chose to like him for what he was, a damned good fighter pilot, they found a man packed with integrity, devotion and a high-minded idealism. Because of this mixture of awe, charm and integrity, spiced with extremely good command of the King's English, he tended to dominate any company he found himself in.

His subordinates were always amazed at his capacity for

work. He seemed to be able to survive long, back-breaking periods which would have driven lesser men into the grave. He never waited until the morning to write his flight records. He could go for days without sleep, and often did.

During the periods of intense activity – and they were many – he always seemed to be straining for some goal or ideal he could not determine. It was as if he could not rest until the war was over. Not only the obvious war, but the war within himself. This made him impatient and when he barked an order, it was always at the double.

Throughout the war he remained seemingly and surprisingly very well-balanced and a delightful companion. He was visionary but not an eccentric. In conversation he was witty, easy, sensible, intelligent, and stimulating. As an officer he was democratic, but he could never suffer fools gladly.

He was extremely shrewd and sharp. It was impossible to deceive him. His kind of mind, which sometimes worked in devious ways, could spot deviousness immediately, almost as if he were psychic.

He was never at a loss for words. When in an entertaining mood he held his audience spellbound. But his mastery of language also meant he could be quite ruthless in his speech. A telling off from Townsend almost felt like the Cat o' Nine Tails. He could wield words like a lethal weapon. He always had an almost instinctive sense of another's vulnerable points and he would zoom in and destroy him as if he were a Messerschmitt.

He was immensely secretive about things he thought were no one else's business and your own secrets were always safe with him. Somehow he could always ferret secrets from his fellow RAF officers.

He was generally first-class at whatever he was doing but he could have periods of being penetratingly brilliant and determined. This made him one of the finest flying officers in the Second World War.

By April 1940 – as the Germans staged air attacks on the British Fleet lying off Scapa Flow – Townsend had already become an ace pilot to be reckoned with. He went out on several sorties and was formidable as a dog-fighter. In one encounter he disabled a Heinkel and flew alongside it as it was riddled with bullets. The obviously terrified German crew were hopelessly trying to keep the stricken aircraft in flight. Townsend pursued them until he was sure they were doomed. He made no bones about it. Had they had any chance of getting back to a safe area, he would have had another go and finished them off. This was the kind of action he had hated before the war. But because of the circumstances he simply had to accept it. He could not afford not to.

To the few men who had known him before, Townsend was now as different on the ground as any man could be. To keep morale up and to celebrate victory he devised a wild dance called "La Cachita". Part rumba, part sheer madness, Townsend would start it off standing on the main Mess table wildly swinging a beer tankard. Then he would leap down on the floor and fellow officers would form a snake behind him. They would dance all round the Mess, and often right out on to the airfield itself. "La Cachita" became the symbol of the Townsend squadrons. When in the air one of the airmen would yell into his intercom "La Cachita" – signifying a hit. When enough of them had been called, Townsend would sing down the cracking radio "Himmel, Kimmel, Achtung, Schpitfeuer." The planes would then wheel towards a formation, head for home and another dancing night in the Mess.

During the summer of 1941 the now Squadron Leader was himself shot down after a dreadful dog-fight in which the RAF had been outnumbered about four to one. He had taken a Messerschmitt with him but suddenly about six of them were on his tail. No amount of defensive action could shake them all off and several series of bullets ripped through his fuselage. He was wounded in four places by shrapnel and was covered in petrol. At any second the plane could have blown up and he would have landed in a state more reminiscent of a charred biscuit than a human being. He dived out of control until he got to 1,400 feet above the patchwork of fields around Hawkthurst in Kent. Then he managed to bale out.

As he landed he was almost unconscious from loss of blood. A small force of police and local Home Guard rushed him to a makeshift cottage hospital where he had a blood transfusion.

An ambulance arrived and took him North to Croydon hospital on the outskirts of South London. They operated immediately and removed a fragment of jagged cannon shell from his left foot. His big toe was so badly affected it had to be amputated. He was in considerable pain yet ignored the advice of his doctors and reported back on duty – with his foot still in bandages – a fortnight after his Spitfire had crashed into the fields of Kent.

By August he was back in business and flying again, though still a little sore. He was posted to a unit in Hertfordshire near the oddly-named village of Much Hadham. It was a fateful posting. Nearby lived a retired Brigadier and his family. Part of the Brig's work for the war effort was to entertain young serving officers in his sprawling mansion. At least a dozen or so would be invited to drinks on Sunday mornings. Townsend soon found himself on the invitation list.

Townsend readily accepted the invitation and, amid the hazy glow of morning gins and whiskies, he was introduced to the Brig's beautiful daughter. Rosemary Cecily Pawle was gay, vivacious and keenly attractive. Every young man worth his salt in the area was after her favours. As usual, Townsend dominated the scene and soon found them. He became a regular, sometimes even nightly visitor to the Pawle household and the Brig thoroughly approved of this brilliant and dashing young man.

In the Second World War there was a great and natural tendency to fall in love and get married as quickly as possible. With hindsight the psychology behind it is obvious. There were few opportunities for falling in love and sometimes it all happened during a week's leave. There was also a sort of ferocious fear that the love would not be the same the second time; or that, flung into some far corner of the world for a long period the serviceman would find love elsewhere. Or the girl, lonely at home, would seek affection from another lonely serviceman. Thirdly there was the passionate desire for the woman to be involved with the fighting itself, by having a loved one actually taking part. Each battle took on a new significance if their man was in the middle of it. There was always a great sense of urgency to everything in war-time

Britain and love life was no different. They fell in love under difficult and unique circumstances and they naturally wanted to sleep together. Sex outside marriage was still frowned on desperately in a Britain still suffering from a Victorian hang-over. Marriage was the quick and obvious answer. (Despite this some 10% of war babies were illegitimate.) There were thousands of war-time marriages, most of them madly hurried affairs. In the cool light of peacetime many of them broke up. Thousands of men died without knowing what real married life was like. But during the war itself, few people thought of the long domestic years of peacetime ahead.

Clearly influenced by all this, Townsend and Rosemary fell desperately in love and married the following month, July, at the tiny village church of St. Andrews, Much Hadham.

Probably because of these complex reasons the marriage became less than ideal at an early stage. But the reasons were not entirely tied up with the rigours of war. Townsend was an almost impossible husband. This was partly to do with his duty to the RAF and partly because of his own personality. As soon as they had wed, with as much pageantry as the war would allow, he was away from home most of the time. During the times he *was* home they at first enjoyed a blissful happiness. Their eldest son was born a year later and Townsend was incredibly proud of him. There were certainly happy times during the war years but they were necessarily few and far between.

Soon Rosemary began to see a different side of the man she had fallen in love with. He seemed like a shooting star in his attitude towards marriage. At the start he was all aflame and alive, promising everything, excited, loving, enthusiastic and romantic. They soared off on this great wave of love and enthusiasm. Then, like a star, it dimmed and faded and the passions dwindled along with it.

This seems to have been somewhat of a pattern with this soon-to-be-famous personality. When he was in a good mood he could be devoted and loving. He was often exceptionally amusing company, even in the home, and certainly if they were entertaining guests. Only those who knew both of them very well could spot the sudden moods of tension which could spring up underneath the supposed gay spirits. For he was a very demanding husband, not so much sexually, but in the standards he set his household.

His nature was tough, ambitious, and sometimes ruthless. Some of this brushed off in the home and he could at times be a domestic tyrant. He was very sure of himself and always believed his decisions were right. As such he continually demanded his own way and always got it. Very few people succeeded in going against his wishes for any length of time. Not even superior officers, let alone a mere wife.

So it was then, that after the first few years of bliss had passed, life in the Townsend household started to have strains and tensions which neither man nor wife ever succeeded in putting right.

Sexually, it was obvious from a very early age that he exuded a great and magnetic appeal. Girls fell head over heels in love with him at first meeting. As a young man he was moderately good-looking, fairly dashing and always excellent in his repartee. But he also had that quite indefinable thing called sex appeal and was quite spoiled by the attention women continuously gave him.

However, it seems that, for a while, Townsend was capable of very passionate and overpowering love. While the star shone brilliantly all was well and he was the most considerate and passionate of lovers. But it was always so impermanent. His temperament finally lacked the warmth to keep the emotion shooting to the heavens. His love became odd and mercurial.

As a person Townsend always seemed high-spirited and refined. He demanded those qualities in any woman he took an interest in and this must have been one of the main attractions he had for Rosemary. But his standards remained impossibly and selfishly high. If he found any flaw in a woman, or any indelicacy, he would suddenly lose all interest. However hard that woman tried to regain his favour, she would suddenly find his feelings cold and inpenetrable.

His character confused several women who knew him, because in friendship, he displayed the highest type of loyalty and affection. To those who became close to him, and there were many, he was the epitome of kindness and consideration.

But it was almost impossible for him to extend those virtues towards someone he fell in love with. He was never able to find real satisfaction in any romance. It was as if he *had* to remain partnerless in order to stay faithful to some ideal he had locked deep down in his mind.

To the women who loved him Townsend seemed to have deep inside himself an ideal he could not identify. He appeared as a lone voyager in search of the perfect romance. One that was almost untainted by human hand. One that was impossible because it *was* so ideal. His pursuit of this ideal was completely separated from his pursuit of lust. He could manage to prise the physical from the mental. This made him appear the complete chauvinist, willing to take the physical pleasures, but unwilling to accept the mental processes that went with them.

He also detested, very emphatically, being tied down. This was also true of Townsend the fighter pilot who was forever reckless and daring, always ready to move on to the next sortie, continually bored if he stayed in one billet a week too long. In the air, however hard they tried, they could rarely pin him down. Against the most fantastic of odds he would find an avenue of escape and shoot down it as if it were a helter-skelter.

So it was with women. None of them who knew him in his early life could get him into the corner. When they did so he always searched, and finally found, the nearest avenue down which he could swiftly depart.

The Townsends' lives together soon became a more and more curious existence, typical of wartime newly-weds. For some time Peter lived with his in-laws. Then he went on a series of difficult postings which had no married quarters and his wife followed him around trying to get accommodation as near to her husband as possible. It seemed that, no sooner had she billeted herself and her baby, than Peter was moved on and she had to pack up all over again. They never did settle down into even a semblance of home life, not in fact until Townsend reached Buckingham Palace.

He seemed forever dashing and exciting but in love he lacked the power of endurance. For the various women who have fallen in love with him, including the wife he finally divorced, this always led to the most unfortunate of relationships.

It was this complex man who caught the King's eye in 1943 and immediately became a force in the corridors of power at Buckingham Palace. It was this dashing war hero, full of magnetic charm and brilliance, but hiding an assortment of intricate personal quirks, whom Princess Margaret first had a crush on when she was just thirteen years old.

It was a chill morning in February 1944 when Group Captain Peter Townsend entered the gates of Buckingham Palace to meet King George for the first time. He was especially well turned out that day with a pin-striped suit and a sombre RAF tie. He knew the morning's meeting was crucial. Two other officers had been on the short list and this was to be the final reckoning. He did not know that, for reasons known only to His Highness, the King had already selected him. All the three names had been similar in rank and war service. All three had been one of the "very few". They had been chosen by the War Ministry at the King's request. The King was moving well away from tradition in this. Equerries normally came from the families of other equerries. King George was determined to give his fighting heroes the recognition they deserved. On a personal basis he felt he did not need just another courtier, trained and suitable as he may be for the duties required of him. He wanted a tough outsider who had proved himself as a man of courage and strong character. He wanted someone who really knew what it was like out there, someone whom he could speak to on a man-to-man basis. Someone who could give him truthful assessments of things like the real spirit of the forces. He had already spotted Townsend as his man. This was a mere preliminary meeting to introduce himself and find out, above all, whether Peter Townsend really wanted the job or was just obeying his own sense of duty, or direct orders from above.

Despite the King's nervous disposition and shyness at meeting someone for the first time, the two took to each other from the moment they shook hands. With a faltering voice – for the King had aged visibly throughout the war and his speech impediment had got even worse – he asked Townsend question after question about the Battle of Britain, how the war was going and what his personal ambitions were. Townsend showed him infinite politeness and respect, yet was clear, able, and confident in his answers. He gave a truthful analysis of the situation as he saw it, rather than saying things he thought the King might want to hear.

The King wanted to know everything about his family. He established beyond doubt that Townsend was, at that stage at least, a happily married man. "Family" was one of the most important words in the King's vocabulary.

When Peter Townsend left the Palace early that evening he told his wife he thought he had pulled it off. He was quite excited about the prospect of being close to his Monarch. It was indeed – at a time when the monarchy was considered almost sacred by the British – an honour to have ever been considered. And Townsend was an ambitious man.

The King was very interested in the Townsend family which, on both sides, had had a long and distinguished record of senior army life. He had also married a Brigadier's daughter. While the King was careful to note that he was not looking for someone who merely had a good birthright, he knew that Townsend's could not be faulted.

The King paced the dark green carpet for a long time, sometimes stammering but, when he had asked his question, always listening attentively for the answer. He liked what he heard.

By all accounts Townsend impressed the King from the word go. He went on to become a close friend and confidante of his master and to make himself indispensable to the royal household generally. Nevertheless, that night when he got home to his joyous wife, neither of them could possibly know of the terrible strain the job would put on their marriage. They saw only the honour and charisma of the position. From now on Townsend would be allowed only one true devotion – the King. He would be expected to be married to his work night and day, and as a married couple they would have to meet like lovers and catch a fleeting night together.

A week later Townsend was sitting at his desk at the Instructors' Flying Training School, Montrose, on the east coast of Scotland. An official War Ministry despatch arrived at mid-morning and Townsend, almost certain that he had got the job, put it to one side for a few minutes while he finished a telephone conversation. Minutes later he was on the phone again to tell his wife he would be moving into Buckingham Palace within the week.

Early on the morning of March 16th he bought a copy of the *Daily Express*. It was full of the allied successes the day before in the bombing of Cassino in Italy. He read briefly and, tucking the paper, as he always did, under his arm, he side-stepped the sandbags outside Buck House, showed his special pass to the policeman on duty and marched briskly across the wide parade ground into the humming bowels of the Palace. As he walked through the door he stepped into a new and different world: one that would take him from being a heroic war ace to being a Princess's lover. It would take him from the news pages of war coverage to the gossip columns; and when the full, true story broke, it took him to the front pages of every newspaper in the English speaking world.

No one who would later give immense thought to the matter could remember the first meeting between the King's equerry and Princess Margaret. At least, they remembered different things. Whenever it was, it occurred in the corridor of Buckingham Palace very soon after Townsend joined the staff. The two were formally introduced and chatted for a few minutes. They were re-introduced several times later and each time neither let on they had met before. Margaret had in fact introduced herself two days after Peter had become an equerry. Later she was introduced formerly by her father. And then again by her mother. Margaret teased the equerry slightly by pretending they had never met and a rather amused Townsend played along with the game – even to the point of exchanging the same pleasantries three times over as the introductions recurred. Already it seemed Margaret had singled out the dashing war hero for her special attentions and as a recipient of her rather impish sense of humour.

At first he was benevolent and fatherly towards her. In some ways he had to be, but he had also become quite struck by the nerve and vivacity of this regal and precocious Royal scalliwag. It was not difficult to see why. For a start there was little he could do to curb either her wit, her temperament, or her rank. He was an Equerry of Honour to every member of the Royal family. She was, in effect, his employer. Secondly, far more sophisticated and senior than her actual years, she was a young lady who genuinely caught a man's eye. Whether she be panting with exasperation because she could not get her way; impishly fooling around; or quite openly flaunting her blossoming womanhood; she was irresistible as a person and charmingly affectionate as a girl.

As her sister Elizabeth entered more and more into the adult world of official duty, Margaret came to Buckingham Palace for ever longer visits. But by the end of the war the King was trying to spend more time at Windsor as well, so he could be with his beloved girls. Now the allied invasion in Europe was well under way, keeping the heat off England (this was before the notorious doodlebugs changed the London situation again) it was no longer quite so essential to keep the flag flying in the centre of the capital. He consequently brought many officials to Windsor with him and was able to carry on working within the lap of the family. They were gayer days, despite the anguish and hardship, than any other since the family had left 145 Piccadilly.

Townsend, whose job it was to be on hand whenever the sovereign did so much as blow his nose, had the best of both worlds. He had a small flat above the King's drawing room at Buck House – and a cottage called Adelaide Cottage in the grounds of Windsor Royal Park. This was the first place the Townsends could call home and they settled in with some relish, hoping that things would now get better.

The famous love affair which was gradually to grow between the equerry and the Princess was still a long way off. There was no point at which anyone can say it definitely began. But from a very early stage in their relationship it was obvious to anyone close to the royal household that the blooming Princess soon became deeply affected by the presence of the fighter pilot. In the beginning Townsend found this gently amusing. It was years before he allowed himself any informal liaison with the Princess, but even in the first year he found he could be a lot more informal than most other members of the court. The King often, and quite openly, used him as a sort of honorary uncle to the girls. Both of them had an affection for him. He maintained a considerable influence over both of them. He was bright and breezy and from the big, brash outside world which Elizabeth would never really see and which Margaret was bursting to find out about. It was in this prestige position that Peter Townsend became the perfect Royal Equerry.

Chapter Six

The transformation from the rough-house world of the forces into the sedate, but uniquely political, powerhouse of affairs at Buckingham Palace, was an exacting business for the budding young fighter ace. He soon found that the tasks facing an equerry can be infinite, tedious and challenging.

Each member of the Royal family requires individual and very separate things from the men and women they choose to help them perform their duty adequately. Companionship is always a foremost essential.

The equerry is the bridge between the common servant who feeds them and dresses them and the blue-blooded aristocrat who may mastermind any major operation. The relationship between the Monarch and the equerry is a highly personal one. The servant will quickly learn his master's every little whim and fancy.

It is almost impossible to define the many duties imposed on any royal equerry. But he is someone with wide responsibilities, a spokesman for his master who understands the Monarch's personality and character to the *n*th degree. He looks after the little details others may have missed and he is expected to be a loyal and entertaining companion and aide during long and tiring trips.

The catering department at Buckingham Palace, for instance, is used to putting on four huge garden parties a year. Some 8,000 people regularly attend each one. Despite the hundreds of other activities each year, the department, with an annual tea party budget of £30,000, manages to produce 52,000 sandwiches, 40,000 bread rolls, 20,000 strawberry tarts, 28,000 other cakes, 24,000 ice creams, 1,600 gallons of tea and 1,680 gallons of coffee. It is an incredible task.

The Head of the Household, the Lord Chamberlain, is given

the gigantic job of selecting the guests each year with a great deal of help from the various government ministries. The Metropolitan police have to reorganise the whole of London's traffic for the day. They also make sure no uninvited guests get into the Palace and they organise the visitors' parking facilities.

When the whole thing is completely set up the equerry then goes to work. He carefully peruses all the arrangements. He will make sure for instance that no one is standing too near the balcony where the Monarch will appear for the National Anthem. He helps select the few dozen people out of the crowds who will actually be presented to the Monarch for a conversation. He personally primes each of them that the conversation will last no longer than four minutes. (Some people haven't got four minutes' conversation in them and have to rehearse. Others try to demand twice that much.) If there is anyone of really special interest the equerry will find out about them and appraise the Monarch of the facts. That person then becomes quite flattered when the sovereign seems to know so much about them.

If the Monarch has got a headache, the equerry will order an aspirin. As the King dresses for the occasion the equerry will answer the phone. His tasks range from the immense to the petty and he must be prepared to be on call twenty-four hours a day.

Townsend's function as equerry to King George VI was no different to any other in this esteemed office. While the family was together on tour he might suddenly be asked to spend an hour amusing the two Princesses while the King and Queen held an audience elsewhere. He did endless little personal jobs for the King, like vetting theatre and cinema programmes to make sure they contained nothing offensive towards the crown – or anything that might upset the Queen's sensitivities. For several years he was the King's shadow, always ready to light his cigarette, open the door for him, or re-direct an eager subject who wanted to shake the King's hand.

During Royal Tours he was a whirlwind of activity. It was the valet's job to make sure the King had a fresh clean shirt for each engagement, but it was Townsend's job to make sure the

King's jacket carried a black arm band if the people he was visiting had had a death recently.

In effect, the royal equerry not only acts as a constant nursemaid to his royal master, he becomes also a buffer between the sensitivities of the throne of England and the outside world at large.

The men in the British Royal family tend to be rather worldly. Most of them have been in the Royal Navy and little is hidden from them in that all-man's environment. But the ladies of the House of Windsor tend to see a very different world from the one ordinary folk inhabit. They are continually sheltered from the rough bruises of life.

Part of the equerry's job is to keep it that way. And in this the people of Britain themselves go to extraordinary, even eccentric lengths to make absolutely sure no member of the Royal family is ever offended. Much of the extraordinary hive of activity which goes on before a royal visit is the direct result of a visit by the equerry a week or so before. Though even the equerries never failed to be amused by the number of eccentric things British people think will offend the crown.

Some typical examples which turned up in an equerry's notebook included: the opening of the Mersey Tunnel by a Royal when the entire staff took their shoes off for the whole day so they wouldn't take the sheen off the floor; the farmer who was asked to move his cows in case they offended the Royal nostrils; a school janitor who was ordered to get new false teeth because his old ones tended to fall out when he got excited; saplings which were planted in front of an old shed and carefully uprooted and returned the next day; hoardings which were put up to hide a hot dog stall in case the royal corgis had ideas about an early supper; the staircase which was boarded up at a youth club in case the youths tried to catch sight of the royal panties; the reformed alcoholics who were dressed in borrowed suits – and returned to their old garb that evening; and so on. It was a royal equerry who said to a fellow confidante that he was sure all royalty were convinced the world smelled of new paint.

The most extraordinary part of this typically British eccentricity is the nation's attitude towards lavatories. It appears the British believe the Royals do not have bodily functions the same as the rest of mankind. Lavatories are regarded by minor officials as something almost pornographic and which must, at all costs, be hidden from the Royal view.

One council, for instance, put in special devices which quietened the flushing in the Guildhall loos. In almost any town the Queen visits the local council will take down all the "Gentlemen" signs outside the public lavatories. This had an appalling effect in Stirling, Scotland, one day when a bunch of well-oiled miners dashed around for nearly an hour trying to find a "Gents". In sheer desperation they found a wall on which they could relieve themselves – only minutes before the Queen's car passed.

But the equerry is well aware that the Royal party may feel the call of nature. He makes sure that at strategic places along any route, toilet facilities are available. In nearly every case, a new seat is fitted beforehand and in some towns the tank containing water for washing hands is changed for treated water used in hospitals.

Years after Peter Townsend had left the Palace, another equerry, working for Princess Margaret, visited a hospital to put the finishing touches on a royal visit. One poor man in the middle of an operation on his foot was quietly but quickly hurried out of the operating room and into another building. Margaret was due to visit the nerve centre of the hospital and may well have stopped for a chat with this unfortunate patient. Had she done so she would have almost certainly wanted to know his name. As this happened to be Townsend, the equerry thought it prudent to remove him rather than bring back unwanted memories to the Princess. It is typical of the kind of detail an equerry has to look after.

Townsend himself was quite brilliant at his job. He made himself absolutely indispensable to the Royal family.

He showed very quickly that he had grasped the fundamentals of political knowhow. His subtlety and intelligence gave him the necessary gift of being able to handle people and situations expertly. When troubled Palace officials wanted to let the King know of a problem which might displease him, it was Townsend to whom they went to present the case.

Equally, the Group Captain would interpret the King's feelings and favours to those beneath him. It did not go unnoticed by the rest of the Palace staff when the King turned to Peter Townsend one day, after he had just smoothed over some difficulty or other, and said: "Peter, I simply do not know what we would do without you."

But Townsend also had strong convictions and a lot of original ideas to back them up. He had the ability to turn dreams into ideas and convince other people he was right.

He had a great musical interest and was moderately successful as a musician. This was always a feather in the cap if you wished to impress the Royal House of Windsor. He impressed them profusely. The King treated him almost as a younger son. The Queen Mother was, and still is, tremendously fond of him. The Queen, then Princess Elizabeth, treated him as a favourite uncle, and her sister eventually fell madly in love with him.

The long corridors of Buckingham Palace – there are nearly two miles of them – are traditionally carpeted in deep red pile. They are gloomy, for little natural light penetrates from the small windows at either end. They are sparsely furnished, yet each small chair or cabinet is a collector's item. When Peter Townsend first walked the corridors he had been used to a decade of gruff, rough-and-ready, sometimes riotous, living in the RAF. It took him about a week to adjust. He spent the first few days being rather awed and subdued. He told his wife he felt like a bird with clipped wings stuck in a gilded cage.

But a week later his ambitious and practical streak was coming to the fore. He grew his wings back and started flying in every direction. He treated the job as he would have treated a new posting at an RAF station. He read the household accounts; saw the menus; talked to the gardeners; found out the huge rambling geography of his new home; asked about the King's special habits and idiosyncrasies; inspected the stables and garages and generally made himself familiar with everything that was going on.

When he had done this he pursued a typical Townsend course. He looked for more responsibility. He quickly mastered the normal working life of an equerry and looked about frantically for more work. In wartime Britain this was not difficult. The Palace staff was at a minimum because most of them had joined up. But it was essential to his scheme that the family liked him and he went out of his way to talk to each one in a language they could understand. With the King he could talk gravely about the war and the services; with the Queen he could talk about flowers, the estates, London society, horses or even domestic issues. The Queen took a special interest in his children and the King even became a Godfather to his second son, Giles.

The King was especially grateful to Townsend for helping his family get through the long evenings when he was away on duty. Townsend made himself most personable as a sort of "family sitter". He could play the piano and sing, and he played an excellent hand of canasta, the Queen's favourite game.

But it was the girls to whom he showed his special talents. Well aware of his own sex appeal and conscious that nearly everyone was attracted to him when he turned on the charm, he worked hard at establishing himself deep in their affections. He was a man of the world, which was in itself immensely attractive to both girls. They had been suffocated by courtiers steeped only in the art of living with Royals – and protecting those Royals from the world at large. Here was a man with good breeding and excellent conversation who had no such inhibitions. He talked to them as an adult, never insulting their intelligence, and they loved him for it, especially Margaret, who still had a complex about being older than her years.

At twenty-nine Townsend was twelve years older than Elizabeth and sixteen years older than Margaret. Without ever losing his own dignity, he managed to close the age gap considerably so that the relationship between the three of them became almost contemporary and pally. Townsend went to some lengths to find out everything that could be known about corgis, for instance. Knowing full well Princess Elizabeth was crazy about them, he looked up all the previous champions, learnt about the various strains of breeding, made himself fully conversant with their history and became somewhat of a specialist on how to look after them. Nothing could be more calculated to appeal to Elizabeth.

One of his special allies in the Palace quickly became Margaret MacDonald, the Queen's dresser (she has now been with the Royal family for forty-six years). She is the daughter of a Scottish railwayman and, as a principal lady-in-waiting, she is known by everyone as Bobo. She has a small flat above the Royal family's private residence in Buckingham Palace and works with two assistants. When the Royal family go abroad she supervises up to six changes a day. She was one of the Queen Mother's closest confidantes outside the family itself, and the same relationship was later inherited by her daughter.

As Crown Equerry, Townsend enjoyed tremendous power in the politics of Buckingham Palace. Only the Lord Chamberlain himself was above him in the hierarchy of nearly 500 which keep the royal household going. The Monarch's private secretary, the Palace Treasurer and the Master of the Household shared equal rank with him.

The Crown Equerry was also responsible for the Palace garage and stables. There are twenty-two Palace cars – four of them official maroon Rolls-Royces. The stables housed ten greys to draw the Queen's coaches and twenty bays for other members of the family. Townsend quickly made himself conversant with every aspect of Palace life below stairs.

It was he, for instance, who found out there was a quarter of a mile of corridor between the kitchens at Buckingham Palace and the family's principal dining room. The meals were brought up on a heated trolley. (Prince Philip later had a small, modern, family kitchen installed in their "flat" at Buck House to try and improve matters, but it never caught on with the Palace staff. They are very reactionary in their habits.)

There were also 100 full-time maintenance men in the Palace alone – electricians, plumbers, engineers, builders and so on. More than 900 gardeners were responsible for the 8,679 acres of Royal Parks – almost one for every ten acres – although the Palace employed nine for the forty acres of garden which now sprawl under the Hilton Hotel.

Townsend also made it his job to get on with Peter Page who has been on the Queen Mother's kitchen staff for thirty years. He started as a kitchen boy and worked his way up to take over from the retiring Palace Head Chef, Ronald Aubrey, a huge rosy-cheeked man who became almost psychic about the royal appetite. Every morning a menu was sent up to the Queen Mother with suggestions for all the day's meals. There were very few alterations to his choice. Townsend and he often worked together in trying to please the royal palate. In this, and all sorts of other ways, Townsend firmly insinuated himself into the whole spectrum of Palace activities.

While he was at the Palace, Peter himself ate in the household dining room, among the ladies-in-waiting and the private secretaries. They were in turn waited on by the Palace servants and looked after very well by the Palace kitchen. The dining room was a big circular place with a high painted ceiling. Once it was a library and it still had shelves all around the walls.

Peter's office in the Palace was a high-ceilinged, very old-fashioned room on the ground floor, which he reached by going through the Privy Purse office in the forecourt used by all members of the royal household. The office had dark green walls, a marble grate with an open coal fire, an ancient mahogany desk and long windows overlooking the gardens. It was nearly below the main drawing room where the King conducted his business. At night he slept in a small Palace bedroom immediately above the drawing room. Consequently the equerry was never more than a few feet away from the King. Townsend liked his quarters at the Palace but hated his room when the court went to Balmoral. It was still furnished with Queen Victoria's hideous tartan upholstery.

Adelaide Cottage, where the Townsends were now officially quartered, was a "grace and favour" establishment a stone's throw from Windsor Castle. It was surrounded by rose gardens and had a picture-postcard quaintness. The Townsend family adored it on first sight. But it was hardly habitable. It lacked all the modern amenities and with two small children Townsend felt he had to convert it if they were to live there for some time. Castle electricians were employed to wire the house up. Plumbers put in water and built a new bathroom. Palace handymen spent their weekends daubing the house with new paint. Within two months they had it looking exactly as they wanted it.

The cottage had been built in 1832 for Queen Adelaide, wife of William IV, as a garden house close to the castle. Later it was used for pregnant ladies of the court who perhaps should not have been. The cottage was excellent as a hideaway as it sat behind a ten-foot-high privet hedge nestled in a by-way of the park. The significance of this aspect had not yet been realised by anyone. But it was one day to play a crucial part in the situation long after the war had ended.

Towards the end of the war, while the King found it increasingly possible to spend longer periods at Windsor, Townsend was also able to live most of the time at Adelaide Cottage.

But when the Doodlebugs started, the King returned to Buckingham Palace full time, and Townsend went back to snatching the odd day with his family. Ideally, an equerry spends some three months full time with the Monarch. Then he takes six weeks off. But this was wartime and Townsend was conscientious and highly ambitious. He rarely took the vacations due to him.

The slight strains the Townsend family had felt earlier, now became rather more neurotic. Rosemary Townsend was not at all happy with the situation. She rarely saw her husband, she was stuck in a small cottage on her own with the baby for long stretches at a time without any let-up from the chores of motherhood. And when her husband did eventually come home it seemed he only wanted to see the child. He had started to become increasingly cold towards her. The shooting star of his original love had burst and the relationship was already fizzling to a standstill.

On the night of September 8th 1944, the first massive V2 raid plunged London back into fear and gloom. It was a year in which the war had seemed to turn favourably towards the allies. In January the Americans had landed at Anzio. The Russians were not only holding their front but driving the Germans back. Caen had been captured in the allied invasion, the allies were in Belgium; Warsaw had fallen; and even the day before the allies had entered Boulogne. On every front the allies seemed to be winning. Now Hitler was pulling one of his last master strokes – and succeeding in striking terrible fear deep into the heart of the British homeland.

Once again Townsend's special talents were required by a King who became more and more edgy as each whining bomb cut out and whistled down on to his Kingdom.

Chapter Seven

Had a mariner from space descended into the offices of Buckingham Palace on the day the Reuter machine nearly went beserk, he would probably have reported back to his alien headquarters that the species known as humans were all insane, volatile, unpredictable and extremely odd in their behaviour.

On the face of it the day had started off very much like any other. The King and Queen had breakfasted, Townsend and the Private Secretary had been in attendance during the morning as usual, and in the rest of the Palace things hummed along smoothly as they always did.

Then, suddenly in the ground floor press room, a series of four bells rang out of the Reuter news agency machine followed by a wild clattering as a single sentence punched itself out on to the paper. The bells were to signify an ultra-important news flash. The words were very simple. The war was over. But the operator on the other end of the machine could not control his jubilation. As the paper bounced out of the machine he kept the bells ringing for nearly a minute.

The result of this small scene was glorious chaos. The news room itself exploded and Vince Tillotson, seconded to the Palace from the Central Office of Information, tore the paper from the machine and let out a loud and involuntary whoop of joy. He could not contain himself. He could not find either a secretary or an equerry and took it upon himself to inform the King. He almost ran down the corridors until he got to the King's office. He was breathless as he knocked. The King was surprised to see him without a formal summons, but Tillotson merely said: "Your Highness . . . the war's over," and handed him the message. The King jumped up from his desk and wildly grabbed the paper. It was what they had all been expecting, but it was marvellous to see it in print.

As a prelude to this happy event, in the early days of February two things had happened to brighten Townsend's world. His second son was born and the Yalta conference was called in the full expectation of the end of the Second World War. The allies were pressing from the West and the Russians were gaining ground daily from the East. As Rosemary convalesced, the bombing of Dresden had got underway, and when she returned to Adelaide Cottage the Americans were fighting on the beaches of Iwajina Island.

In March Cologne was captured by the allies who were now relentlessly pushing the German armies into total chaos. On April 12th Townsend was called to see the King and help him draft a note to Mrs. Roosevelt whose husband had died that day. It was a sad event in an otherwise jubilant month. As the Russians and Americans linked forces in Germany on April 27th an ecstatic King called his favourite equerry in for a celebratory sherry. "Do you know, Peter," he said. "I do believe we've done it."

They were to drink several more celebratory sherries over the next few days and on April 30th, when Hitler committed suicide, the King allowed himself to get quite tiddly. Townsend kept him company for most of the evening. He had never seen the King so excited or happy. As the war closed it was as if a massive weight was being lifted from his back. Although he was still worn, and seemed twenty years older than at the start of the war, he became quite jolly and jovially cracked jokes all day.

On May 5th the Princesses were formerly recalled to Buckingham Palace to re-establish their personal headquarters there. The German army had crumbled and the Armistice was under way. Margaret was not yet fifteen. Elizabeth, who had joined the ATS Women's Auxiliary Service, wore her uniform at all times. On Sunday the whole family gathered and were in great spirits. The King had been told that the war in Europe would officially be over the next day. They prepared to celebrate with their nation.

The King planned a victory broadcast on the radio. The whole family were to appear on the balcony of the Palace to receive the adulation of an ecstatic crowd. The Palace itself buzzed with excitement. The servants' quarters rang with cheers as the cooks kissed the valets and the chambermaids danced with the butlers. It was a scene going on all over the country and in many other places of the world. The Prime Minister, Mr. Churchill, came to the Palace that morning to brief the King and receive his congratulations. Townsend was all over the Palace that day sorting out all the minor details of a major event. Already crowds were gathering outside the huge wrought-iron gates that guarded the Palace courtyards.

As the King went on the air – noticeably jubilant, despite his still-chronic speech impediment – Margaret was hatching a plan. It seemed ludicrous to her that they should be stuck all the time in the Palace while the whole of London was ablaze with gaiety. There must be some way in which they could take part. Elizabeth was brought into the conspiracy and agreed. It would be fantastic fun to go out into the streets and join in. They jointly asked the King's permission and for a long while he demurred. They would all have to be on the balcony at midnight but soon after, he eventually agreed, they could go out for an hour. As long as they went to great pains to hide their identity and stuck very close to Peter Townsend, the man given the job of looking after them. So it was then, that as church bells chimed across the nation and with the lights of the Palace blazing away for the first time in six years, the family came on to the balcony as the first stroke of midnight hit Big Ben.

At about a quarter past twelve, three shadowy figures left a side door by the mews on the Victoria side of Buckingham Palace. The girls had make-up on and pulled scarves tightly around their heads. The man held both of them by the hand. They wandered round to the front of the Palace and mingled with the shouting, dancing, joyous and ecstatic crowds. They even got kissed by a jubilant sailor and Townsend had a real job making sure one of them wasn't whisked off dancing down the Mall. Margaret in particular got stuck in. Eventually she got her way. Townsend and Elizabeth had to dart through the crowds as Margaret got caught up in a huge mob of people who had formed a human chain and were coiling up and down the street almost crying with laughter and happiness.

The end of the war heralded a whole new era for Princess Margaret. Conscious that they had been cooped up for so long the King became very adept at turning a blind eye when Margaret started sorting out a selection of friends and going off to such things as theatres. She was now a gay and vivacious fifteen-year-old and the King benevolently felt it was probably time she spread her wings a little. Elizabeth, on the other hand, did not feel the same inclinations to go out on the town. She was by now deeply in love with Prince Philip and marriage was most certainly on the cards. The King had given her far more responsibility and, as a nineteen-year-old, she attended no less than forty official engagements in her father's name that year. The King was obviously in poor health and ailing fast, and while it was never mentioned as such by any of them the whole family knew it was only a matter of time before Elizabeth would be taking over the throne.

With no such responsibility hanging over her, Margaret was determined to get out and about and enjoy life to the full. At this stage, if Elizabeth was her father's pride, Margaret was certainly his joy. He felt her happiness keenly. She was able to sing, dance and be gay, something that by now the King himself found very difficult.

Occasionally the King and Queen liked to join Margaret for a visit to the theatre. When Danny Kaye came to England just after the war, Margaret became an immediate overnight fan. She bought all his records, learned his dance steps, and could even mimic him as a comic. She begged her parents to let her see him in person at the London Palladium. The King decided he would quite like a night out and asked Townsend to arrange the Royal Box. When Margaret heard about it she insisted they go in the front row instead because she said she couldn't see anything from the Royal Box. She laughed and clapped throughout the performance and later went round to see Danny in the dressing room to offer her congratulations.

They soon became firm friends – a friendship which was to last a lifetime.

In the following year her parents were to visit the first Royal Ascot since 1939. Margaret was beside herself with anger when they decided she was just a little too young to go to the races. She begged and cajoled to no avail. After they had set off for the day she calmly called the royal garage, and pretending she was her own lady-in-waiting, ordered a car for herself. She got the driver to step on it and arrived simultaneously with her parents. An angry father could hardly chastise his daughter with thousands of loyal subjects looking on, and by the time they had arrived home Margaret had charmed him out of his anger completely.

By this time Margaret felt completely at ease with the equerry. She depended on him considerably for all sorts of things and he never treated her like a child. When going off to one of her parties, or to the theatre, she would seek him out and ask him what he thought of her clothes. Most of the time he complimented her, but if he said they did not suit her, they were quickly removed and never seen again.

Whenever Margaret expressed a wish to see a certain play or film, Townsend was sent scurrying to the theatre the night before to vet it for Royal viewing. So when Margaret asked him about a certain play, an actor or an author, he mysteriously knew everything about it. He seemed to have an immense knowledge of things far outside his world in the Palace and Margaret found this intriguing.

Townsend was being drawn nearer and nearer to Margaret whether he liked it or not. One of the special duties the King bestowed upon him was to, more or less, become Margaret's Guardian Angel. The King was not averse to her going to a party, or even staying weekends with approved friends. But "PT", as he often called him, made sure that only "desirables" would be present and "non-desirables" would suddenly, and without explanation, receive a "regret cancellation" note arranged by the Palace. Because of this Townsend got to know every facet of Margaret's life and he saw the slightly hesitant schoolgirl blossom into a sophisticated young woman-about-town with a striking personality and a dominating character.

What had started off as duty had become friendship. As the months went on this developed into a genuine affection, in the best possible sense, where all kinds of little details built up to a situation where Margaret was becoming more and more dependent on and influenced by her father's favourite aide. At this stage there was no romance as such. While it may have crossed Margaret's mind, it was nothing more than childish whimsy. It had never occurred to Peter Townsend. His affection for her was linked to his ambition. If he kept her happy, he kept the King happy. If he kept them all happy, he kept his job and headed steadfastly towards the honours list. Nevertheless, it helped greatly that they got on so well and Townsend went to considerable lengths to make sure it stayed that way.

Life in post-war Buckingham Palace was a tranquil affair. While the household stayed efficient, it hummed its daily routine and the work became less and less arduous. Towards the end of that year, on November 3rd 1945 to be exact, Townsend's second baby was christened George Hugo Peter. George after the King, Hugo after his father and Peter, obviously, after himself. The child was christened in St. George's Chapel, Windsor Castle, and the King asked to be the child's godfather. Peter stood proxy for him at the ceremony. Both Princesses attended and, afterwards, went back to Adelaide Cottage for tea. It was one of many visits they enjoyed during the post war years. It was a place where both girls found they could completely relax. Princess Elizabeth chatted pleasantly to Rosemary about all sorts of everyday things. Rosemary never indulged her and always talked to her on a woman-to-woman basis.

As Margaret played with the eldest Townsend boy on the lawn, or chased the family dog around the rose trees, Peter would relax in a deck chair and either read a newspaper or simply sunbathe. Whole afternoons were spent like this regularly during the summer months when Townsend was on leave. They were afternoons both girls cherished. Sometimes their parents dropped over to pick them up, more often Peter would drive them the few hundred yards to Windsor Castle in his own Austin saloon. When it was very warm he walked with them through the flower beds and across the lawns of the Royal park.

King George was more than happy to see his children at Adelaide Cottage. He had always called the family "the Royal firm" and considered himself to be "one of the very few men in the world who never gets a complete holiday". He constantly told his page, Maurice Woods, how lucky he was to have people like the Townsends around to help the children get a more balanced view of life than he could provide himself.

The press followed Margaret endearingly wherever she went during this period. She had become the darling of the nation. This was a role she enjoyed immensely and she was forever thinking of new ways of living up to it.

Any hitch or confusion at an official engagement would irritate the King, and Elizabeth would get nervous. But Margaret found it extra exciting when something went wrong. She once went to an exhibition on homemaking at the massive Olympia exhibition hall. To the excruciating embarrassment of all the officials present the lift carrying the small royal party jammed between floors. The lift was open-fronted and the thousands thronging the hall could see and hear the Princess. Giggling profusely, she said if the worst came to the worst the people could hand them food from a nearby stall and they could eat as if they were in the old Newgate prison. The picture of Margaret in Newgate was a natural for most of the world's papers the next day.

Margaret the teenager was quickly establishing herself in the eyes of the country as the gay one of the Royal family. For many years it was to stand her in good stead with the British public. They loved her for it and were able to forgive her many indiscretions over a long and involved lifetime.

During the late forties things settled down to a steady routine in the royal household. During 1946 alone, Princess Elizabeth did at least sixty public engagements for her father. These were to increase to about 100 – or two a week – by 1950. During the same period Margaret was enjoying her teens with post-war relish. While most of the country was sighing with relief and trying to build their lives into a pattern again, Margaret was getting set to take society by storm.

1947 was a significant year for all concerned. It was the year when, in November, Elizabeth would at last marry her childhood sweetheart, Prince Philip. And it was the first time that Princess Margaret and Peter Townsend began to realise their friendship was getting a little more than a good working relationship. This was the year when Margaret blossomed out into full womanhood and her father thought her old enough at seventeen, and capable enough, to accompany them on a three-month Royal Tour of South Africa. It can be safely said it was during this tour that the foundation of a long and passionate romance was laid.

Before they all left on the HMS *Vanguard* that spring, a strangely odd, but significant incident occurred between the two sisters. It was an incident which would have been impossible for non-Royals, and one which Elizabeth would remember many years later. Margaret one day found her sister sobbing heavily in her private dressing room at Buck House. She tried to soothe the distraught Princess but was unable to do so. It appeared that a trivial incident in the street that morning had caused the distress. Elizabeth, who had always led a closely sheltered existence, had been quite unable to hide her emotions and when she had fallen in love with Philip, it was very obvious to all concerned. But she had no way of knowing this and was quite oblivious to the fact that everyone had guessed she was madly in love. She sincerely believed it was her own very private little secret. That morning she had visited a factory. As she left, a crowd of factory girls had shouted and waved. Some of them, in a rather lewd way, asked her where Philip was. She kept her composure right until she had got to her own quarters. Then she just burst into tears. Margaret was sympathetic. She remonstrated with her sister: "Nothing is your own in this business. Not even your love affair."

The girls consoled each other and Margaret told Elizabeth that she was going to fall in love, but absolutely no one was going to find out about it unless she announced their engagement. There were several targets she had in mind and she would fox the world. She went into long details about how she could get away with it. It was obvious to Elizabeth that her sister was far more self-possessed than she was herself. As the plan unfolded two things were quickly obvious: Margaret was determined to fall in love with a man that year; and she had already thought out just about every way in which the *liaison dangereuse* could be hidden from everyone, even her family. "They'll probably know I'm in love. But they'll never know with whom," she vowed. And with hindsight, it was a remarkably prophetic statement.

Chapter Eight

The opportunity to put her plan into action came sooner than even she had expected. Ever since the war had ended and things had become more relaxed, the King had wanted to take his family away on a real holiday, right away from the affairs of state. His remedy was simple: they would combine business with pleasure and go on a Royal Tour. The battleship HMS *Vanguard* was commissioned to take them to Africa. Once there they would do 5,000 miles by rail and another 5,000 by air, before relaxing on their way back on the battleship again. The minimum of staff was to accompany them and the whole atmosphere was aimed at being informal. Townsend was the inevitable choice as the family equerry. It was a fateful decision.

The long, slow luxurious trip by sea was everything the family wanted. No one was in a hurry. Their quarters were small but comfortable – the *Vanguard* had a special suite which could be converted into a floating palace for such occasions. It was built with the fact in mind that British kings are traditionally sailors and at some such stage such quarters might be needed.

On this trip Townsend really became one of the family. He was always careful to be respectful, but now he could relax in their company, and more important, they relaxed completely in his. They could depend on him at all times; they could lean on his shoulder in times of stress; they could cheer themselves up by conversing with him; and they could rely on him to have a sixth sense about their daily needs. It seemed as if he was almost psychic. No sooner had one of them thought of something than they found Townsend had done it or was about to do it.

Days were spent largely sunbathing, although the King took a keen interest in the running of the ship and kept in touch with the affairs of state via the radio. They cruised the Mediterranean – so lately an arena of fierce conflict – and headed lazily towards the Suez Canal. In the evenings they had family get-togethers in which they invited their own staff and top members of the crew along to their quarters for general amusement. These were nearly always musical evenings, dominated by the Princesses taking it in turns to play the piano and sing, though most of the people present played a number or two, including Townsend.

This trip was most conducive to romance and Margaret had just chosen her target. The obvious one. Right in front of her nose. One that she knew she could keep a deep secret because it was quite normal for them to be seen together. She had decided quite emphatically to fall in love with Group Captain Peter Townsend, the man they all treated like a second cousin.

Townsend had little idea of the fate decided for him by a woman who was very used to getting her own way. He was flattered by the attention she seemed to shower upon him, but still thought of it in terms of his own ability to be personable to his employers. However he got an inkling that Margaret was being extra-specially interested in him. During the voyage she would join him on deck for long talks, especially in the early evening when there was likely to be a sunset. She had also developed an uncommon interest in his married life and continually asked him questions about his wife and how the marriage was working. Later it was Margaret who specifically sought him out to invite him to the Royal drawing room. She always sat next to him, or near him and coaxed him to play his favourite piano pieces. It was towards Townsend she looked for approval when she got up from the piano herself.

Later when they had reached South Africa and were heavily involved with official duties she would persuade her father that Peter should take her somewhere while the King and Queen were engaged at a function. During a family trip up Table Mountain, Townsend had hung back so the family could be together. Margaret made a point of hanging back to be with him. In the evenings she wore a dress which was of a quite dramatically lower cut than royalty usually wears. Despite remonstrations from the family, she, as usual, got her way.

Without ever actually declaring her interest she managed to flirt with Townsend in all sorts of little ways. In this she was being a teenage minx, for Townsend was really quite helpless against her.

He must have been a little perplexed by her behaviour and probably, at that stage, a little concerned. He was always polite to her, but never awed, and he was one of the few people – men in particular – who could tell her if something displeased him. But he never did tell her that her behaviour displeased him.

The Royal family stayed at various farms in the bush during the tour and Margaret adored the early mornings. Then, she and Townsend would go riding across the veldt. This became a regular habit and they would race each other for an hour or two until they returned, flushed and hungry, to the farmhouse. Despite this kind of familiarity, Townsend was still very much an equerry. During the tour of East Africa, Margaret and a basic contingent of servants plus a few reporters went off for a single night to a small thatched cottage on the Amboseli Game Reserve. On arrival Margaret found the royal household had failed to pack the special Royal Standard which must fly over any residence where a member of the Royal family is staying. Townsend was haughtily sent to fetch it.

In fact, what had started off as a holiday turned into something of a nightmare for Margaret and Elizabeth towards the end of the official tour. There were endless rounds of handshaking; countless people to meet and smile at; and the girls found they had very little time to themselves. It was the first post-war tour and everywhere they went they found jubilant crowds pushing each other to get a view of them. At first Margaret loved the limelight and acclaim, but gradually it began to wear her down. To Townsend, who had been used to flying aircraft in impossible conditions night after night with hardly a wink's sleep, this kind of hardship was child's play. He was always on hand with sympathy and advice, or merely there for a pleasant chat to cheer them up. Each day held its own nerve-racking experiences for young girls who had never been on tour before. At the end of each engagement (they always were determined to follow Queen Mary's advice and *never* show their emotions in public), Margaret in particular just had to let off steam. She would get back to the ship, throw her handbag or hat on to an easy chair and exclaim: "Thank God that's over for another day."

She would join the family for an evening pre-dinner sherry or Campari, and from an early age this small tipple became a sacred ritual. (Nowadays, it is more often than not whisky and soda.)

Townsend, in a very pleasant and soothing way encouraged her all the time and Margaret found herself seeking him out more often as the tour progressed. The trip back to London after two months of engagements was a godsend to everyone. They immediately flung themselves into life on board again and all of them relished the total relaxation.

"PT" again became the favourite cousin and the musical evenings continued with much gaiety and amusement. During the trip the King agreed to an official engagement between Elizabeth and Philip Mountbatten and this caused the whole journey to have a romantic happy-go-lucky atmosphere. She could at least stop hiding her love for this handsome young Greek Prince and declare her affections to the world. Margaret was certainly caught up in this revelry and was very conscious of how her sister's love gave her a radiance and beauty unique to such times. It was the same radiance which led President Truman to be so enchanted by Princess Elizabeth when he met them next year. He called her "My Fairy Princess". Margaret hoped she exuded the same kind of radiance when she glanced towards Townsend from the piano.

In the months that followed the tour the Royal family, and consequently Townsend, saw a great deal of Prince Philip. The young Mountbatten was what you might call a very poor relation, and at first Margaret tended to be rather haughty towards him. However, he was very quickly able to establish who was on top of the situation. He became haughtier towards her than she was to him. He never took any nonsense, and after the wedding he kept her well and truly in her place.

Margaret was used to lording it over her escorts and friends, but she never got away with it with her brother-in-law. Soon after the wedding they all went to a party. Margaret wanted to stay on. Philip wanted to go home. A disgruntled Margaret was bundled into the royal car. Weeks later Margaret was staying with them on a short country holiday with Lord Neville. Margaret, who was always late to bed and late to rise, demanded breakfast in bed. Philip ordered the breakfast to be placed on the table with everyone elses's. Then he sent her a message saying she must get up and eat it before it got cold.

Philip never did wholly approve of his sister-in-law. She was altogether too fly-by-night in her attitude towards life. Philip, with the temper of a Greek and the bearing of a British aristocrat, was always a little on the right side of upper class convention. He seemed even more royal than the Royals themselves and had a very proper idea of how they should conduct themselves. Margaret, who had always been spoiled and who was used to being in the centre of attention, was not at all sure she liked this treatment from such a new member of her family. Ever since, they have more or less tolerated each other, but Philip's influence over Elizabeth was one of the major contributing factors to Margaret's behaviour later on.

There were only a handful of early occasions when Princess Margaret went out into the Big Bad World incognito; nearly all of them were with Peter Townsend. The first of any real significance was on VE day, the others were nearly all during 1947. (In the following year she would hardly ever be at home.) It started early in the year when Townsend found Margaret scurrying down the stairway at Buckingham Palace dressed to go out. She had make-up on, a headscarf and a deep woolly overcoat. He politely asked her where she was going and she said: "Out, I'm going out. I can't stand any more. Being cooped up *all* the time just drives me crazy. I just want to walk around for a bit as everyone else does."

Townsend, who by now had acquired a superb diplomacy in dealing with such situations, carefully tried to talk her out of it. She remained determined. She stalked off down the stairs and was about to head towards the back exit of the Palace. It was not only unusual for a Royal to leave the Palace without any escort – lady-in-waiting, or detective – it was, considered Townsend, rather dangerous. Margaret stalked on towards the exit. A voice suddenly rang out and echoed down the long corridor: "Princess Margaret."

It stopped her in her tracks. Townsend composed himself. "If you are really determined to go out, Ma'am, then at least do me the honour of letting me come with you."

It was the first of many such ventures outside the Palace gates. They marched happily down through the rather sleazy areas of Victoria until they reached the Thames. On another occasion they walked in St. James's Park and along the Mall to Trafalgar Square. Whenever Townsend thought Margaret had had enough, he hailed a cab and they headed home. But as the success of each venture became imminent, Margaret insisted on being more daring. They once caught a bus down the Strand to Fleet Street. They fed the pigeons in Trafalgar Square; they window-shopped in Oxford Street and once even had a drink in a pub next to Charing Cross station.

During the following year, 1948, Prince Charles was born, one of the great events of the decade and one of the great moments in the last years of King George. In a gay mood Margaret rang up her friend Mark Bonham Carter and told him she would kill the first person who called her "Charlie's Aunt". But the event was a blessing to Margaret for another reason. The birth now made her third instead of second in line to the throne. It took her one place away from the dreadful responsibilities of the crown. As with every member of her family, the monarchy was a burden which had been placed upon them, not one which they had sought for with any ambition. Like the others, Margaret would have faced the responsibility if it had been thrust upon her, but she was more than happy to remain a Princess.

So the birth gave her the excuse she wanted to stop being dominated completely by her role as a Royal and branch out into the Big Bad World where she knew many delights must await her. She was eighteen and still her father's favourite. She had many suitors and she got on with the business of enjoying herself in a very big way.

1948 was the year of the parties. She would go to at least five and sometimes seven or eight a week. A night rarely went by when she was not dancing to the early hours. It was the year she spread her wings and made or broke nightclubs with her presence. In the next two years her name was linked romantically with no less than twenty-two blue-bloods, playboys and even a handful of rakes. Princess Margaret had been locked up long enough. Now she was getting her own back with a vengeance.

She played merry hell with her escorts and, if they displeased her in any way she would ditch them and find someone else. She was quite uncompromising: she wanted fun, fun, fun. Escorts, and they queued up for the job, had to be witty, amusing, good company, handsome, excellent dancers, aristocratic, fun-loving, and continually gay.

Elizabeth had not been allowed out until she was nineteen. Margaret had wrung a year's grace from her father and by the end of 1948 a "Margaret Set" had sprung up which was unprecedented in British history. King George looked on his daughter's newfound escapades with part concern and part gentle amusement. He was very conscious that the new young, gay life of London was a consequence of the gruelling war years. In his personal diary he noted "Poor dears, they have never had any real fun yet." He was forever conscious that most of the young men Margaret sought out had been serving officers in his forces. They had fought valiantly sometimes for six years and now they were reaping the real harvest of peace. They were entitled to let off some steam. But he did become concerned by the gossip columnists and Philip positively frowned on the goings on. This was *certainly* not Royal behaviour. He constantly expressed his disapproval to his wife and, when his father-in-law would listen, to him too. Desperate to do the right thing, the King, as he often did, turned to Townsend for advice. Townsend was happy to give his wise judgement. Margaret was allowed to go on living it up with her new set.

The Princess tasted the gay life and quickly developed an insatiable appetite for it. She heard about the magnificent revelries of Britain in the twenties and thirties and was determined that her set would revive them. It was, in a country still laden with ration books and shortages of everything, a peculiar thing to do and the people of Britain had mixed feelings about it. On the one hand they resented the fact that all these blue-bloods could dance the night away, drinking endless bottles of champagne, popping caviare tit-bits into each other's mouths, and generally living a life of over-indulgence and rakishness. (Britain had emerged from the war with a general populace which had a deep resentment for the "officer class" and was very socialist-orientated until Churchill came back to power in 1951.) On the other hand, stories of their revelries livened up dull news pages. At least someone was managing to have a good time. Women cutting up old bits of material to make some trousers for their kids would muse how lovely it would be to dance the night away covered in silk and diamonds. It was the fairytale world, untouched by the constant rigours of post-war austerity. If Margaret could find a bit of gaiety and madness in this dull age when the common housewife queued for her weekly ration of eight ounces of butter, then good luck to her.

Even if the King had disapproved, it would have made no difference. Margaret was a determined young lady. Had she not got her own way, she would certainly have given him merry hell, something he was loath to encourage in his "little girl".

The Margaret Set grew out of boredom, idleness, and desperation. The end of the war was a dramatic anti-climax. Britain had fought a gallant and weary six years egged on only by Churchill's voice echoing around the snug kitchens of a thousand little houses and the memories of pre-war Britain where roses grew in the garden and one ate cucumber sandwiches for tea. When Churchill had been deposed ("There is no gratitude in politics") and when they all came home they found the roses had withered and if they wanted a decent cucumber they had to grow the vegetable themselves in the back garden.

The country was wallowing in a national debt which seemed so colossal it was impossible – and to this day it can only afford to keep up with the interest payments. The ration book dominated life. Within its pages were the only tiny pieces of happiness available to the British public.

There were very few families in the country who had not been exposed to a death of some sort. Every British clan had been exposed to severe hardship. It seemed there was very little reward once the war was over. A feeling of gloom settled over the country, based on a sort of hopelessness. They had fought so hard for absolutely nothing but the satisfaction that life under Hitler would have been worse.

To the mass of the working classes, life was remedied somewhat by the Attlee government who started to nationalise everything and put the officer class firmly in its place. The officer class, on the other hand, found itself with very little to do. Their stately homes had been broken up; London life had been taken over by the Salvation Army, and Westminster was spitting at them.

As a kind of glorious reaction against, not only the war, but life as it then was in the late forties, they rebelled into a mad frenzy of gay activity. They ranged in age from Margaret's eighteen, through the twenty-year-olds to the raffish early thirties.

In this mood nightclubs sprung up everywhere. Through bribes and bartering they got the necessary sustenance to please their new guests. Young bloods started to flood into the West End of London in search of this naughty but nice way of spending an evening. To Margaret, who had never known real hardship and possibly had never even conceived of it, this seemed like the paradise she had always imagined. To her, in her childhood fantasies as she sat the war out at Windsor, everyone else was living like this all the time. Now it was her turn to join the fray.

No one knows what happened inside Townsend's mind except, of course, himself. But one thing is manifestly certain: he showed no reaction at all to Princess Margaret. She, finding the outside world diverting enough anyway, and forever moving on to new amusements, more or less put Townsend out of her mind. She was still brash enough to seek his opinions on her new dresses, or ask if he knew a certain Marquis with whom she was to dine. Expertly, Townsend answered her quietly, to the best of his knowledge, and sent her on her way.

During this year Townsend accompanied the Royal family for their yearly holiday in Balmoral. Staying close by was an erudite Fleet Street veteran called Noel Whitcomb. He was convalescing with friends in the valley of Deeside after a serious illness. That Sunday, as they always did, his friends and their guests went to the small village kirk called Crathie Church. The Royal family was attending the same service. Whitcomb, a specialist in royalty, was well known to the Royal family. Margaret spotted him first and nudged her sister. Elizabeth nudged Philip who looked over and frowned with one of those special, penetrating frowns he reserves for people he is really annoyed with. Margaret spent the rest of the service half-smiling and looking at the roof. The Royal family were not at all amused to see a reporter in their hour of prayer.

Whitcomb later repaired to the local hostelry where a grizzled old Scottish warrior was roaring into his pint. For fifty years, he explained, he had been seeing various monarchs to their seats in the tiny kirk and reckoned he could spot a reporter a mile off. Margaret, he told the sympathetic bar, including Whitcomb had, taken him to one side and told him he was slipping. "There was a laddie called Whitcomb did me in the eyes. If I lay ma hands on him I'll break his bluidy neck." Margaret, of course, had found the whole thing amusing. And even more so when Whitcomb was eventually to take Townsend to one side and explained that their dual visit was pure coincidence. "Poor Mr. Whitcomb," she told Townsend. "Remind me next time I see him to ask him how his neck is."

Chapter Nine

In her nineteenth year Margaret decided she would like to expand her social horizons to include a few of the hot spots of Europe. She literally looked at the map and talked to several people, including Townsend, about where she should go first. She could more or less take her pick of Europe. After all, she had relatives in most countries. She wanted it to be the Mediterranean and she, above all, wanted it to be "completely carefree". The consensus of opinion – and the King wanted to know who she would stay with before he gave his final permission – was that Italy offered the best social and practical facilities for a real holiday. She and her advisors had obviously not considered the "paparrizi", that unique band of brigands with cameras, who stick like limpet mines to any subject which might present a picture. Margaret presented a usable picture getting off a plane. So she was the most natural target for these ingenious devils, when they learnt she was going to be informal during the visit.

From the moment her plane touched down in Rome she was followed with an ardour she had never encountered before. Much as she loved the limelight, she found these gentlemen just a little too much.

Margaret conceded that part of her time abroad would have to be spent on official engagements. She dutifully went to British Embassy cocktail parties and on an official sight-seeing trip around Rome. But Margaret had gone to Italy primarily to get away from it all. Various friends, both English and Italian, had offered whatever comforts they had in Italy. She could pick and choose between a dozen magnificent villas, half a dozen seaside hideaways, even a castle or two. But wherever Margaret went, the paparrizi followed. As she relaxed by a shaded swimming pool, the wiry little Italians were clicking away from the bushes. As she ate supper by candlelight on a veranda lapped by the sea, the night would suddenly be ablaze with flash bulbs. Nothing could stop them pursuing her despite every elaborate precaution.

After ten days of this Margaret decided to call it all off. She returned to Rome and went to say goodbye to the British Ambassador. She was so pleased to see the restrained and genteel behaviour of the British press in Rome that she gave them a whole twenty minutes to take pictures. At one stage the Ambassador's wife tried to pick a rose from the overflowing gardens. Unfortunately she pricked her finger and a *Daily Mirror* photographer, Henry How, clipped the rose with a small penknife. By doing this he missed his picture of the Princess. Margaret took him to one side and posed, sniffing the rose just for him. She told him it was so nice to get away from all "those dreadful little men". At that minute an Embassy security guard was calling for reinforcements to stop a group of them scaling the garden wall.

Italy was by no means the only country which had taken an insatiable interest in the gay Princess. The whole of the European press followed everything she did with an interest not known again until Grace Kelly married Prince Ranier. They speculated continuously about her boyfriends. In one year, a single French magazine had her engaged to no less than thirty-five separate eligible bachelors. In the USA the Artist League of America voted her the girl with the most beautiful eyes in the world. That night, while dancing with a shy young Guards officer, she impishly commanded him to look deeply into the most beautiful eyes in the world. As he flustered with embarrassment she fluttered her eyelids. "They are indeed, Ma'am," he managed to stutter eventually. It was Margaret's payment to him for being a clumsy dancer.

Margaret's nightclubbing had by now become quite notorious. She was just coming up to twenty and her nightlife was unceasing. She rode the public storm by going out even more often and staying out until after dawn. She cared little for the stuffed shirts who frowned upon her nocturnal activities, including Prince Philip. She would startle onlookers at important society balls by opening her handbag, getting out a packet of twenty cigarettes, and chain-smoking them between dances.

There was only one rule upon which the King was absolutely firm. He did not approve of young ladies tarting themselves up with make-up. A touch of lipstick or rouge, maybe, but he detested mascara or heavy eye-make-up. Margaret's answer was simple. She had a special bag fitted out with everything she needed to make up her face. She would say goodbye to her father in the Palace with just the hint of lipstick on her face. Then, in the car with the lady-in-waiting holding the mirror, she would carefully do up her eyes and perfume behind her ears. On the way back in the early hours a quick operation with cotton wool and cold cream restored her to her natural condition again. When the King saw a picture of his daughter at a nightclub, he was convinced the picture editor had touched it up. There she was, sitting with a glass in one hand and a cigarette in another, with men all around her, wearing eye-make-up. He had actually never seen her with such make-up and simply did not believe she ever wore it.

But one incident really put her on the map as a Royal raver. Just before her birthday in July 1949 she took some pals to meet her old friend Danny Kaye, who was by now on the friendliest of terms with the admiring Princess. Laughingly the girls persuaded Danny to teach them how to dance the can-can. They could not have had a more expert mentor and within an hour or two they had got it off to a fine art. The girls rehearsed in secret, both at Buck House and other places.

The opportunity to show off all this diligence came when they were invited to a party at the home of Sharman Douglas, whose father was the American Ambassador to the court of St. James.

The champagne flowed all evening and just before the official cabaret was about to begin, Margaret and her five friends disappeared into a back room which had been specially prepared for the occasion. Only Sharman Douglas and the stage manager, the Marquis of Blandford, had been told the secret. The mingling guests began to gather about the stage as the band played an overture for the cabaret. They were completely startled to suddenly find Princess Margaret and five other shapely girls take the stage dressed in short black dresses, net stockings, frilly white panties and huge bobbing feathers in their hats. They ran on stage as the band struck up the can-can and Blandford whispered to remember they must put their best leg forward. The 200-odd guests then roared their approval as – at exactly the right moment – the royal knickers were put plainly and provocatively on view. Someone in the audience remarked it was a pity great-great-grandfather Edward was not there: the can-can had been his favourite.

Throughout all this gay activity Peter Townsend had by no means been forgotten. They were still deep friends and that year the Group Captain piloted Princess Margaret's personal aircraft in the King's Cup race around Britain. He skilfully flew the blue and gold Miles Whitney aircraft around the whole course but did not come in the first ten. The following year he came second in Margaret's sponsored Hawker Hurricane.

He was still, more or less, Margaret's unofficial watchdog, keeping an eye on her friends and finding out details of where she was going, for the King.

But whatever deep ideas of romance had been aroused in the royal heart during the South African tour, they were now considerably cooler as Margaret went on and on widening her set of influential fun-lovers.

Top of the list was still the Marquis of Blandford, a playboy with a lot of money to burn and a lot of energy to burn it. There was a young roustabout called Billy Wallace who, most consider, had too much money and not enough sense. He was the son of a former cabinet minister, Euan Wallace, who had died in 1941 leaving his son several millions. Wallace's whole life seemed to be devoted to getting through the family fortune as fast as he could.

He and "Sonny" Blandford were the male bastion of the Margaret Set. They called the shots and selected the company. If they did not approve of a party, the party was a washout. If they decided to give it their patronage, with the almost certain promise that Margaret would turn up, it was a sell-out. Obviously they were top of the list of any society function.

Both of them took it in turns to escort Margaret, though her preference was for Sonny Blandford.

As the decade of the war turned into the diffident, soulless and unnoteworthy fifties two young blue-bloods managed to flutter a little more than Margaret's eyelids. For a while she took to both of them in quite a romantic way but they were later to share notes and agree they had been played off against each other. One was the rather portly Lord Porchester, eldest son of the Earl of Caernarvon, and a man with a penchant for good food and roulette. The other was the fabulously rich Earl of Dalkeith, a rather more serious man who tended to frown a little as dawn sprayed itself across an almost silent Piccadilly.

Margaret, always a woman of moods, found just what she wanted by keeping both men in tow. When she felt madly gay she would prance forth into the night with the young and ebullient Porchester. With everyone but her, he was completely irreverent, keeping her in stitches as he often wittily, sometimes even rudely, put them down. To Porchester the night was always young. He was not a great romantic, he was too rumbustious for that, but he was bags of fun. He never tired of trying to find new ways to amuse his prestigious girlfriend. After a night at the theatre they would dance until dawn in the various nightclubs around Jermyn Street and St. James's which had sprung up after the war. Then they would go and watch the dawn rise over the Thames, or even mingle with the crowds in Covent Garden and have a bacon-and-egg breakfast with the market porters. With Porchester, Margaret enjoyed carefree happy-go-lucky nights of abandon and the young Lord was a specialist in hunting down the various scenes which sprang up in the late forties.

But moody Margaret occasionally wanted something more artistic. She came from a family to whom music was both a serious subject and the mainstay of their recreation. She was intensely musical and when she felt like a night at the ballet or opera it was the Earl of Dalkeith to whom she turned. With the young earl she enjoyed a completely different kind of evening. They would go incognito to the theatre and then on to a small and exclusive bistro which served excellent food and wine by candlelight. These evenings would be full of pleasant, informal conversation, which always had an element of romance, for the young Earl was spiritually opposite to Porchester. He was manly in the British male aristocratic sort of way, but far more old-fashioned and staid than his buccaneering counterpart. He had a great deal of charm, but it was concealed behind his mask of good manners. Whereas Porchester could reduce the Princess to uncontrollable giggling by blowing a raspberry at a taxi driver, Dalkeith would please her by being sure to pull her chair out before she sat down. Whereas Porchester would make an ugly, ungainly mess of kissing her goodnight, Dalkeith would hesitate shyly and eventually give her an affectionate peck on the cheek. With the two men in the stable she could pick and choose her evening's entertainment by the mood of the day.

While Townsend looked on loftily from the Palace; and while Blandford and Wallace manoeuvred people in and out of the "PM Set"; and even while she created amorous situations with Porchester and Dalkeith, no end of other suitors were coming in through the back door.

She encouraged them to keep trying and occasionally, when she was bored with the company she had been keeping, or when she felt like exploiting new situations, she would allow other young blue-bloods the undoubted privilege of her company for an evening. To get through to Margaret for an appointment was an immensely tricky business. It would be less tricky when Margaret moved to Clarence House with her mother after the King had died, but in the forties and early fifties any suitor had to go through the whole rigmarole of Buckingham Palace protocol. Margaret had a private line to her own personal living quarters, but for various reasons only a handful of people had the number. If, like Blandford who was in the Palace Guards, you had access to the house phones, it was easy to get through to her by merely dialling Margaret's personal Palace number. But an outsider who had met Margaret and had been encouraged to continue the contact, making an actual date with her was desperately difficult. They were first apprehended by the Palace switch-board, a team of highly trained young ladies who have heard every single story you could think of to try to get past them. If you were able to convince them of your intentions you would probably get through to the lady-in-waiting, which at this time was Miss Jennifer Bevan. You would then request, carefully, politely and in the third person: "Lord X presents his compliments to Princess Margaret and would be honoured if she would accompany him to so and so." The lady-in-waiting would tell him that she would indeed present his compliments to Princess Margaret. Then she would put the phone down. It was completely up to the Princess whether she bothered to answer or not. Most of the time she simply ignored the request. When she genuinely could not make the appointment but did wish some kind of liaison with the caller, the lady-in-waiting would call him back. (The Palace had a special contacts file because it is thought of as too much encouragement to ask for the gentleman's telephone number.) She would say: "Princess Margaret presents her compliments to Lord X and wishes to say she is sorry she will be unable to attend so and so. However she is available on the following dates." In this way the hopeful young fellow would know she was not averse to spending an evening with him and that he must plan something spectacular which fitted in with her diary.

When he had done so and Margaret had accepted, he was passed on – without ever speaking to PM herself – to an equerry, probably Townsend, who would request a full, written detailed record of what the young suitor had in mind. Where they would go, what the transport would be, who would also be in the party – officially Margaret was not allowed out with one man all night – and he would then be given a small lecture on the dos and don'ts of taking a Princess out on the town.

A small file would be opened on this gentleman and everything known about him – such as his own, or his father's entry in *Who's Who* – would be scrutinised by various people. The King would want to know, briefly, the name of any man taking an active interest in his daughter. The police would be alerted, in a general way, of the Princess's plans. And even the press secretary would read the file, in case a news hungry reporter bumped into them late one night and wanted an item for his gossip column.

So a young man of good breeding who had danced with Margaret at a society hunt ball, and been given the impression by her that she would be agreeable to further contact, was put through a considerable experience before he was allowed through the Palace gates to collect an occasionally flippant and often non-caring Princess.

She got her emotional and physical freedom from the apron strings of her heritage in mid-1948 and managed to cling on desperately to this new-found and exquisitely exciting way of life throughout the whole of 1949. She had got London thoroughly taped by the time she was twenty in 1950, so much so that she was able to build up an intimate set within the set at large.

Before the psychologically important age of twenty-one, when she veered back into some kind of sensibility, she had a mad and catastrophic fling during her twentieth year, which left many a red face in Whitehall and Westminster and which gained her important enemies in the Palace itself.

It was as if she had to over-indulge to such an extent that she got over it, rather like employees in a chocolate factory who are allowed to eat as many chocolates as they like during the first week because the management know they will never touch another one. The now desperately ill King would not hear a word against his daughter. But in this year she laid the foundations of important political intrigues against herself which would come to fruition when she sorely needed influence and not censure.

For these three glorious years she cared nothing for what she considered to be the stuffy forces working against her. She well and truly expiated herself from the obvious frustrations of being so involved with royalty. She got up bright and early after the nightmare of the war years and was determined, almost with sheer brute force, to get her childhood out of her system.

Only the absolute loyalty of her lady-in-waiting, the constant turning a blind eye of her detective and the ever-faithful cover-up operations by Townsend, allowed her the real freedom she craved. She abandoned herself to the dubious glory of every new experience. She spoiled herself and learnt how to giggle until her heart ached; she learnt how to love and, more especially, how to deal with the men with whom she temporarily shared a liaison.

In these halcyon nights – for by now she did not see much of the day – she experienced some kind of physical, mental, emotional, spiritual, or social contact with nearly all the most eligible bachelors in Europe. They only went to clubs where the management, for good reasons, would ensure their uninterrupted gaiety.

The men who drifted in and out of her life during this period tried to give her everything they had. They amused her, they taught her the ways of their world; they aroused all the gay sensuality and sexuality which had been forced down inside her by the protocol of her position and rank.

There was not, for these three years, a young-blood or roué in London worth his salt who did not try to court her. Many succeeded. Many failed. But they closed ranks to protect her reputation. The British press *never* had any kind of go at her although sometimes they were straining at the leash. The continental press were less hamstrung.

They printed every last detail they could get their hands on.

Margaret drank too much, smoked too much and stayed out too often, too late. Everyone knew but her father, who remained oblivious to his daughter's outrages. Much of this was because Townsend protected her in the King's eyes. Very little of the truth actually filtered through to him and he refused to believe that which did.

He rose at eight a.m. sharp and regularly went to Margaret's bedroom and found her sleeping peacefully. He did not ever discover that she was often shamming sleep and had arrived home and dashed through her toilet only minutes before he arrived.

Margaret had become sport with several of the favourite escorts. Mark Bonham Carter, one of her oldest favourites, actually tried to fight a duel with Lord Porchester one morning because Porchester had talked openly about "sharing the same pillow" with Margaret. They ended up in Hyde Park and Porchester got off with a bloody nose.

On another occasion Lord Rupert Nevill had to get Margaret back to his town house and fill her with black coffee because she had tried to dance through Trafalgar Square looking for the pigeons. She and Sonny Blandford had only narrowly missed being taken to West End Central Police Station by a couple of very young, inexperienced policemen.

So it was that she loosened up from the tight, inbred, precocious world of an overindulgent childhood into the fully promiscuous world of post-war Britain. She discovered at least that her previous experiences in love had been but childish whimsy. Now she found new passions which could only be quenched by something more than a goodnight kiss at the Palace gates. She now knew she could control men with all the guile and ingenuity of the female species – in fact, what most full-blooded women find at that stage in their lives. She found there was a lot more to men than a dancing partner or an arm to hold.

Many men flitted through her life and briefly got a mention from William Hickey in the *Daily Express*. Mr. Tom Egerton, a rich young ex-Captain from the Guards who she had known during the Windsor period, escorted her from time to time. Lord Ogilvy, eldest son of the Earl of Airlie, successfully invited her to many a society function. They were on the fringe of the PM Set and went in and out of favour, but they never got really close to Margaret in any romantic sense.

Few of them had the attributes of young Dalkeith, who was not only highly personable, but enjoyed no less than five stately homes sitting in half a million acres of prime farm land in England and Scotland, and a personal fortune of well over a million pounds. This in itself did not unduly impress Margaret, but Dalkeith was able to provide both the setting and the security when Margaret had one of her periodic yearnings to get away from it all.

Out of all of them, probably the one man who got closest to Margaret, perhaps along with Sonny Blandford, was Mark Bonham Carter, a son of one of England's most distinguished Liberal families. He had dual qualities, both of which endeared him to the Princess. He was not only both keenly intelligent and knowledgeable, but also capable of sustained evenings of gaiety and fun. He could switch moods with Margaret and either drink and dance the night away or sit and talk quietly in front of the fire about poetry or music. He was a companion in the truest sense of the word and Margaret often sought him out in preference to any others. He remains a friend to this day and in times of trouble, of which Margaret has had more than her fair share, Bonham-Carter has been one of the few people she could completely rely on to help her back to some kind of tranquillity.

In theory, Princess Margaret Rose was never allowed out of Buckingham Palace on her own with one man alone. Most of the time it was expected that she would go out with a party of people which included at least Miss Bevan and the Princess's personal detective. Much of the time this worked and both these people had quickly to adapt to the nightlife. They would sit discreetly in a corner of whatever club they found themselves and whatever they indulged in during the evening was added to Margaret's personal bill. (The bill was never presented but Palace equerries would make sure of requesting it the following morning. No Royal ever has cash on any outing. But the Palace is highly efficient at paying up any bill within twenty-four hours of its incurrence.)

In practice Margaret managed to spend many hours alone with men without any other escort. Miss Bevan had been chosen personally by Margaret because of her ability to look the other way when Margaret wanted some fun. The detective just had to do the best he could and put up with it if Margaret gave him the slip. A typical example was when Porchester took her to a Guard's ball at Maidenhead on the River Thames. It was a beautiful summer's night with a full moon which shimmered across the silver river. Just after midnight a slightly bemused and perturbed Porchester noticed that Margaret had disappeared. The lady-in-waiting was sent to look for her in the loo and the detective did a short reccy around the building. No one caused any open alarm but within a short while the local police had been informed the Princess was missing. It was merely precautionary – those knowing PM well had got used to such disappearances – but it would be their head on the block if anything had happened to her.

An hour later, as the party was beginning to wind up at about 3.30 a.m. Margaret swept back into the ballroom.

She had, she told them with her most innocent and bland voice, been taken up the Thames by a Guards officer in a canoe. "It was so romantic," she mused as Porchester wagged his finger in her face and told her she was naughty. Miss Bevan smiled at the detective who looked up at the ceiling and whistled lowly. The local police were informed that all was well and an hour later they were whisking down past London airport on their way back to the Palace.

During the following year, when the whole family spent their annual holiday at Balmoral – Townsend was the equerry as usual – Miss Bevan, a generous, indulgent woman who perhaps knew Margaret better than anyone else on earth, smiled significantly to herself when she heard Margaret's choice of song for that evening. The audience was filled with a mixture of dignitaries and church elders. They looked forward to the dulcet strains of a Scottish hymn or traditional ballad. Instead she sat down at the piano and with a completely straight face, but a definite glint in her eye, sang *I'm Just a Girl Who Can't Say No*.

Miss Bevan mused later that the audience did clap, but very uncertainly.

It was during this same trip to Scotland in the summer of 1951, when Margaret had her twenty-first at Balmoral, that she re-kindled her affection for Peter Townsend. By now the Group Captain had gained promotion. From equerry he went on to become Deputy Master of the Household under the Master, Sir Piers Liegh. As second-in-command his new duty was the domestic administration of all the royal households, a very considerable responsibility. And, as with most master and deputy situations, it was the deputy who did most of the day-to-day work.

One of the things Townsend had to contend with, and he was brilliant at it, was Palace politics. His new appointment, over the heads of many others, some of them clearly more senior than he, caused a great deal of bickering and Palace jealousy. He quite clearly and coolly took command of the situation, as he had after every promotion in the RAF, and anyone who gave him trouble, after he had tried to work with them, was quickly and efficiently removed.

Despite his new position, he was still far too indispensable to the Royal family itself to be allowed merely to sit at his desk at Buckingham Palace. He was given a larger staff than ever before, received a much higher salary, much prestige, and was still required as Equerry-in-Waiting (in itself a promotion) when the family went to Balmoral.

Prince Philip was now firmly implanted into the way of life of the Royal family, and he was present this year at the family's Scottish home. He never did entirely approve of Townsend who he felt had insinuated himself rather too much into the affections of his parents-in-law. Indeed, it seemed to him sometimes, they treated Townsend as a closer member of the family than they did himself. Townsend himself noted Philip's coolness, and was wary of it, but not perturbed. While he shared the King's confidence, and while he had the obvious affection of the Queen and Margaret, he knew that any indignation from Philip would be quietly ignored as "bad form".

But with this in mind he was very happy to find how PM sought out his company more and more each day. Away from the lights of London, Margaret was frankly bored stiff. Her father was ailing in health and her mother's attentions were continually aimed towards him. Elizabeth was ecstatically married to a new husband and they kept very much to themselves, going for long walks with Baby Charles. Miss Bevan was a bosom-pal, but hardly stimulating as a constant companion, and Balmoral was just as restricting as any other royal household.

So for diversion she turned to the ever-willing Townsend. They walked a good deal, but more than anything else, they spent long hours on horseback seeking out all the glorious nooks and crannies of the estate and beyond into the tors, lochs and forests of the Scottish countryside. "PT" was considered completely "safe" by the family and one of the very few men she was allowed to go out with unescorted.

During this trip Townsend was amazed to find out how much the Princess had changed. She was clearly years older now than the Margaret who had shown him such obvious affection during the trip to South Africa. No longer did she need to flaunt those little acts of femininity which he had found so childish but endearing. For the first time she made it clear that she wanted a little more from the equerry than kind and indulgent sympathy and companionship. Despite his first nervous reactions Townsend found himself responding to the new situation with an alarming zest. At last they knew they were physically attracted to each other.

The estate workers at Balmoral are super-secretive about anything to do with the Royal family. But during this year even they could not help talking among themselves. It would be ages before the rest of the world woke up to learn of the romance. But those rustic and intrepid Scotsmen knew all about it almost certainly before the Queen herself.

They got very used to seeing the two canter off for long hours by horseback into the most inaccessible areas of the wild Scottish countryside.

Woodsmen turned away when Margaret and Townsend suddenly appeared through a copse, walking hand in hand, or running after each other as if he were a squire lecherously chasing a young dairymaid. The gamekeeper swore under his breath when he knew the loving couple had visited a clearing made out for the feeding of game. They had disturbed hundreds of birds.

In the local pub they quietly swapped yarns and all came to the conclusion that the affection between the couple had suddenly become a lot more serious.

Apart from these memories there is only one monument to their love in this period which still exists. On the top of a wind-swept tor there is a cairn, now some six-foot high, which the couple assembled during this holiday at Balmoral.

The locals, who are fiercely proud of the Monarch's traditional links with the estate, will remain silent if you ask them which one it is. But they know. Each year on Margaret's birthday a small, hand-picked bunch of them climb the mountain and add a few rocks.

Cairns were the traditional way in which any Scottish highland family – in the rural areas at least – remembered any serious family anniversary. It was a small monument of loose rocks to which they added some more every year until, after generations, it became quite a size. Young lovers would traditionally start one during the year they fell in love. They would add to it on each anniversary of their betrothal. Margaret and Townsend put the first stones together during their stay in Balmoral and added rocks to it. Occasionally, just very occasionally, on her now infrequent trips to Balmoral, Margaret has ridden out to the same hillside and, looking a little wistful and perhaps a little sad, she has picked up a rock and added it to the pile.

The first time the "PM Set" really knew something had changed was at Margaret's twenty-first birthday party when she was on her finest impish form. Her parents gave her a lavish do at Balmoral where the whole Margaret Set descended in force for a weekend of revelry. The three most hotly tipped bachelors, Billy Wallace, Lord Dalkeith and Lord Ogilvy, had all been invited and Princess Margaret got immense enjoyment out of seeing them vie for positions close to her. As she walked on to the dance floor she had requested the band to play *Diamonds are a Girl's Best Friend.* This was a "thank you" to the three men, all of whom had bought her diamonds. But it was the last thank you they would get during the visit. Margaret spent the rest of the time ignoring them and as they tried to get close to her to ask her to dance, she would flit off and find another unsuspecting partner. She did manage the last dance with someone who was certainly not tipped as a hot favourite, Peter Townsend.

Because of this her new affection for Townsend did not catch the public eye for a long time and the press continued to speculate about the "men in her life".

During November 1951 the latest beau in favour was Lord Plunket, known to Margaret and all his other friends as Patrick. He was a traditional fun-lover of the old school and managed to keep up with Margaret's late nights in London. He was not at all sure he liked Margaret's habit of suddenly ditching him during the course of the evening and rushing off to dance with any one of the dozen young men who had set their eyes on the Princess. Lord Plunket thought he would steal one over all of them. One evening he romantically asked Margaret if she would go to Paris with him on a spree. It was a daring venture and one which Margaret took to immediately. Poor Plunket had no idea what he was letting himself in for. He thought he would introduce Margaret to new pastures. He was a known face at such "In" establishments as Jimmy's where a fellow guest was often the Duke of Windsor. He pictured himself squiring Margaret around the Paris he knew so well and impressing her with his worldly knowledge. Things went wrong for him and his little tête-à-tête from the very beginning.

The King was very happy to agree to his twenty-one-year-old daughter going off to Paris, but he did not quite see the trip as Plunket did. Margaret's aunt, Marina, the chic Duchess of Kent, said she hadn't been shopping in Paris for years and wouldn't it be fun for them both to go. Margaret was delighted. The British Ambassador in Paris, Sir Oliver Harvey, immediately set about making up a comprehensive programme for the British Princess and when the party finally left London, Plunket found himself accompanied by Margaret's personal maid Miss Robina MacDonald, the Queen's lady of the bedchamber, Lady Jean Rankin, the Queen's secretary, Capt. Oliver Dawnay, two Scotland Yard detectives and two servants for the Duchess. The party numbered eleven in all and Margaret seemed so excited by the trip she ignored Lord Plunket most of the time.

The Royal group literally stormed Paris for four days and Margaret had a whale of a time. The two detectives took it in turns to go with her because she hardly slept for a minute during the visit. It genuinely took two of them to keep a guard on her and they did it in twelve-hour shifts. There was at least one official engagement each day and sometimes two. Margaret, for instance, lunched with the President one day and attended a Charity Ball with the British Ambassador that evening.

But between the official engagements Margaret flung herself into Paris society with a vengeance. The French press immediately dubbed her *La Petite* (The Little One) and her every nod and wink was captured on the pages of all the French newspapers and magazines. On the third day she had a small engagement in the morning and the rest of the day was her own. She devoted herself to getting the best out of Paris. She lunched at a small Bistro with the Duchess and her sister, Princess Olga of Yugoslavia. Then on to the Eiffel Tower for a wind-swept visit to the top. She whisked down the Champs Elysées to visit Dior where she quickly ordered four evening dresses, three day dresses, two hats and some perfume. Then on to a private supper gathering at Chantilly where Sir Duff and Lady Cooper entertained her. It was a night they all remember. The hit tune in France at the time was *La Ronde de l'Amour (Love's Roundabout)* from the film *La Ronde*. Everyone was singing it and Margaret could not get the tune out of her head. It was so typically Parisienne and entirely fitted her mood of the time.

The champagne flowed in a night-club atmosphere and French guitarist Jacques Fevrier and coloured blues singer Gordon Heath played French, Scottish, English and Welsh songs all evening. They all sang a hearty chorus of *Green Grow the Rushes O* and *Auld Lang Syne* as the clock struck midnight. As the singing died down Margaret made sure the party did not come to an end by sitting down to the piano herself to play *Love's Roundabout*. She told them she just had to play it. It was like a compulsion. She had not been able to get the tune out of her head. She had no music and experimented a little before plunging right into the song. The other musicians struck up with her and someone even found an accordion to give it that Parisian touch. Margaret played for an hour. Greta Garbo slinkily lounged against the piano and Cecil Beaton, the photographer, passed the drinks around. At four a.m. Margaret was flushed with happiness and was still determined the party would not end. Her hosts by this time were running out of ideas to keep the night swinging. But Margaret answered their problems. They all put their mink coats over their evening dresses and piled out on to the extensive lawns surrounding the house. There Plunket and the detective lit a bonfire and Lady Diana Cooper supplied half a hundredweight of chestnuts fresh from the local woods, as the dawn came up over the French countryside the revellers ate a breakfast of chestnuts and warmed their hands on the fire. They sang camp fire songs, like *Frere Jacques*, and when they eventually broke up the party they drove in the early morning rush hour back to their official residence.

Princess Margaret does not generally like to get up early. After one of her usual sprees she would often sleep until 11 a.m. But in Paris she was determined to get as much into the four days as possible. She slept for a mere two hours and was then up, breakfasted and ready to go by about 9.30. After a morning of shopping she had lunch with General Eisenhower who was on an official visit to France, then an afternoon of sightseeing and back home to prepare for the biggest spree of all. It was Friday night. She would return to Britain the following day. Friday night is traditionally the hot night of a Paris week. Margaret selected a party of the most fashionable people in Paris and they all started off at Maximes, the famous centre of Parisian high living in the Rue Royale. Margaret sat down in a stunning white satin gown which left her shoulders bare and did everything to show her feminity at its best. In the party of twelve was the Duchess of Kent, Princess Olga, her husband Prince Paul of Yugoslavia and their son "Nicky". There was also the Comte de Ribes, a dashing playboy with dazzling dark eyes and the Spanish millionaire Carlos de Bestuigi, another amorous and available bachelor. Poor Lord Plunket could not get a look in.

The Comte had already ordered the menu. They started with cold consommé madrilene and cheese puffs; then they got stuck into a filet of sole; lobster cooked in liqueur; roast saddle of lamb with artichoke hearts stuffed with asparagus tips and served with cheese sauce; to top it all they had an omelette surprise. Throughout the repast they gulped down two cases of the best pink champagne and finished the meal with large brandies. For a while none of them could leave the table, they were so full. But eventually Margaret's feet started tapping to the music and she danced with each male member of the party.

When they had fully digested at about one o'clock it was time for hotter stuff. In three huge cars they went to Jimmy's where they danced the rumba for nearly an hour. Then the cars sped across an almost silent Paris to the Monseigneur Club, one of the plushest in the world, with its thick blue carpeting, blue velvet walls, tiny red table lamps and bunches of deep red roses in big black vases on every table. As they entered the club the band struck up *Love's Roundabout* and Margaret immediately swept on to the dance floor with Prince Paul before the party had even got to their tables.

Margaret was clearly in her seventh heaven as she samba-ed with the Comte, and rumba-ed to *Temptation* with Prince "Nicky". At Margaret's special request, as the night came to an end, twelve Hungarian violinists gathered around their table to play *Love's Roundabout* just for them. All the party hummed with the violins and Margaret sang the tune all the way back to London the following day.

The British press carried dozens of pictures of Margaret letting her hair down and, while Prince Philip tut-tutted, the King's attitude remained: "Jolly good luck to her." Townsend looked on from a distance, rather amused.

To the handful of people who were close to the King, it was obvious he was dying slowly and painfully. He now spent most of his life on painkilling drugs and was intensely short of breath. In the autumn of 1951 he had an operation for the removal of one of his lungs. After the operation the surgeons quietly told the Queen that it was only a matter of time. He would not be able to hold out much longer. The King himself was not unaware of the oncoming disaster and was now doing everything he could to make sure Elizabeth was prepared to take over. She and Prince Philip left on a tour of Canada, a carefully conceived exercise in which she would learn all she could about the workings of a Royal Tour. She would endear herself completely to the Canadian people, and later to President Truman, who raved about her to his friends for years afterwards.

It was the year, also, of the Festival of Britain, an exercise in British pride and prestige which was supposed to herald the end of the fighting forties and the beginning of the fortunate fifties. It was close to the King's heart and all the Royal family were pressed into giving it great interest and support. The King bravely visited the Festival several times, including the official opening, and very few of the British public knew what intense pain he was really in.

By now, off duty the King had become an almost unbearable companion. His pain and lack of breath made him immensely tetchy and irritable. In the end only his wife, his daughters and Peter Townsend could talk to him without getting a grumbling reply. He relied more and more on his equerry to carry out his personal wishes to the rest of the Palace staff. The King planned a health-restoring trip to South Africa, a place for which he enjoyed a peculiar affection and affinity, early the next year. King George and Townsend spent long hours talking about it and Peter was assigned to go out to South Africa immediately after Christmas to find a suitable house, away from it all, and generally set the whole thing up. During this period PT became extremely close to the King, in a personal way rarely enjoyed by any member of the royal household. In this capacity his favour with the Queen became concrete. She was very grateful that someone could handle her husband, and even make him happy during these trying times.

That Christmas the whole family went, as usual, to Sandringham. It was a touching Christmas for the Royal family. They were all aware that it would probably be their last together. It was during these two emotionally charged weeks that the friendship between Townsend and Princess Margaret even got closer and deeper.

Despite her fun-loving late nights, her hosts of boyfriends, her teasing and her reputation, Margaret found herself extremely pleased to be back in the company of the elder equerry. He gave solace, encouragement, affection and worldly wisdom. Margaret had flitted with him, flirted with him, flaunted in front of him and eventually found in him the kind of man she had always really craved. During that Christmas she found herself inescapably falling deeper in love with him. And, more important, for the first time, Peter Townsend himself was beginning to realise that his own future was being inexorably drawn to hers. During that Christmas, Queen Elizabeth and Princess Margaret had a "mother-and-daughter chat", the subject of which the King was never told.

Chapter Ten

In the unlucky thirteen years of the tempestuous relationship between Princess Margaret and Peter Townsend, 1952 was remembered as the year in which the storm clouds gathered. The breezes of flirtation and the soft winds of love were blasted away by the black sombre clouds of oncoming gloom.

The year dawned bright for the lovers and the early months would signify probably the first and certainly the last of their true halcyon days. It all started well enough. On January 2nd Princess Elizabeth and Prince Philip left for a long tour of the Commonwealth. King George and the Queen were spending the winter at Balmoral with Margaret. Townsend was as usual the equerry-in-waiting. Each day had fallen into a pattern. The King would go shooting each morning as Margaret and Townsend attended their duties. Then the two would go riding for an hour or two and meet up with the royal shooting party for a picnic lunch on the grouse moors. The Queen would join them by Landrover. Then Townsend would ride back to the castle to continue his work. He often dined with the family.

On these rides they became the young lovers they had always yearned to be. As they sped and galloped across the moors they shrieked with excitement, raced each other, and finally stopped to fling themselves into each others' arms for a loving embrace. They said nothing to the rest of the family but it was obvious to everyone that they had become the closest of affectionate friends. The King was, as always, delighted to see his daughter so happy. The Queen Mother wisely decided on a course of discretion. The Queen, who knew Margaret extremely well and had been party to her vow of secret love, guessed exactly what was going on and at this stage was even gently amused by it. But not one took it seriously enough to even contemplate a further marriage. And the reason the couple simply *had* to try and cover their relationship was that Peter Townsend was still very married. Innocent flirtations on a "cousin" relationship were one thing. Falling in love was completely another.

Neither knew, in their wild Scottish embraces, that the whole thing was fast coming to a head.

On the night of February 5th Townsend had supper with the family and, seeing they all seemed more exhausted than usual he retired early to his "hideous" Victorian bedroom.

The King amused himself with a jig-saw puzzle as Margaret played the piano. At about 9.45 p.m. the King got up without finishing the puzzle. His daughter stopped playing and fitted the last few pieces into place for him. The King said it had been a long day and kissed his wife and daughter goodnight. He retired at just a little after ten. The following morning, at just after seven, the royal valet, James McDonald, crept stealthily into the King's bedroom and pulled back the curtains. He had no need for caution or quietness, as he found out when he got to the bed. King George VI, the reluctant monarch, had died in his sleep and a new Elizabethan age was about to begin. McDonald was immediately struck with emotion. He had been a loyal servant to the Royal family for most of his life. He quietly covered the King's head with bedclothes and went to wake up Peter Townsend. Peter Townsend took immediate charge of the situation. The family physician was called for and the equerry woke up the Queen's lady-in-waiting and told her he requested an immediate and urgent audience with the Queen concerning something of the utmost importance. By the time he was ushered into her drawing room he knew she had guessed what he was going to say. It was a moving moment and the Queen sobbed silently for several minutes. She would tell Margaret herself, but would Townsend please make the necessary arrangements for informing the Prime Minister and, later, for an official statement to go out from Balmoral after the doctor's visit. Townsend quietly and efficiently did all this within the next twenty minutes. He then helped the Queen draft a telegram to Elizabeth, giving her the bad news and recalling her to England. Despite the gloom of death over the castle, it hummed with activity as the royal household made all the necessary preparations for the announcement of the death of the King.

For some time Princess Elizabeth had carried a small buff envelope around with her wherever she went. In it were personal instructions from her father in the case of his death. There was also a copy of the formal declaration she would have to make on the day of Accession, and draft messages to both houses of Parliament. Elizabeth and Philip had been given a hunting lodge in the tiny native town of Sagano in Kenya as a wedding present. At the time of the death they were visiting it for the first time. They were trying to have a second honeymoon virtually on their own in the lodge. The news of her father's death was not completely unexpected. After the first initial grief Elizabeth and Philip opened the envelope and read the contents. They were clear and simple, without any kind of personal touch or message. She and Philip made the necessary arrangements to fly back that night. As they touched down at London airport she was still wearing one of the light summery dresses she had packed for the tour. The Queen changed into mourning dress at the airport. She sped into central London after saying only: "This is a very tragic homecoming."

Winston Churchill came immediately to extend his condolences. He was unashamedly weeping and this set the new Queen off herself. They sobbed together for several minutes before Churchill took his leave. Then Queen Mary came into the room. She was a very old lady by now, but still extremely grand with it, as she had always been. Almost like a psychic she had predicted this day. Even at the age of eighty-four she was regal and sprightly. She curtsied to her grand-daughter. "I wanted your old granny to be the first of your subjects to kiss your hand, Your Majesty," she said proudly but sympathetically. All her years of painstaking coaching and tuition were now bearing fruit. After offering her respect to the Monarch, Queen Mary became a grandmother again. She told the Queen her dress was a little too short for mourning. Even as she spoke, the first despatch box had arrived from the Foreign Office.

After lying in state for a week there was a funeral at Windsor

Castle and a Commemorative service at Westminster Abbey. Margaret's fun life had come suddenly and quickly to an end. She was withdrawn, beside herself with grief and could hardly picture a life without her "beloved Papa".

Peter Townsend was a pillar of strength. He was himself deep in an emotional chasm as his marriage broke up. He had a deep and genuine sympathy for Margaret and she turned to him constantly for solace. She gave up the nightlife for months and turned instead to the Church. She became so devout that many speculated she would actually become a nun.

Margaret was by now every inch a fully-developed woman, both physically and emotionally. She had had her sprees and knew how to enjoy herself. But her father's death signalled a time of reckoning. For a time it cut her down, suddenly, from the pedestal of her own importance. Elizabeth was by this time so involved with the tremendous responsibility of assuming the throne that her anguish became stilled by the overbearing hand of duty. Margaret, on the other hand, had simply lost a father, and one to whom she was incredibly close. The gay "La Petite" became pensive, sad, glossy-eyed and truculent as the events of history teemed on around her. Margaret was her father's angel; and, equally, he was her ultimate hero. She felt his loss perhaps more than anyone else on earth and for nearly a year, it took its toll. As "Daddy's girl" she had been spoilt and pampered. King George had often told his closest aides – and Peter Townsend was one of them – that his "Meggy" could have got away with murder. She could never do any wrong. She would pout her lips, cajole a favour, smile sweetly or endear him with her eyes; he succumbed gracefully to all and any of these girlish charms with an indulgent approval. Margaret, on the other hand, returned this kind of relationship by doting on her father. This was part ambition. Margaret always wanted her own way and having father on your side was as good as getting it. But it was mainly because she genuinely and dearly loved him. As a father he was extremely lovable and Margaret, unexposed to the world outside as she had been for most of her life, showered affection upon him.

So when George died there was a sudden and massive gap in the emotional life of the young Princess. No longer did she seek the fly-by-night happiness of drink, dancing and *risqué* affairs. The gap was too wide for that. Her security and emotional stability had been wrecked. None of the young men with whom she had danced away the night were able to give her even a little of the strength she had gained by returning to a house governed by the stability of her father.

It was in this mood that she turned, finally and irretrievably, to the only other man on whom she knew she could depend: Peter Townsend. One day, in a moment of extreme grief she hugged him close to her and, with her head on his shoulder in classical style, she cried bitterly as he consoled her. He was tender and sweet, in a fatherly way, he pecked her affectionately on the forehead and tried to dry her tears with his hanky. Townsend was immensely tough and had never once showed any signs of weakening, but he was by no means an unsympathetic person when it came to the emotions of a lady. He was himself deeply hurt and upset by the breakdown of his own marriage. In a sense both Townsend and Margaret cried on each other's shoulders and for a while created strength for each other. This was a new kind of contribution to their ultimate relationship. Townsend was now no longer merely the man of fantasy for whom Margaret had had secret desires; he was no longer merely a companion with whom she could ride into romantic sunsets; he was no longer the always-dependable dogs-body who could be trusted to make sure Margaret's favourite brand of cigarettes had been packed before any journey. Now Townsend was also desperately needed in a truly emotional sense and for a while Princess Margaret actually replaced her affections towards her father with those towards the Group Captain.

Of all the stages of their unpredictable romance this was the one that really sealed their love together. She had cocked a flirtatious eye at him as a teenager in the corridors of Buck House; she had whimsically flirted with him on Table Mountain; they had tested their affections by building a cairn on a Scottish hillside; they had held hands on runaway nights through London town; they had declared their love for each other at a Balmoral Christmas; now, on the King's death, they flung themselves into the very depths of emotion towards each other. She no longer needed him merely as a man, but as a mentor and a father figure. The secrecy of the affair had built the wall, now the desperation and sadness provided the cement.

Townsend now wholeheartedly acknowledged something which had given him many a sleepless night. He knew that whether he liked it or not, he was falling madly in love with the young Princess. As it happened, he liked it not. For a start it was political and social suicide, and Peter was always ambitious. While he was sure Margaret would return the love, he was bitter over the whole question of marriage. He was also well aware that he was married and had two sons. This made him impossible as a royal choice, even after a divorce. Whatever way he looked at it as he tossed and turned during countless worried nights, the whole situation was a mess.

It was in this mood that they had embraced to console each other over the death of the King. Margaret told him, significantly, as she was to tell a close friend in a letter later, that the only way in which she could see life in the future without her father, was with Townsend being close to her. He told her that it was his earnest wish to stay close to her for the rest of his life. It was the first time they had actually spelled the possibility of marriage itself.

There was another small element which contributed to Margaret's immediate loneliness in the distraught period after her father's death. Her lady-in-waiting, Jennifer Bevan, married Captain John Lowther and the couple went off to live in Chelsea. Miss Bevan had an immensely important place in Margaret's household. Margaret had tended to rely on her for almost everything. But she was also a valuable confidante and companion, probably being closer to Margaret during her late teens and early twenties, than anyone else on earth. She had shared her doubts and anxieties, helped cover up Margaret's indiscretions, looked after her when she was surrounded by bores, kept the detective entertained when Margaret wanted to go off somewhere at a party, and generally mucked in and helped whenever something went wrong. The two giggled together like schoolgirls, discussed the various boyfriends, went shopping for make-up and other female necessities, and generally behaved like a couple of young ladies out on the town.

When Jennifer Bevan married it was another sad loss to Margaret. Miss Iris Peake took over as principal lady-in-waiting, but no one was to ever get as close to Margaret as Jennifer.

Margaret also turned, wholeheartedly, to the Church. To the nation it seemed as if she was mourning her father. The Queen Mother knew that she attended services because she was also rather confused, even a little guilty about her deep love for Peter Townsend.

The Queen Mother saw her daughter's terrible consternation in all sorts of little ways. She is an extraordinarily sensitive, sensible and sympathetic woman. At first she had a heart-to-heart chat with her daughter, talking of Townsend and the situation, in the third person and never using his name. It was clear to Margaret her mother had guessed her feelings. Margaret was still emotionally upset, but she made it very, very clear indeed that she was determined to get her way.

The Queen Mother, as she often did, went to see Princess Alice at Clock House. The Princess advised her to do nothing. To forbid their relationship was merely to foster it. Margaret, added the Princess, would come to her senses soon enough when she saw the obstacles against such a liaison. She advised the Queen Mother to have a frank talk with Townsend and she asked her to send her daughter over for tea one day so that they could have a sensible chat.

The Queen Mother was herself extremely fond of Peter Townsend and under normal circumstances would have welcomed him dearly as a son-in-law. But she found her own chat with him rather difficult. They did not mention Margaret but Townsend let it be known that his marriage was on the rocks. He said that he thought his wife wanted a divorce and that they had only deferred it because of embarrassment to the Royal family. The Queen Mother told him that if the marriage was irreconcilable, they must, of course, be free to divorce, but he would have to leave Buckingham Palace. With a great deal of political sensitivity, she told Townsend he could take over as head of her own household at Clarence House where she and

Margaret were about to move. This took Townsend away from any damage to the Queen, and put him well and truly under her mother's nose.

But more important it meant that he could go on seeing his beloved Princess. Indeed, they would be living in the same house for now Townsend rarely went home to his wife.

Thirdly, he could divorce. This had been hanging over him for more than a year and he was now aware that his wife was having an affair with John Adolphus de Laszlo, the famous painter's son whom she later married.

He was indebted to the Queen Mother for all this sensible and sympathetic action. And it was his regard for her, fostered more than ever at this time, that finally made him listen to her when the crunch came.

The Queen Mother's idea, backed by Princess Alice, was to let the whole thing explode and blow itself out. With hindsight they could not have been more intelligent about it. At the time Townsend's shooting star was soaring to the heavens. He could not imagine a life without Margaret. But, as usual, the halcyon days were numbered and, as it always did, the rocket would one day explode and fizzle into a damp squib as Townsend had second thoughts.

Margaret's devotions continued. She saw two priests regularly for private study and she discussed with them the whole question of adultery and divorce. It was clear she was trying to reconcile her ambitions with her devotion to God. They helped her all they could but there was no way in which they could find a way out of her problems. The issue was cut-and dried. Adultery was banned in the commandments themselves. Canon law, to say nothing of the civil laws affecting royalty, did not recognise divorce once the marriage vows had been spoken in a church. It was a troubled time for Margaret and she suffered greatly as she tried to battle it all out in her mind. Townsend himself had great misgivings and told her about them constantly. With him, she had no doubts. They *must* be allowed to love and that was that.

After the funeral at Windsor on February 15th 1952, Townsend was fully employed managing the changeover at Buckingham Palace. Elizabeth and Philip were moving from Clarence

House to Buckingham Palace, the Queen Mother and Margaret were moving from Buckingham Palace into Clarence House. There was a lot to be done before the official residences were taken up on May 5th. Just after the move had taken place Townsend went and had a long, frank talk with his wife. They both agreed they wanted a divorce and Townsend pressed home the fact that he should divorce her, not the other way round. Because she was, in fact, having a relationship with de Laszlo, and because she fully understood Townsend's relationship with the Palace, she agreed.

As it was done in those days, the "evidence" was set up, a private eye employed and Mrs. Townsend's adultery was witnessed and proved. By August the case had been prepared and just before Christmas a small item in *The Times* announced that Peter Townsend had been granted a divorce because of his wife's adultery.

An order for the custody of the two sons was granted to Peter Townsend, but by mutual consent their care and control were to remain with the mother until further order of the court. This meant, in effect, that Townsend had it his way. He was not able to look after them there and then, but could call upon the court to release them from their mother's care, if and when he married again.

To the outside world Margaret seemed to eventually recover from the doldrums after her father's death and continue being the gay young Princess they had always known and generally loved. She put on a great public façade and kept the gossip columnists guessing almost every day as she got back into the swinging nightlife of London. Her words to her sister when the crowd had teased her about Philip, now had great significance. She was having a full-blown adult affair and absolutely no one outside close family knew about it. And even they were not sure. Only Jennifer Bevan, confidante and lady-in-waiting, had been brought completely into the conspiracy.

The only noticeable change in the Princess was that she did not stay out all night. After an evening at the theatre, she would perhaps enjoy a bite to eat and maybe a dance, but she rarely stayed much after midnight. The Margaret Set, which had been in abeyance since the King died, thought she had grown up a lot in the interim period. They put her early nights down to reform as she grew older. In fact she was scurrying back to the sanctity of Clarence House, where Peter awaited her.

The British Court, any Court in history come to that, is by nature incestuous. Even during Queen Victoria's day it was where the real politics in matters of state were played. Her son Edward had little interest outside the boudoir and lost the Monarch's grip on political influence. The job of his equerries was, frankly, to secure an unending line of licentious young ladies for his pleasure. He was a libertine of the first order and the scandals surrounding his monarchy still reverberate around his Dominions.

George V did much to try to regain political influence in his court and, certainly, Queen Mary was regally old-fashioned and a continual reminder of the old adage of a woman behind every great man. But times were changing. Under George VI, the monarchy lost all but a semblance of real power. Under Elizabeth the power is ritualistic and symbolic rather than influential. She still functions as Head of State and is technically important both as a passer of laws and a creator of foreign influence. But, in the corridors of her various households, the intrigues of old are seldom heard. No longer can a young and dashing Earl of Buckingham intrigue for his family interests by getting close to the throne. No longer can an Archbishop of Canterbury start wars against the Catholic nations. And no longer can the Queen order political opponents to the Tower of London if they speak against her.

Yet her court is remarkably similar to the courts of old in everything but its intense national political activity. This still exists, but it is now seldom realised outside the buildings themselves. The Monarch remains head of a small village, numbering a few hundred people, to whom she is the absolute matriarch.

As all villages do, it hums with gossip. Everything that happens in the Palace gets reported down through the line to the last kitchen helper. If the Queen asks for an aspirin there will be endless speculations through the entire Palace power structure, as to whether she has a cold coming, or whether that glass of port last night had given her a headache.

A worried look, a frown of temper, a smile or just a simple nod, will produce post-mortems and induce explanations as to what any of them could have meant.

A few words of wisdom, as Prince Philip is helped to undress, can be reported back down the hierarchy until it has been thoroughly digested by the last page and footman.

And so it was that, by the smallest actions, hardly discernible to any outsider, Margaret and Townsend revealed their love to the rest of the Palace staff. The way they smiled at each other. Or touched hands briefly as they passed; or the fact that she suddenly, in a moment of weakness, called him Peter to a third party. Each tiny speck of tittle-tattle got outrageously consumed until it was simply understood that the couple were in love.

By the time the Townsend divorce came through, just before Christmas 1952, it was no longer rumour but a firmly established fact in the minds of the staff. However hard she tried to live up to her childhood dream of keeping her love affairs secret, neither she nor Townsend could escape the gossip of either Clarence House, or the Palace.

There is a small, almost élite corps of Fleet Street veterans who do little else but keep their ears cocked towards Buckingham Palace and the Royal family. In the main they follow them on official engagements and tours and merely report what happens. But they make it their duty to inhabit the various pubs around Victoria and Buckingham Palace, and come to that, the other households, and drink with Palace staff. Often they don't even introduce themselves, sometimes they strike up a working bargain with an underfootman or a kitchen porter.

And it is in this way that the nation gets to know about the inside workings of Buckingham Palace. By the time any official press statement is made, these men and women have already built up a useable dossier on the event about to take place. The marriage of Mark Phillips and Princess Anne was a typical example. Fleet Street knew it was on the cards, despite a Palace denial, months before the official announcement.

By the time 1953 had become a month old, the Townsend–Margaret story had got into dossier form. The tittle-tattle had filtered down through the grapevine to the Star and Garter public house near Victoria Station where it was picked up by a young lady who worked for a glossy woman's magazine. Bit by bit the gossip columnists started to take an interest in the Group Captain. Foreign magazines, not hampered by libel laws and enjoying a curious circulation among people who have an insatiable desire to read about the British Royal family, plastered the story over an incredulous continent.

The difference between British and Continental magazines in their handling of a Royal story is quite immense. For various reasons the British Press will gloss an anti-Royal story over with lots of banal and seemingly loyal statements and sentiments. This is mainly because newspapers found very early on that if they attacked royalty in even the most vaguely mundane way they lost circulation immediately. The British population would not tolerate it. A photograph of Princess Anne, for instance, publicly whipping Mark Phillips with a riding crop at a jumping event where he had criticised her round of jumps, was looked at with fascination in newsrooms, but *not* printed – even in the communist *Morning Star*. In the popular press they merely remarked that her marriage to the young Captain seemed to be "rather tempestuous".

Because of all this Fleet Street sat on the Royal story for as long as it dared. The Continental Press, however, had a field day with the Margaret–Townsend Affair, to the acute embarrassment of the British Court, which had already shown great reservations about Margaret's earlier nightclub existence.

While the British newspapers played it down, the European media overdid it. Not content with the story as it stood, they printed every little piece of tittle-tattle they could find, much of it made up. There is, for example, an infamous journalist who specialises in royal stories for the foreign press who to this day openly boasts of his prowess in this field. Suddenly, in the middle of a drinking session with others at a subterranean Fleet Street afternoon drinking club he will scan his watch, take out his diary, look up the date and tell the assembled journalists "I thought so. It's time I gave Margaret another abortion." He is by no means alone in the field, and it is to the constant discredit of many magazines that they have never questioned his information.

Continental magazines are also very adept at fixing pictures. For example, they will put two models in a compromising situation and replace the faces with those of royalty as if one of the paparizzi, known as the "lens louts", had startled them in a bedroom.

In Scandinavia, Germany, France, the Lowlands and, in particular, Italy, this kind of publicity about the Margaret–Townsend affair flourished week by week until it caused a crescendo of embarrassment to everyone concerned.

Against this background Margaret and Townsend tried a futile game of playing the whole thing down. She put on a brave face and prepared to move to Clarence House with her mother. He merely got on with the job of being a royal equerry.

But by now the cat had been well and truly let out of the bag and the halcyon days of their romance were absolutely over.

Chapter Eleven

Margaret and her mother had by now spent several weeks getting organised for the move to Clarence House. The move surprised many people for they thought a place as huge as Buckingham Palace could accommodate the Queen Mother and Margaret. They had no idea of the complicated running of the Palace. It was impossible to split the place up into two separate establishments. Although, in some ways, the Palace is like a block of flats, with dozens of separate units (housing, clerical, administration, domestic, royal quarters and official quarters), every inch of it is needed to help the monarchy run smoothly.

The move was a most complicated affair involving, for a start, some £100,000-worth of the Queen Mother's personal furniture. Although Townsend himself supervised every minute of the move, the Queen Mother and Princess Margaret got very involved with setting up the new home. They would go from room to room at Clarence House discussing where they wanted special items placed. They compared colour schemes and organised trips out to such stores as Harrods where they organised the buying of carpets, material, fittings and new lighting.

These trips took on almost nightmare proportions for the authorities involved. For the couple of Royals to go on a simple (informal) shopping spree together needed hours of preparation. The Queen Mother left it to Peter. He put a call through to the store itself, then he organised a police escort and warned the Metropolitan police of the visit (traffic flow would have to be dealt with).

Mother and daughter would arrive at a side entrance of the building and would always be met by the store's highest available employee who would spend the entire time with them while they shopped. Often they were not recognised by their fellow shoppers as they drifted around sampling material or picking up light fittings like any other customer. They constantly asked the price – but no money ever changed hands. The chosen items and the bill would be sent in the store's transport later that day and officials would settle up by cheque the following morning. (When Margaret was very young she passed a sweet counter and asked for a "gobstopper" which cost a single penny. It was the only purchase that day but a bill was duly presented for the copper coin.)

After several foraging trips to London's West End and Knightsbridge, both the Queen Mother and Margaret were satisfied with the new arrangements at Clarence House. As the Queen and Prince Philip began spreading themselves throughout Buckingham Palace, Margaret moved into her own beautifully furnished self-contained apartment within Clarence House. She could use the facilities in the rest of the house, but for her own private use and entertainment she had a large, airy bedroom with the customary royal four-poster; she also enjoyed a small dining room, a large private sitting room and a compact reception room which had a spare put-you-up in case it was necessary for her lady-in-waiting to be close to her at night.

Wherever any Royal is, there will be flowers. All the royal estates have large areas of land given over to growing blooms and a special convoy is sent each morning from one of the estates to whichever residence the family are using at the time.

Each day from Windsor a large van leaves the Royal Park at about seven a.m. It stops at the back door of Buck House, and does the rounds of the other Royal households. So that when the Queen or Margaret get up that day – the Queen usually much earlier than PM – the whole place is festooned with freshly picked flowers. Margaret's preference was always for roses. On her move to Clarence House, special preparations were made so that new rose bushes were planted and outbuildings converted so she could enjoy fresh, scented roses nearly every day of the year.

Margaret entertained informally in her sitting room, and formally in the reception room. In one corner a small bar had been fitted out where Margaret's male friends could dispense drinks for small dinner gatherings. At these occasional and informal soirées Margaret enjoyed pink champagne in some abundance. When the occasion was formal she rarely drank more than a small sherry before going to the theatre, or a single glass of champagne at a Hunt Ball. On formal occasions her glass was rarely re-filled.

From the roses onwards Margaret loved pink. Her bedroom especially was festooned with pink drapes and wallpaper and pink predominated throughout the rest of the suite. The whole place was tastefully furnished with antiques, many of them priceless family heirlooms. Despite her up-to-date and sophisticated tastes in both things, she never had any time for ultra-modern furniture. (She was closely influenced here by Queen Mary, herself a connoisseur and lover of great antiques.)

Her piano, a highly polished Stein, sat splendidly in the middle of her sitting room. And in those days she had a huge veneered radiogram flanked by long cabinets full of records ranging from the classics to jazz. She enjoys Bach and Beethoven, Noël Coward and Danny Kaye (both of the latter good friends of hers in those days). In 1953 she loved playing the hits for her personal guests. *The Harry Lime Theme* had a long innings and so did *Silver Dollar*. She especially enjoyed singing French songs as a duet with Lady Blandford and one young blood at the time managed to record her singing *Y a d'la Joie*. For years royal fans could purchase the disc, at an exorbitant price, from a small and seedy record shop in Charing Cross Road. The only known copy still in existence is owned by the prosperous proprieter of a small and exclusive country club at Remenham, Berkshire, who will only play it if you can prove you are a personal friend of PM's.

It was also the pioneer days of the tape recorder and Margaret was one of the first to realise the benefits of taping her favourite tunes. She set about taping forty of them and they lasted for most of the evening. When they ran out, Margaret turned to the piano. She could mimic most singers and only needed to go to a show once before she could "vamp" most of the tunes. (She came back from *Pal Joey* that year and played every tune in the show after one hearing.) One evening get-together ended with her doing running impersonations of Burl Ives, Vera Lynn, Dinah Shore, the late Fats Waller and even Maurice Chevalier.

During these days the housekeeping itself was no problem. Her mother had a formidable army of aides, most of them old retainers fondly transferred from Buckingham Palace. They looked after everything from laundering Margaret's handkerchiefs to washing her car. But she could give the chefs a hard time. She always took an interest in the food being cooked and served, although she rarely set the menu herself. The kitchen staff went to endless lengths to provide good, basic, nourishing dishes.

Normally Margaret breakfasted alone in her suite having little more than some fruit, cereal and a cup of coffee. She rarely ate this meal before ten a.m. Then she dressed with the help of a maid. At about eleven a.m. she would briskly start the day's business. On most days there would be some kind of official function before lunch, but if the morning was free she would attend to letters and other personal details with her lady-in-waiting. She lunched lightly with the Queen Mother and often walked in St. James's Park with her dog Johnny. Then she would go visiting friends or relatives and often stay for tea. At about five p.m. the evening's events would begin. These started with a round of phone calls ascertaining what might be happening that evening. Then she would change for dinner, nearly always with friends. On the odd evenings when she did not go out or entertain she sat in with the Queen Mother playing cards or the piano or watching television.

Against this background of acute international embarrassment and the face-saving exercise of moving house as if nothing had happened, 1953 sneaked up on the couple when they were hardly looking.

If the previous year had been the one in which the storm clouds had gathered, this was the year in which the heavens broke and rained a tempestuous downfall upon all their hopes and aspirations.

It started off with an article in an American tabloid quickly followed by an even more detailed account in the Paris-based

Samedi-Soir. Both were very well-informed. Neither were written by the parasites of royalty. Neither of them could be ignored.

The gist of both articles was that Princess Margaret was planning to renounce her royal title so that she could marry Peter Townsend. The British press felt it had been held off the story for too long. If the romance was common knowledge throughout the world, it was time the British public got to hear about it.

The trickle of rumour began to be a flood and, in the guise of knocking the foreign press for knocking the British Princess, the sensational Sunday tabloid *The People* splashed a front-page story in the middle of May.

Now the couple's enemies moved into action. They had been planning to do so for some time and had been building their own tactics all along. Now that it was all out in the open, the scene was set for a holocaust. Margaret and Peter had been firmly committed to each other at least since the divorce, and probably before. The exact stage when they actually decided to marry must have been a traumatic experience for both of them. Peter Townsend, the shooting star, at first gave Margaret his complete and undying love. He was a man of keen sexuality who managed to mask it with affection and adoration. It was an intense affair, conducted mainly in secret, frowned on by almost everyone, even the servants. It was an affair of total defiance by Margaret, who was absolutely determined to marry the man. She showed every inch of her stubborn nature. At first she wanted to try and change the law. With Parliament, and with Churchill in particular in command, this would have been exceedingly difficult. The Archbishop of Canterbury made it be known through his own channels from the very start that the Canon Law could not change. Then Margaret threatened to renounce her titles – at least as Princess. Each of these brought a flurry of doubt into Townsend's mind, quelled only by Princess Margaret's insistence of their love.

Shortly before the story hit the British press, unearthing an avalanche of speculation, Townsend had gone to see Sir Alan Lascelles, chief plotter to his eventual downfall, to declare his love and his intentions. Sir Alan, Townsend's actual boss, was not at all amused, though it was his clear duty at that stage to put the petition before the Queen. He did so the following morning and couched his diplomatic introduction in such a way that the Queen was in no doubt as to his feelings. He was the absolute staunch epitome of the ardent monarchist.

He was positively angry about the proposal. To him a presumptuous servant was trying to marry the Queen of England's sister and it was all quite outrageous. He saw Margaret as a thoroughly irresponsible young lady for whom no affair of the heart should interfere with the affairs of state. In all this, for the next two years anyway, the law was on his side. It was actually illegal for the marriage to take place.

A lot was made of the fact that in the divorce itself Townsend was outwardly the innocent party. And this did much to put the nation emotionally on his side. But it meant that, while controversy was raging, Townsend had to move out of Clarence House and back into Buckingham Palace, where he was now absolutely miserable. He did everything he could to help prepare for the Coronation and he continued his duties much as before. But he could see the writing on the wall.

Margaret, on the other hand, was presenting her own petitions to the Queen who gave her a very sympathetic hearing. Elizabeth pledged that she would look into the situation carefully and see if there was any way at all in which the marriage could be made possible. She doubted it, rightly, but at least offered to try. She warned Margaret that she should at least keep it in mind that she might have to wait until she was twenty-five when the Queen's permission was not needed. Even then, however, the marriage was by no means an easy project. Margaret had to give a year's notice to the Privy Council – and get the overwhelming approval of both houses of Parliament. Sometimes it is not so easy being a Royal and Margaret wilted visibly under the strain of restriction. All this emotional activity was being played out against the massive organisation for the Coronation.

At the Coronation itself many saw Margaret and Townsend together for the first time. It was in Westminster Abbey, during a pause in the ceremony, when Margaret was able to slip over to where Townsend was standing. It was a brief encounter in which they merely touched each other in support and encouragement.

When the main ceremony was over each member of the Royal family had gone to their own robing rooms to spend a penny, freshen up, down a small glass of orange juice and prepare for the magnificent procession through the streets of London. Margaret shared the robing room with her mother. They had only a few minutes but Margaret seemed withdrawn and anxious. She suddenly left the room and wandered in the Great Hall of the annex to Westminster Abbey. Courtiers were standing around under the fabulous cerise ceiling illuminated with a myriad of silver stars. They chatted quietly to themselves beside the heavily draped walls. Margaret looked around the great hall intently. Suddenly she spotted Townsend in his Royal Air Force uniform of sky blue and aiguilettes – the gold lanyard and tassels worn on the right shoulder only by Equerries to the Monarch. At almost the same time Townsend caught sight of the Princess and almost like a Hollywood movie, they moved through the richly robed people towards each other. The bells of Westminster Abbey were pealing. Music swelled from the Abbey organ enveloping the Great Hall with music which reverberated in every nook and cranny of the ancient building. As the couple came together through the throng the Princess's white-gloved hand rested for a second on the airman's sleeve. She saw a tiny thread of cotton on his left breast pocket and gently removed it. For a moment they were oblivious to the bedlam around them. They looked intensely into each other's eyes and for a few seconds did not care whether the world knew about it or not.

It was the beginning of the end, for a lot of people did see them, and a lot of people cared.

The selection of Maids of Honour at the Coronation was a surprising choice. They were all chosen from the fringes of the former Margaret Set. At the very least they were young women who knew Margaret, and some of them knew the Queen just as well. Like Lady Rosemary Spencer Churchill, they had gone to dances and dinner parties at Windsor during the war. But others, like Jane Heathcote-Drummond-Willoughby and Lady Jane Vane-Tempest-Stewart, they were originally two of a large number of debs selected from a book and whittled down to those who knew either Margaret or the Queen. Lady Anne Coke who was to marry Colin Tenant was very much part of the exclusive PM Set, as was Lady Mary Ballie-Hamilton, clearly of Scottish ancestry.

Although they were there in the Queen's honour, it became clear why they had been chosen. As Margaret continued to linger close to Townsend, three of them broke away from their conversation and quietly guided the Princess back into the care of her mother.

That night Townsend and Margaret, tired but jubilant after the ordeal, stole out of a side door at Buckingham Palace and mingled with the crowds. Heavily disguised in coats and scarves, they held hands as they wandered down the Mall and the side roads around the Palace. Thousands thronged the streets hoping to catch yet another glimpse of the newly crowned Queen and her husband. At about ten o'clock they found their way to the statue of Queen Victoria just in front of the Palace. They joined with the crowds in singing and cheering. Mass calls demanding the Queen should come on to the balcony again went up from a thousand delirious throats. The Queen showed herself for a few minutes and waved to the spotlights and the multitudes. After that the couple threaded their way back to the Palace. Just inside the gates as they walked beneath the outer arches of the huge building they met Princess Alexander of Kent who was returning from a similar clandestine outing with her lady-in-waiting. All four were a little startled at first and then giggled when Margaret pointed out they were now all the Queen's subjects and entitled to cheer her along with all the millions of others.

They all hurried back into the Palace. It was the last time that Townsend and Margaret would get lost in a crowd together.

After the Coronation Townsend was, more or less, put out to pasture. He found suddenly that his attentions were being discouraged little by little until he felt ostracised and an outsider. This was far more Sir Alan's doing than the Queen's, but

Elizabeth did not argue when it was suddenly decided Peter Townsend should not be the equerry on the coming tour of Margaret and the Queen Mother to Rhodesia.

Behind the scenes a small but powerful political intrigue was being played out to put pressure on the Queen. This was headed by her own secretary, Sir Alan Lascelles, who had persuaded Winston Churchill, a man with great influence over the Queen, to join forces with him. On their side also was Prince Philip who was firmly against the romance.

This powerful lobby – the Queen's husband, her secretary and her mentor, Churchill – did everything they could to have Peter Townsend exiled. For long unbearable months of indecision during which Elizabeth also had to face the ordeal of the Coronation, she demurred and put off the fateful day.

In this whole episode there was also a powerful lobby which favoured the romance. Opinion polls showed that ninety per cent of the British population, for a start, was agog with approval. Both the Queen Mother and Princess Alice, always influential over the Queen in times of family crisis, approved of Townsend. Princess Margaret herself simply told her sister that nothing would make her change her mind and some way would have to be found of interpreting the tricky constitution so that a marriage was possible.

But the critics were gaining ground fast. Churchill had his staff prepare a full dossier on the consitutional problems. The Chancellor of the Exchequer, Mr. R. A. Butler, introduced a bill to Parliament which made Prince Philip, rather than Margaret, regent, should the Queen be unable to carry out her duties before Prince Charles became eighteen. He made it clear to Parliament that the bill was approved of by all members of the Royal family.

Churchill's dossier made it perfectly plain that marriage between the Princess and a divorced man was impossible until Margaret was twenty-five and able to choose a husband without the Queen's consent. As head of the Church of England she could not give her consent to a marriage which the Church could not recognise. It was a clear-cut argument which left little room for manoeuvre and the Queen finally decided that she could not give her permission. She knew she could not stop the couple seeing each other and, indeed, did not want to do so. Despite Philip's general disapproval, Elizabeth could remember the tenuous year it took her father to make up his mind for her own marriage. She had been deeply in love and on tenterhooks as King George kept putting the decision off, month after month. She knew exactly what Margaret was going through. She also had more knowledge than perhaps anyone else of her sister's stubborn determination. She did not want to be instrumental in forcing Margaret's hand.

Everyone concerned in the matter who had any influence at all, courtiers, politicians, family, Palace advisors and so on, worked out a formula which they hoped would please most parties concerned. The first thing, they decided, was to get Townsend out of the way until Margaret was twenty-five and their direct jurisdiction over her became considerably less. The family would do all they could to help Margaret get over the parting and would gently encourage her to find other escorts in the hope that her love would recede over the months. If, in two years' time, the Princess was still determined to marry the airman, everyone would have to look at the situation again. The Queen made it clear that, if Margaret still did want to marry, she would favour the liaison despite her personal doubts. Margaret, she reasoned, could not simply be locked up. But for the moment, the plotters got their way.

A senior civil servant, Sir Lionel Heald, had prepared a long memorandum for Churchill which was to give the Premier abundant ammunition when he visited the Queen for his weekly audience on Wednesday afternoon. It clearly gave the Queen no option but to ban the marriage for at least the time being, despite Margaret's stubborness. Churchill spelled it out and quickly showed he had done his homework.

The Cabinet was unanimously against the marriage. Should Margaret wait until she was twenty-five, Parliament was most unlikely to grant permission unless she renounced her rights of succession and those of her children. This would require a special act of Parliament and under the provisions of the Statute of Westminster, which virtually governed the constitutional law, similar acts would have to be passed in the major Commonwealth countries such as Canada and Australia where the Queen was still constitutionally Head of State.

At the meeting of the Commonwealth Prime Ministers which was going on at the time, Sir Lionel had sounded out each foreign PM as to his attitude towards Margaret's possible renouncement. They were clearly uneasy. To a man they argued that the hereditary principle of the monarchy had already been threatened by the abdication of Edward. They said another within such a short time would do immense harm to the British monarchy as a whole. If it was so easy for one member of the close-knit Royal family to just wash their hands and give it all up, then it seemed equally possible that outsiders could get themselves in line to the throne. While the system, now well over 1,000 years old, was adhered to, it simply could not be tampered with.

In short, even if the British Parliament were to give their permission, the Commonwealth Parliaments would not.

On the day after this important decision, Winston Churchill personally took over directions from Number Ten Downing Street. He summoned the Air Minister, Lord De l'Isle, and asked him to select several postings suitable for Peter Townsend, and give him a choice as to his career over the next couple of years. Churchill left De l'Isle with the parting shot that there must, under no circumstances, be a delay. The Group Captain had to be in the country of his choice before Margaret came back from Southern Rhodesia. De l'Isle hastily considered the situation. Townsend's post would have to be that of Air Attaché at a British Embassy abroad. Churchill had stated the farther away the better. But there were only three places which could be arranged at short notice without causing international flurries. (It was difficult to replace an Air Attaché overnight in sometimes sensitive areas without a great deal of comment. Lord De l'Isle was also anxious not to embarrass or endanger the career of any of his men.) They were the Far East Headquarters in Singapore, which could accommodate several Air Attachés; Johannesburg, which was then vacant; or Brussels, where the present Attaché was overdue for recall. It was inevitable that, when summoned by De l'Isle, Townsend should choose Brussels. Ostensibly he said it was because he had two young children at school in England and wanted access to them during the holidays. This was undoubtedly true. But it must have been in his mind that Brussels was only an hour's flying time from Heathrow Airport and that, if he could slip into the country, he would be able to spend many weekends with Margaret.

This was a tricky one for Churchill and Lascelles who had become quite determined Margaret should marry someone else. They were now deeply implanted in the web of intrigue which was built specifically to keep the airman out of her affections for as long as possible.

The Townsend Affair only reached Cabinet level briefly and on purely constitutional grounds. Churchill wanted to be sure he was right when he said the whole Cabinet was against the marriage when he went to see the Queen. But Sir Winston had long consultations with senior civil servants at the Foreign Office in which he laid down some hefty instructions which were designed to keep Townsend well and truly in his place. Prince Philip had by now left the conspiracy. He had nodded his approval when he heard of the arrangements, and left it at that. He was more than aware that the Queen was most upset about the whole affair and did nothing to aggravate the situation further once this delaying tactic in the marriage plans had been established.

But Townsend, who almost welcomed the obscurity of a foreign embassy now that he had become a household name, had no idea of what he faced in a Brussels closely watched by the plotters at home.

The succession of events which led up to Peter's hurried departure showed firstly that the Queen still wished to express her faith in the equerry who had served her family so well for nine years. Secondly, it was obvious that, when the court, the politicians and civil servants wanted to do something she was virtually powerless to intervene without a direct command.

Margaret and Peter had by this time accepted the fact that they would have to part for a while. But Margaret had extracted two promises from her sister. Firstly that they would meet again briefly when she came back from the tour in a month's time, and secondly that throughout his exile, they could communicate both by letter and phone. The plotters decided to move fast to thwart both these concessions.

Margaret made her tearful departure from Townsend at Clarence House on the evening of June 28th while the Household was still attending to the last details of packing. They supped together with the Queen Mother and formally said goodbye a little before midnight. Margaret's last words were that they would have three or four wonderful days together before his posting and begged him to try and find a retreat where they could be alone for a while. (They both had close friends who had offered secret accommodation should the need arise.) The next day June 29th, Margaret and the Queen Mother flew off to Africa.

On the very next day Townsend flew with the Queen and Prince Philip to Northern Ireland for an official visit. It was the Queen's way of publicly showing Peter Townsend was not in *her* doghouse at least. But conspiracy was afoot. While the Monarch and the equerry were safely in Ireland at a civil reception (as it happened, eating roast duck) Buckingham Palace made a brief announcement which rocketed around the world. Peter Townsend would take up a post as Air Attaché in Brussels on July 14th – a few days before Margaret returned from abroad.

Because of the events of that day, Townsend himself did not hear of the announcement until later that evening. Deep in the heart of Africa a concerned Queen Mother heard the news first and decided that only she could break it to Margaret. Certainly she did not want to let her daughter read about it in a newspaper. They were staying in a luxurious hotel in Umtali. Outside, the harsh African sun beat down on the white streets. Inside the Queen Mother was most uncomfortable despite the pleasant air-conditioning. She dreaded the interview she knew she must have with her daughter. When she was finally able to tell her, Margaret was absolutely distraught. She broke down completely and a physician was summoned. He gave her sedatives and Margaret retired to bed for twenty-four hours. Everything was cancelled for the next day or two but Margaret went through the rest of the tour barely able to stand the strain. She became withdrawn and her eyes welled with tears at the slightest show of emotion.

Townsend protested to no avail by telephone from Belfast. He tried to call Margaret but could not get through. Later, as the plane touched down on the tarmac of London Airport a gaggle of pressmen were waiting. This time they were hardly interested in the Queen. They wanted to picture the supposed agony of the Group Captain. In order to save the Queen embarrassment Townsend stayed on the aircraft as the Queen and the Duke walked to the Rolls-Royce awaiting them. However, to her everlasting credit, the Queen waited until Townsend finally showed himself. She then walked back to the aircraft – a distance of nearly 100 yards – and shook his hand. She said simply: "Goodbye, Peter," as a dozen cameras clicked. Townsend nodded curtly and said: "Goodbye, Ma'am". It was the last act in Townsend's life as a member of the Court of England.

When Margaret finally returned to Clarence House the only material evidence that Townsend had ever been there was an old coat he had given a footman for his off-duty wear. She found the Palace lonely and her determination grew.

Buckingham Palace had been so keen to get the announcement out of the way, they even took the Foreign Office by surprise. This was almost certainly engineered by Churchill and Lascelles and the FO knew about the announcement only the day before.

Sir Christopher Warner, the Ambassador in Brussels, was openly furious. He felt he should have been consulted before any posting as important as this was made and he let the FO have some extremely terse despatches over the following day or so. He called his old friend, journalist Norman Barrymaine, and asked him to fly over to Brussels immediately. Barrymaine knew Townsend fairly well and left the very same day. Sir Christopher wanted to know everything about the affair and about Townsend personally. The two drank port well into the night and Barrymaine told him everything he knew. None of it put Sir Christopher in a better mood. A sudden new posting without his knowledge was almost unprecedented, but this posting filled him with fury.

However, he could do little but register his protest in the strongest possible terms. This brought an immediate apology from the Foreign Minister who, off the record, blamed it on "The Boss" – Churchill. Sir Christopher, satisfied that he would have to make the best of it, prepared his embassy for the arrival of their new diplomat.

On July 14th Peter Townsend drove to Kent and stayed the night with friends. He smoked a lot of cigarettes and, unlike him, drank a fair deal of brandy that evening. He looked gaunt and unhappy though his temper improved as he enjoyed his friends' company and the brandy softened his senses. The next day his friends bade him farewell. His eyes were bloodshot and he looked very haggard. He drove to Dover and on a clear summer morning boarded the British car ferry, the *Lord Walden*. He mingled with the passengers, had lunch in the restaurant and drove his car off the ferry in Calais. The crossing had been pleasant but in France he ran into heavy rain. He was very depressed as he drove the whole two hundred miles through Lille, Saint Omar and eventually to the outskirts of Brussels. He reported immediately to the embassy on his arrival that evening. He found the building flanked by a dozen pressmen and twenty policemen (there were normally only two on duty). He found out the arrangements for his accommodation, introduced himself to the on-duty diplomats and an embassy chauffeur drove him through the drizzle to the Grand Hotel for his first night of exile.

Chapter Twelve

The move to Brussels plunged both Margaret and Peter into a deep depression. Margaret blamed all the people who had conspired against her. Peter felt the world was against him. But he was not as unhappy as Margaret.

He viewed the move rather differently than Margaret because he had already begun to have some serious doubts as to their relationship. Not, at this stage, any doubts at all that he loved her dearly, but doubts about whether the whole thing was actually possible or not. Townsend had got very used to being a backroom boy. Now he was an international celebrity and he did not like it one bit. Secondly he could see what Margaret would not admit to herself, that from the very beginning they would be put under immense strain and pressure. Peter Townsend, already recoiling from a marriage which initially had all the ingredients of happiness but which became eroded because of official duty, was quick to realise that the official side of his new marriage would increase tenfold if he married Margaret.

He wanted to collect his thoughts; he wanted to get out of the overwhelming limelight; he wanted to really know whether he loved Margaret as firmly as he thought; and he wanted to know whether Margaret would be quite so determined to marry him after the strain of a long absence.

It was because of all of these reasons that Townsend left England without any real show of protest. There must have been moments of dilemma but really he had no choice. For a start it was the Queen's wish. He was duty-bound to follow the wishes of his Monarch. He also knew that protest would merely aggravate the situation. He genuinely felt extremely protective towards Margaret and he wrote her long, passionate letters trying to cheer her up. He promised he would live life in exile as quietly and devoutly as possible, and he promised that, as soon as the immediate heat had died down, he would find ways of seeing her again. These letters reached Margaret at various stages of the Royal Tour. They did little to cheer her up. Never had she hated the restrictions of her position so much. But a combination of the inbred training, the early education from Queen Mary, the memories of her father's wishes, the constant advice and sympathy of her mother, her own undoubted feelings towards her sister's position, and her inimitable brand of survival helped to keep her relatively sane during the long days in Africa. She wrote letters back to the family which were described as "missiles of disapproval". She cajoled her mother that nothing would change in the two years of his compulsory banishment. She wrote long letters to Townsend telling him of her love and describing the agony of being away from him. She told him what she had told the others. No amount of political intrigue would make her change her mind. She implored Peter not to give up hope and begged him to try and get through the two years without depression.

As she did at the time of her father's death, she prepared to turn towards the Church to help her get through this trying new period. After she arrived back in England, visibly stricken and depressed, she sought out her old religious tutors and once again the newspapers speculated she would take orders and become a nun.

During Lent she drove with her lady-in-waiting every Tuesday (except once, when she had a cold) to St. Paul's vicarage, in London's Knightsbridge, where she joined thirty or more other young people at post-Confirmation classes in the drawing room. Her teacher was the vicar, the Rev. Edward Barry Henderson, who found her a devout pupil. Even on the morning of her departure to Norway to attend a royal wedding in May, she received communion from Rev. Henderson. Wearing a black suit and a small black beret she mingled with the small congregation at St. Paul's and was not noticed until she went to the altar rails. She arrived at just after eight a.m. and slipped into her usual pew in front on the left-hand side.

On Sundays she attended church at least twice, unusual even

for a Royal – although only very exceptional circumstances would prevent them attending once.

But her real religious influence during these days came from a young curate she had met while at Windsor. He was the Rev. Simon Phipps, a very good-looking, vibrant ex-Major in the Coldstream Guards. He had been one of the young officers at Windsor Castle and had attended many of the royal functions while he was there. He had eventually taken holy orders and become curate of St. Peter's in Huddersfield, Yorkshire. His removal from the Guards did not remove him from the affections of the Royal family. He regularly escorted Margaret to Hunt Balls and other society functions. He was a principal guest at her twenty-first birthday party at Balmoral and had a privileged seat at Westminster Abbey during the Coronation. On these occasions they enjoyed themselves, but when it came to Margaret needing advice and wise counsel over her own emotional problems, it was to Simon Phipps that she turned. He saw her countless times over the long months of Peter's banishment.

Life for Peter Townsend in Brussels quickly became unbearable. The European press pursued him wherever he went; he was under constant guard from the Belgian government "for his own safety"; and he was under regular surveillance from his own embassy. It meant he could only lead the most restricted of lives. And for a time he rarely left the confines of the embassy building, or his own luxurious flat in the Avenue Louise, locally called Millionaires' Avenue. For reasons of security not even fellow diplomats could get to him direct. His address was a secret, his phone number was never added to the inter-embassy listings and on many occasions he felt his line was being tapped.

Virtually his only friend in Brussels, outside the acquaintanceships he made in his job both within the embassy and in the diplomatic community, was the sophisticated and quite brilliant Countess Aline van Limburg Stirum. She was a bright, witty, commanding, yet utterly feminine aristocrat of mid-European descent who immediately took the forlorn and lonely Peter under her influential wing. In her own right she was one of the leading socialites in North Europe at the time, especially the

Low Countries. She was a brilliant horsewoman and, on her own level, managed to insinuate herself into any ongoing political intrigue of the time. She had known Townsend casually before, but she got to be actual friends with him when he joined the famous and exclusive Brussels Riding Club just outside the city. She lent him her champion chestnut gelding Tourbillon which Peter exercised every day. He felt at home at the club where all the members enjoyed an informal atmosphere. Many of them, like Townsend himself, were hiding from a certain notoriety. No one ever had the bad manners to mention Margaret and it was virtually the only place in Brussels where he could relax completely.

The Countess proved to be a staunch friend, ally and counsellor throughout the time of Townsend's exile. Through her influence all sorts of little things were arranged for him: exclusive house parties where he was untroubled by either the snoopers or the gossip columnists; and away-from-it-all weekends where he could talk for an hour with Margaret on the telephone knowing that the line was not tapped. She would choose select little restaurants for him to dine at, always in the right, very exclusive company.

Apart from the secretaries – one for home and another at the embassy – Townsend had a specially hand-picked English chauffeur/valet/bodyguard who was with him virtually all the time. For most of the time an armed-guard in plain clothes stood around the entrance to the flats where Townsend lived vetting any unknown newcomers. Embassy security was especially hotted up. Townsend could be a huge security risk.

Within this pitiless atoll in the middle of a bustling city, Brussels tried to lionise him. He became as furtive as Greta Garbo at dodging the press and eventually the rest of society too. He was obviously a major attraction for the upper-crust hostesses of Belgium.

Even though he was in the doldrums he was still highly attractive, and the air of fantasy which the tragedy of the parting had given him was almost irresistible. But Townsend was extremely difficult to entertain during the period. He went to parties only when it was relevant to his job or to those especially engineered by the Countess. To the rest his secretary gave the invitation a polite refusal. Soon, when people began to understand he was unavailable, the invitations dropped off and Peter was able to lead a rather more peaceful life.

He was to be in Brussels for two years and three months and he was to hate every single minute of it, with the exception of his riding and the odd weekend with the Countess. Their regard for each other was completely mutual. She adopted him like a mother hen and he not only used her shoulder occasionally to cry on, but used her influence when he wanted to do something in complete secrecy. There was no question of Townsend being unfaithful in his love for Margaret during this period in Europe.

When it was all over and Princess Margaret was twenty-five, she had agreed to marry him. But on this his lips were completely sealed. Only the Countess had any inkling of his true feelings. To others, even those close to him, he would say: "The word must come from someone else."

After Sir Christopher Warner had got over his initial annoyance and met Townsend personally, the two became well acquainted. Townsend did his job perfectly well and that was most of what Sir Christopher had to worry about. But they often talked at length about many things and Sir Christopher always had it in his mind that Townsend, if nothing else, had been a brilliant and brave fighter pilot.

Because of the Ambassador's regard for him, the Countess's influence, and the conniving of Margaret, Townsend made at least a dozen trips to Britain during the period he was abroad. These trips were carefully arranged in great cloak-and-dagger style and Townsend always stayed at Clarence House. It is certain there were other trips in which the couple rendezvoused outside London. At least one of them was spent with Colin and Lady Tenant. Another hideaway was provided at least once by Margaret's former lady-in-waiting Jennifer Bevan. There may have been many more. On the trips he made to Clarence House everything was done secretly, but officially. Both Brussels and London airports were dealt with by the Special Branches of each country. Townsend merely passed through both with the minimum of fuss and without ever going into any public sectors. Townsend's own black Austin Princess would be waiting unattended at the airport and he would drive himself unobtrusively into London. The return journey on Sunday evening would be made in much the same way.

The plotters frowned on these clandestine exercises, using the excuse that, if ever the press should hear about them, the whole thing would explode again. But they could do nothing about them. The invitations came from the Queen Mother herself. When diplomatic objections were made to her, she would merely say she would wait until such a disaster occurred but that surely Her Majesty's Government was capable, with its vast resources, of diverting such a disaster. H.M. Government obviously was. Because no inkling got out until Peter was officially in London again.

In the embassy itself Peter Townsend worked in a rather dreary back room on the second floor which had austere service furniture in veneer and oak and a small carpet. On the bare walls was a prominent picture of the Queen and Prince Philip – standard equipment in every embassy room. His total staff was a single RAF Staff Sergeant who was rather like an equerry. The embassy itself was a peculiar old building and the way to Peter's office had a strangely sinister effect. From the entrance he made his way up a long and grand red-carpeted stairway to the first floor. He walked past the Ambassador's suite almost to the end of the corridor where he found a narrow stairway which gave the effect that he was working in a turret. Townsend once remarked to the Ambassador that no place could be more appropriate for a banishment. But Norman Barrymaine was to find out later he did not mean this with any sense of humour. His walk up to the "turret" everyday became a heavier burden as the months dragged on.

Despite the opulence of the area, Townsend's flat was very modest. It was small and pleasantly furnished and cost him about £30 a month. It had a living room which also served as a lounge and dining room, a small but modern kitchen, and two tiny bedrooms. It was a standard bachelor pad.

On the mantelpiece over the fireplace were two photographs of his sons, both looking impish. There were no pictures of Princess Margaret on display but in a small cabinet beside the door he had two photograph albums, and nearly all of the photos were original pictures he had taken of Margaret over the years.

In the evenings, after his ride, he would spend a lot of time at home reading or writing letters. He set himself the task of learning French. He could already converse in it but decided a diplomat should be utterly conversant with every aspect of the language. He mastered it in two years and now he speaks it like a Frenchman.

Outside her mother and a few old friends Margaret's only constant companion was her short-haired Sealyham Scotty, Johnnie. He went everywhere with her except to private dinner parties and official functions. The dog stayed in the room while Margaret dined, and slept at the bottom of the bed. There were many nights, as Margaret sobbed herself to sleep when little Johnnie came and licked her face in sympathy. Often, during summer evenings Margaret would put on the compulsory headscarf (for incognito travelling) and take the Scotty across to the local park. She talked to the dog constantly. Had he, in turn, been able to understand, it is certain every last secret of the Townsend Affair would have revealed itself. But the dog could only whine in sympathy when he knew his mistress was in the depths of depression.

Chapter Thirteen

1954 was a quiet year for a vigilant press. Roger Bannister cracked the four-minute mile; all food rationing ended and Winston Churchill reached eighty. But newspapers still had a lot of space to fill and they turned to the Romance for satisfaction. There was also a sort of happy hangover from the Coronation and all the rigmarole that went on afterwards. People were Royal-orientated with an insatiable desire to consume every morsel of tittle-tattle about the family. So while both heroes of the saga kept a low profile, no person in Britain, barring the odd possible Stornaway hermit, was allowed to forget the romance.

In the second year of his exile little changed in the routines both he and Margaret had been forced to adopt. He dug into Brussels society and was rarely seen outside the embassy or the riding club. She went to small dinner parties with friends or entertained at Clarence House. They corresponded frequently, often as much as once a day. They spoke on the telephone, mostly late at night. And Peter made frequent incognito visits to England where he would meet up with Margaret for the weekend.

In London, Townsend would often stay at the town house of his old friend the Marquess of Abergavenney, in Lownes Square. More often they would meet up at the home of Margaret's cousin Mrs. John Wills and her husband, an ex-major, at Binfield in Berkshire. They would spend evenings in Sloane Street with their friends the Blandfords. But most of the visits were spent at Lord Rupert Nevill's farmhouse at Lewes in Sussex.

These clandestine meetings were known only to a handful of friends and relatives. Although Townsend was officially quartered elsewhere, he invariably spent most of the time with the

Princess. The detective and lady-in-waiting (the Queen Mother insisted they should go with Margaret for the weekend) were quartered separately at various local hostelries. They rarely saw much of their charge during the weekend itself.

The meetings were tinged with great sadness and always came to an end far too quickly. But for both of them, they were a godsend. There was a terrific cloak-and-dagger atmosphere to the weekends and both went to fantastic lengths to cover their tracks. Some kind of transport was always laid on for a quick getaway should the press get an inkling of what was going on. (In Sussex an army helicopter was always available but the pilot had no idea why he was kept on alert every now and then.) In London there would always be a car available at the back door of any house they stayed in. It was all very necessary and, in the funny way that it often happens, the secrecy had a way of making the whole relationship between them far more intense. They had to get the most out of every minute they were together.

After supper they were invariably left alone by their hosts and they talked right into the early hours of the morning. Forbidden love ensured the meetings were always exciting, as if they were prisoners let out occasionally on parole, but knowing they must be back behind prison walls before sundown. It was a less than satisfactory arrangement, but one which, under the circumstances, they were more than willing to put up with.

By coincidence a journalist was staying at the same inn as Margaret's detective one weekend and by careful ferreting he found Townsend was there too. He tried to confirm this with the detective who told him it was rubbish. But Princess Margaret was told and she personally called the journalist and begged him not to divulge the information. He did not, but from then on he kept a close eye on her activities and because of this Fleet Street kept up an avid interest in the romance. It was not allowed to die down as many people, especially the plotters, had hoped.

This year of secret and illicit love had its difficulties, but it also had moments of sheer bliss. Margaret filled their moments together with adoration and a burning love. She reminded him constantly that in the following year, 1955, she would be old enough to marry him. They must wait patiently. Margaret was still very determined indeed that the marriage would take place. But Townsend, alone in his Brussels flat at night, gradually felt the cobwebs of doubt spreading across his mind.

As Margaret's twenty-fifth birthday loomed she agreed to go on a Royal Tour to the Caribbean. The plotters saw this as a clear sign that she was getting over her love for Townsend and getting back to being the gay young Princess she had always been. The Queen Mother knew differently, and so did the Queen. They knew she was time-wasting in the most pleasurable way she could think of. She seemed gay and her old self because of the birthday. They knew that her determination was as strong as ever and that her happiness was because she was getting closer to Peter, not farther away from him. The British press speculated daily on the reasons for the tour. Was she going to get over her love, to celebrate it, or just for a holiday to get away from the oppressive atmosphere of London without her lover? While, as usual, she would have several public engagements on her tour, there would be many days free to enjoy the sun, sand and congenial atmosphere of the tropical islands. Even some of her old set, like Colin Tenant, had property out there and promised exotic evenings of calypsos and barbecues. So, firmly convinced this was the year of the accomplishment of her great love, and after saying a fond farewell to Peter, she set off absolutely determined to enjoy herself.

In Brussels a different story was beginning to emerge. As the fateful birthday got nearer he began to feel a slight disenchantment with his future. In his own mind the doubts had started already. But more than this, an anti-marriage lobby had been set to work in the most subtle way, and they were at last breaking down Peter Townsend's confidence.

It was virtually impossible to work on Margaret herself. They could control the situation only in a legal and constitutional way. And while Princess Margaret enjoyed the patronage of her mother and sister, no politician, civil servant or Palace official could hope to sway the mind of the determined and stubborn Princess. But Peter Townsend was a different matter.

The issue was tricky and while they could not order him not to pursue the marriage, they could work on him. And they frequently did. The security he was put under was abnormally strict. He was virtually a prisoner in either his flat or office. Even taking into consideration who he was, and the circumstances of his exile, the "protection" was stifling and overdone. Embassy officials would point out gently that this was nothing to what it would be like when he married the Princess. They used a policy of the utmost gentle persuasion by planting little doubts like: "Only you know whether you will be able to stand being in a glass cage for the rest of your life, Peter. But I'd give it some thought."

Townsend, to be fair, knew only too well that this was sound advice. He genuinely hated to be in the limelight and found publicity offensive and reporters irksome and irritating. He knew full well that if the marriage went through he would be pursued and spotlighted for the rest of his life.

There was no question about his love for Margaret. It was still there. But much of the actual passion had died. Unlike the Princess, to whom secrecy was an essential ingredient of their love, even enhancing it in certain ways, he had found the whole business nerve-racking. (Not that he was not very good at dealing with his own nerves. But he did not find the atmosphere conducive to the ideal romance he craved.)

He had long conversations with the Countess, and some of her friends. He expressed his doubts, not on his love, but on the situation as a whole, and the consensus of opinion was that the marriage should not go ahead without the greatest possible thought and soul-searching. The Countess believed that a determined young lady and a divorced man sixteen years her senior would find it difficult enough to spend the rest of their lives together anyway. The fact that their marriage would be so highly controversial and they would be put under the spotlight for the rest of their lives made the odds against its success incredibly high.

In his own relationship with Margaret he had been almost startled by her fierce determination. If this was translated into a marriage situation he knew there would be huge clashes of personality. They were both strong characters, both used to getting their own way. They both liked to lord it in the home, being something of domestic tyrants. Townsend was more than aware that any marriage between himself and Margaret would be a stormy one. There was no clear point at which Peter Townsend finally made up his mind, but as the birthday approached, it was obvious to his close friends that he wanted a long, frank talk with Margaret before they went any further.

On August 21st, as they published her birthday photograph, the press unanimously asked if she were about to announce her engagement. The journalists, several of whom knew what was going on, were straining at the leash and would not allow Buckingham Palace to remain complacent. The Royal family spent the day quietly at Balmoral. Peter was in Brussels with his two sons on holiday from school. Margaret and Peter spoke briefly on the phone but they did not mention the marriage.

The speculation in London was getting unbearable and embarrassing for the flurried staff at Buck House who tried to put off the constantly inquisitive press. The Queen's secretary duly informed Her Majesty that some kind of statement must be given out to the hungry world. On the following day Buckingham Palace made a statement which was one of those typical epistles from civil servants to the press. It said simply that there would be an announcement today. What it certainly seemed to signify was that she had *not* decided *not* to marry and the romance was still on.

In September Peter Townsend flew into London officially for the annual Air Attachés' conference at the Air Ministry. This was carefully timed to coincide with the Farnborough Air Show two days after the conference ended and most of the military diplomats were away from their embassies for at least two weeks. Townsend took some leave as well and was still in England when the Prime Minister, Sir Anthony Eden, was suddenly and unexpectedly demanded for an immediate audience at Balmoral. The press thought it was what they had been waiting for. An announcement which would settle it all one way or the other.

They were on the right track although the situation had been over-dramatised. Sir Anthony and his wife had been informally asked to Balmoral to spend some time with the family. The

Queen had always had a very close affinity with Sir Winston. She was anxious to try and get to know Eden in the same way, but they also had many things to discuss. Eden had to cancel the first visit at very short notice because of affairs of state. He had come as soon as he was free.

A few days before he arrived, the Queen discussed the Townsend affair with her sister. Margaret remained as adamant as ever. She was still determined the marriage would go ahead and she firmly believed Townsend was of the same opinion. She would not know of his doubts until they met when he was on leave later in October.

It was now no longer vital that the Queen give her permission for the marriage and Margaret said she intended to renounce her title. The Queen felt she must sound out the Prime Minister and tell him of Margaret's decision. This discussion was head of the agenda for the informal conversations lined up for the week.

What the Queen did not expect was that Eden himself would have some additional information about the affair. The Foreign Office had let him know in confidence that Townsend was not desperately happy with the situation. This was carefully presented as the off-the-cuff personal view of the Ambassador but it made its mark. Eden and Queen Elizabeth agreed not to start making any plans until Peter Townsend and Princess Margaret could meet and thrash it all out. Only days later the Group Captain made the first of many visits to Clarence House.

Just a few weeks later it was all over and Peter Townsend was off around the world.

Chapter Fourteen

By a strange quirk of that unaccountable thing called personality, a chemical change took place in the aftermath of their relationship. Both had agreed, like secret conspirators, to wait two years before they made the absolute and final decision. Peter Townsend had roamed the world seeking his revenge in dark corners and using months of jungle driving as an anaesthetic against the sorrow and remorse. Princess Margaret had, more or less, sat it out. Now, after thirty months, the final reckoning was overdue.

Like a soldier in a trench far from home, perhaps reminiscent of his days in sordid service camps, Townsend often thought of the girl back home. Like a prisoner who is denied even the comfort of a weekly visit, he began to yearn again for the soft touch, the gleam in the eye, and the forbidden fruits of the love he had once known.

As he plunged headlong through Africa or stopped in primitive South American tribal villages, he found a gradual awareness that he was missing Margaret very deeply.

He still had, locked deep in his heart, her solemn pledge that she would never marry anyone else. On lonely nights as he drank a solitary Scotch and swatted the mosquitoes, her words must have run through his head time and time again.

Margaret had managed to keep a very low profile during the time he was away. But she had been reunited with her old friends, many of whom were by now much older, wiser and less adventurous. Most of them were even married and had settled down to some kind of domestic bliss.

Her passion for Townsend had blossomed now for almost a decade and his exile in Brussels had only contributed to the longing in her heart. During that time, of course, she had seen him almost every month and they were never apart long enough to let the fires dwindle.

While Townsend spent his lonely frustrated years in his second exile rethinking his position, Margaret was getting used to life without him again. While she still nursed a fervent desire to see him once more, her desperate love for him had begun to lose its fervour.

In short, she experienced the truth of that old adage "Time heals all wounds" and she had gradually found herself losing the intensity of her passion. In this way their roles had become curiously reversed and it was a bizarre turn of events for which Townsend was manifestly unprepared.

Margaret's curiosity drove her to see Townsend again. She must *know* once and for all whether she loved him or not. But she had misgivings about such a meeting.

When Townsend reached Algiers on the last leg of his journey in 1958 – some two and a half years after the fateful announcement had been made – he desperately wanted to re-negotiate the whole situation. He asked a close friend of his, Norman Barrymaine, to fly out to Algiers to put him in the picture.

When Barrymaine reached Algiers Townsend made it plain he had now decided to marry Margaret against all the odds. The first thing he wanted to do was meet her and find out if she still felt the same way.

By now, most of the plotters had dissolved and the Prime Minister, Harold Macmillan, a sensible man who had great influence with the Queen, was by no means as indignant as Churchill had been. The court was a different matter, but by now the Queen was far more experienced in her job and able to handle her courtiers with a great deal of decorum. All this, thought Peter, gave the idea fresh impetus.

Barrymaine spent four days with Townsend telling him everything he knew about the situation since he had been away. They sat up on the verandah of the St. George Hotel for most of the night, breakfasted together the following morning and slept during the intense heat of the day during the afternoon. Townsend wanted to know everything, not just about Margaret. He had been able to tune into the World Service of the BBC from time to time, and, at odd spots on his journey, had bought a newspaper. But he had an avaricious desire to know more. During this time he also wrote long letters to his sons, apologising for being away for so long and asking them to spend the whole of the Easter holiday with him when he finally arrived home. A call was put through to his lawyer in London asking him to "feel out" the situation and Townsend then rambled on to Barrymaine about his hopes of reconnecting the liaison. It was clear that despite his terrible anxieties about their future, his journey had placated him enough to feel he could now fight with Margaret against the rest of the world.

He was exceptionally fit, bronzed and alert. He seemed determined, resilient, boyish and charming. He was keen to get cracking again. He had expiated all the nervous depression, the self-pity, and the great sadness and inevitability of their parting. Peter asked Barrymaine to go back to London, confer with the lawyer, and report back to him by phone in Algiers. In the meantime he was preparing to pass through Brussels on his way home so he could consult his Countess, a woman for whom he now had so much regard that he would rarely make an important step without her advice. She had booked him into the Astoria Hotel ready for his invasion of British soil and she waited patiently in Brussels as he sat on the beach and waited for the fateful telephone call.

Townsend's lawyer, a man of famous anonymity, soon graced the tables of various dinner parties where he was able to gently prod views on his client's possibility of a return to grace and favour. He got himself invited to a hunting weekend where he knew an equerry would be a fellow guest. He dropped into the Savoy one evening after he heard a personal secretary at Clarence House would be entertaining friends. And finally, when he was sure of his position, he sounded Margaret herself out through a lady-in-waiting.

By the time Barrymaine consulted him on Townsend's behalf he had grave doubts about any future meeting. The court had gently exploded when it heard Townsend's return was imminent. Margaret had curiously not shown the kind of agitated desire to see her lover again that he had anticipated. Indeed she seemed entirely calm about the whole affair, merely agreeing that she would see him and looked forward to his visit to Clarence House. One of the major things against the proposed meeting was that it was planned for when the Queen was away on a state visit to Holland. This, it was agreed, was bad tactics.

The Queen herself privately interjected to say she had no objection to the meeting whether she was in the country or not. All this, so far, had been conducted without the specific interest of the press. They had inklings, but nothing definite. There was not, however, a news room in Fleet Street which did not include the word "Townsend" on its daily conference agenda.

A little after New Years day, 1958, Townsend left Algiers by car ferry for Marseilles. He gently meandered across France and had joined the Countess in Brussels around mid-January. As the politics rumbled through London on his behalf, he had time to spare, though his eagerness was by no means abated by the delay.

He moved to the Astoria in the city centre and spoke at length with his solicitor. The lawyer advised him only that there were difficulties. The court, he said, had already tried to influence the Queen against such a meeting. Beyond anything, no one at Buckingham Palace wanted to resume the kind of "Townsend Affair" publicity they had been used to some thirty months before.

Despite this, Townsend slipped into the country unnoticed and stayed with his friend Barrymaine in Sussex. On arrival he told Barrymaine he was having tea with the Princess that afternoon. The Queen was in Holland and Margaret was due to go on a State visit to Germany the following day. On his arrival in Sussex he spoke to Margaret by telephone. It was the first real inkling Townsend had got that something was radically wrong. He agreed to call again just before four o'clock to check that it was still okay for him to go to Clarence House. He wanted to arrange for the gates to be opened at a certain time so he could whisk through without the waiting photographers taking a picture.

They spoke for an hour. The gist of the matter was that Margaret told him she could not see him at Clarence House that day. He must go back to the continent. The Queen had given permission "in principle" for them to meet again, but this was not the time. The court had been hard at work.

The series of events before the final downfall of their relationship disillusioned Peter Townsend more and more as each day passed. Press speculation was the real downfall because it acutely embarrassed the court and they felt they had to act in the Royal family's main interests. They acted by hammering down Margaret's accessibility to what had now clearly become her "former" lover.

The two did finally have a hurried meeting at Clarence House but the newspapers next day so worried everyone – including them – that Clarence House was ruled out as a meeting place at any future date.

When they spoke by telephone the next day, Margaret told him all meetings were off for the time being. He dejectedly sent her four dozen pink roses. After her German visit Margaret went immediately to Royal Lodge Windsor where she planned to have Sunday tea with her mother. The Queen drove over from the castle and joined them for tea. They spent an hour discussing the situation and at about five p.m. Margaret telephoned Peter in Somerset to tell him officially he must not see her again during this visit. He flew back to Brussels again, despondently feeling he was being exiled for the third time.

Days later Margaret flew to join friends in the Caribbean. It was a flight arranged hurriedly by the court so that everyone could have time to think on how they should handle the new embarrassment.

Two weeks later, when Townsend returned to stay in Sussex, he was no longer the bronzed, excited and expectant man he had been in Algiers. The Sussex village had by now got wind of Townsend's visit and he agreed to move back with his mother in Somerset. There they always managed to turn a blind eye to his presence. He talked to Margaret several times after she got back from the Caribbean, but nothing either of them said seemed to take them any nearer the blissful situation he now craved. Tribes of reporters followed him everywhere and he begged them to leave him alone. He felt, suddenly, he could go on no longer and told Margaret he must see her. He went to Clarence

House for what he called a showdown. He told her the whole question of marriage must wait but he demanded the right to see her when he wanted to – whatever the consequences. Margaret was hesitant and unsure. By now she had been hamstrung by the court and had been ordered to promise nothing. She now had her own very deep, personal doubts about the relationship.

The press all over Europe mis-read this meeting and promised an imminent marriage. The situation had got out of hand and Townsend and Barrymaine sat down at the typewriter and wrote just twenty-nine words:

> There are no grounds whatever for supposing that my seeing Princess Margaret in any way alters the situation declared specifically in the Princess's statement in the Autumn of 1955.

This was not strictly true. Townsend had gone to see her for the specific purpose of re-kindling their relationship.

On May 19th 1958 Peter Townsend met Princess Margaret for the very final time at Clarence House. The meeting was epitomised by Margaret's solemn words: "I think Peter, we must now accept, the party's over."

The meeting lasted less than an hour before Peter Townsend and Princess Margaret shook hands in the great main hall at Clarence House and Peter once again took his leave. As he turned towards the door for the last time, Margaret, in a slightly plaintive voice, said: "Thanks for everything, Peter. It could have been so wonderful."

He did not turn round but slowly let himself out and drove thoughtfully back through London's rush-hour traffic until he found the South Road for Sussex.

Five days later, at a little after dawn, on Empire Day, to be exact, Peter Townsend stood shivering with a handful of close friends in the post-dawn mists at Dover Harbour. Once again he was saying goodbye to England; once again he was boarding the cross-channel ferry for a self-imposed banishment. He was back on his way to Brussels and the handful of friends he knew he could trust. After the sixteen years of the trials and tribulations of being the Palace servant who had fallen in love with a Princess, it was time finally to call it a day. With a few solemn handshakes, Peter Townsend walked up the narrow gangplank to the top deck of the boat. He watched over the side as his car was loaded. The sun started to break through the early mists and warm the frost off the steamy windows of the ship's lounge. He saw the last of his friends huddled in their heavy overcoats on the dock. With a wave to them, which was only just discernible, he turned and went into the bowels of the boat. All of them knew at last that the Townsend Affair had finally come to an end.

BOOK TWO
SNOWDON

Chapter One

The long and emotional saga of Princess Margaret's life is a story of various deep depressions interspersed with mad gaiety, periodic romance and some long and lonely years. Like most people, her life evolved along an undulating line which finally emerged as a pattern. Each time one of these depressive periods came along the antidote has been threefold. She turned first to the Church; second to her public duty; and third to a whirlwind of gaiety. It was as if she had to expiate her sorrow in the first two things which could take the trouble off her mind. These periods always lasted for roughly a year, by which time she seemed gay again and abandoned herself to the fun to be had out of life.

1958 was no different and, as she has done throughout her life, she turned to her old spiritual friend, the Rev. Simon Phipps.

Only days after Peter Townsend's boat went into oblivion, Margaret sighed deeply over the lunch table she was sharing with the Queen Mother. She had seen a doctor that morning but both had agreed there was nothing medical to be done. She was depressed, unhappy and at a loose end. Between courses the Queen Mother gently suggested Margaret should invite the Rev. Phipps to tea one afternoon that week. Margaret quietly agreed and they chose the Thursday, two days later.

Phipps was an extraordinary man to be so close to a royal princess. Handsome and dashing, he was extremely light-hearted and gay as well as being sincere and intelligent. He was a natural choice for the young Margaret when she needed friendship and sound advice.

Phipps was eight years older than Margaret and from time to time drifted in and out of the rumours connected to her royal hand. Before he became a priest he was the exactly the kind of escort King George liked for his daughter. His war record was exemplary. He served in the Guards, was wounded twice and won the Military Cross. He first met Margaret when she was just seven years old in 1937, when his father Captain William Phipps retired from the Navy to become Gentleman Usher-In-Ordinary to King George. Simon Phipps was a teenager at the time. When the war broke he was just eighteen, and he immediately joined the Guards. Soon after being commissioned he found himself in Margaret's company again at Windsor Castle where he was stationed. They continued their friendship throughout the war.

Phipps was a man of many talents, including a profound knowledge of music. He was, as soldier and later civil engineer, a man of the world who could breathe a sigh of fresh air into the stuffy corridors of royal living. With the lads at the end of an exercise he could swear like a trooper. Yet, at the evening balls, he was the epitome of the perfect gentleman.

But more than anything else he treated Margaret like a woman. He never indulged her, yet always respected her. He could talk to her frankly about everything, including her complicated love life. Had they both been born Catholics, Phipps would have certainly been her confessor. Even before he joined the Church.

For when he was not with the regiment, or gaily enjoying an evening of cards or dancing, he could always be found talking theology. He had a profound knowledge not only of the Church of England, but most of the world's other religions. He had some exciting theories about Christ's teachings, some of them not absolutely compatible with the strict doctrine of his Church. And he was extremely human in his approach to spiritual problems.

It was obvious he was a natural person for Margaret to turn to throughout her most depressing moments during the Townsend affair. Now that was over once and for all, she turned to him again for guidance and solace.

He had been ordained at Huddersfield and then went on to become Chaplain at Trinity College, Cambridge, where he could match his bright wit with the undergraduates. He was a lot more urban and cosmopolitan than many of the blue-bloods who surrounded him and he rarely had a seat to spare when he gave a sermon. He was the only Church of England clergyman in his time to proudly boast a union card from the Amalgamated Engineering Union and when outside the college walls often preached on the factory floor.

Throughout 1958 Margaret regularly made the sixty-mile trip to Cambridge where she lunched with Simon Phipps and spent the afternoons talking to him about her problems and her faith. They sometimes prayed together for up to an hour and whenever Margaret drove back to London she was noticeably more relaxed and spirited.

This may well have been because of the Reverend's teachings, but may also have had something to do with the fact that he was a gifted comedian whose favourite pastime was writing peculiar lyrics. He taught many of them to Margaret. Her favourite at the time reminded her of her friendship with the great Noël Coward. After a long session with Margaret when they had talked about the theory of Original Sin – something deeply ingrained into the clergy and something which particularly worried the young Princess – he sat down at his piano in his quarters and sang:

> What can anybody do that is the least bit new
> And hasn't been done before?
> Wouldn't it be nice to discover vice
> That is not just a terrible bore?
> I long to break out and make a sortie
> In a world that is mildly naughty.

For years it was a song Princess Margaret would hum over and over to herself.

The second stage of the Margaret recovery was her total abandonment to public duty. She flogged herself without respite for months on end.

Only twelve days after seeing Townsend for the last time she had set herself a course of events which would take her the length and breadth of the country and keep her occupied for up to twelve hours a day.

The first appointment she had was on a cold, rainy day when she set off from Clarence House for Bulford, Wiltshire, where she arrived in mid-morning. She presented colours to the Highland Light Infantry, of which she was Colonel-in-Chief. She stood sheltered from the rain in a huge transport shed and spoke unfalteringly to the massed soldiers standing to attention. Some observers noted the aptness of the words:

"At no time has there been a greater need for resolute and unwavering service. History is not made by a few outstanding actions. It is made by devotion to duty, by steadfastness in time of anxiety, by discipline in waiting."

If the events of her day finished prematurely she would eagerly cast around for other things to do while she was in the area. Officials had to hastily find a hospital or an old folks home to which she could make a spontaneous visit. Despite the problems this kind of suddenness had for the officials in charge, the visits were fantastically appreciated by the people at large.

A few days after her speech to the Highlanders she found herself opening a school in South London. The ceremony was over at a little after three p.m. and she had nothing to do until seven p.m. So she cast around for other things to see. The nonplussed officials suggested she see the local town hall and despatched a dozen underlings to try and make sure the place was clean and empty. But it was not Margaret's idea of usefulness to go and see an empty town hall.

Then she suddenly remembered that the Lewisham train disaster had occurred less than a week before. Lewisham was only a few miles down the road and within minutes her cavalcade set off south. They found the hospital still in a turmoil from the suddenness of the catastrophe. An equerry hurriedly spoke to the Matron, Mrs. Marjorie Bell, and found out the worst casualty area was ward B2 where twenty-two serious male casualties were licking their wounds. Margaret and her entourage swept through the corridors until they reached the ward and forty-four eyes, many of them black and blue, suddenly lit up in delight.

She spent an hour talking to every single inmate in the ward and even managed to joke with most of them. As she swept back to her car Mrs. Bell said her visit was the best medicine every one of them could have had. She had never seen such a bunch of low-spirited men perk up so quickly.

This was exactly the kind of thing which took Margaret's mind from her troubles and convinced her yet again she still had an important public role to play.

The whole of 1958 was spent like this. She went to the theatre occasionally and dined out with friends about once a week. But nightclubs were out. So were riotous parties and drinking. When she was not with Phipps or at other church functions, she was nearly always to be found somewhere in England showing the Royal flag and expiating her own loneliness.

That Christmas Princess Margaret and the Queen Mother travelled as usual to Sandringham to spend Yuletide with the rest of the Royal family. They all noticed how accomplished and relaxed Margaret had become again. During the long dark evenings she kidded around on the piano with her sister, got back to mimicking her old favourites and gave them some of Simon Phipps's less-daring verses.

She invited odd friends to come to Sandringham for the weekend and everyone was pleased to see Margaret's moping days were over. The Townsend affair had put a considerable strain on everyone concerned and they were blissfully happy that the Princess now seemed to be over the worst.

The Group Captain's name had simply never been mentioned again by any member of the Royal family. They managed to just rub him out of their minds. He disappeared from the face of their earth and during this particular Christmas they went to every length not to mention anything which could possibly remind Margaret of him.

It may not have mattered, for Margaret was genuinely now completely over the romance and ready to start again.

Peter Townsend himself had seemingly got over it as well. He had returned to his old haunts in Brussels and looked up an old lady friend from his horse club days. She was a pretty, twenty-one-year-old heiress called Mlle Marie-Luce, daughter of a Belgian tobacco manufacturer. When they met up again Townsend no longer had to hide himself from public view. They had a brief, but fun-packed courtship, and were married within a year.

That year Margaret turned increasingly to her old friends so that by the summer of 1959 she was again the gay-dog Princess who was such a favourite with the British press. Men streamed through her life, and consequently headlines. She looked up old acquaintances, made a lot of new ones, toyed with various proposals of marriage and generally laughed, joked, danced and shrilled her way back into London's highest society. Lord Porchester came back with a bounce. By now he was rather paunchy and looked decidedly well-fed, but he could still raise a giggle from the Princess even though, by now, prolonged laughing left him red-faced and a little short of wind. (Porchester would eventually marry a pretty American Socialite called Jean and take over running the Queen's riding stables.) He squired her back into the old routine and Margaret again more often than not saw the wrong side of dawn before getting home to Clarence House. This time no one complained. They were all so relieved to see her back on her old form they even welcomed the reports in the gossip columns. Prince Philip actually managed to give her a nod and a wink when she mentioned some unregal event at a nightclub.

Margaret had by now blossomed into an extremely beautiful young woman. She was wonderfully full-breasted and it was a period in which she showed the best of herself through the fashions of the day. Her new clothes reflected her new attitude. They were bright and breezy fun clothes with the emphasis on showing off the full attributes of her womanhood.

Of all the men who flitted through her life during this tempestuous year, only one of them could be called her contemporary in age. He was the young and dashing Lord Patrick Beresford who had first escorted her to Ascot in 1957. When she tired of Porchester's giggling, she turned to Beresford for more subtle amusement. He was an officer in the Horse Guards, with a back like a board, a jingle of spurs to his gait, an old-fashioned twinkle to his eye, and an almost total lack of chin; four of the essential attributes of a young Guards officer. While Porchester roared with amusement, young Beresford had a cynical, almost vicious, yet bitingly witty approach to life. Neither of them were awed by the Princess but while Porchester always kept his place, Beresford enjoyed seeing how far he could go with the Princess. His anecdotes became notorious;

his jokes more blue; and his choice of friends for the evening more *risqué*.

Escorting Princess Margaret gave each young blood of the day overnight status as the present most eligible bachelor. They were lionised by a society which insisted on keeping up the pretence of aristocracy in a world which was diving fast towards socialism.

Amid the news of H-bombs on Christmas Island, the first sputniks sent up by Russia and South American revolutions, the drones of London and the Shires kept an ever-eager eye constantly cocked on Clarence House.

Iris Peake, Margaret's lady-in-waiting, refused an average half-dozen calls a day from every unmarried lion anxious to squire the Princess.

But dozens more got through and found a receptive Margaret raring to hit the high spots again.

Most weekends found her at houseparties organised by the new Margaret Set. Billy Wallace, erstwhile playboy, threw open his house in Devon for the Princess's pleasure whenever she wanted it. Prince Michael of Rumania escorted her to various Royal Film Performances and had a running battle with pressmen at London airport trying to deny he had proposed to her. He had, but had not been taken even slightly seriously.

Mr. and Mrs. Denys Rhodes – she was a niece to the Queen Mother – put on lavish hunting weekends in which all the young beaus came storming down from every quarter of the country. Margaret was the most-in-demand catch for every sporting young rogue from Stornaway to the Cornish tin mines, and she loved every single exciting, flirtatious second of it.

She was the restless soul, yearning constantly for a deep ideal love, for a single man who would be all things to her; yet she could turn as compensation to a dozen in as many days and make every one of them feel, at the time, that he was the only one.

Margaret did not hunt. Unlike every other member of the Royal family, she was never madly fond of the outdoor life or sport. Apart from occasional horse riding, the only exercise she ever got was taking her dog for a walk. Unlike, say, Prince Philip, she had no competitive spirit. She watched and enjoyed a game of polo, but she would much rather be at the opera house. During family Sundays at Windsor she sometimes played cricket with the rest of the family (Royals v. Household) but no one could coerce her on to a golf course or a tennis court. Even at racecourses she took more interest in the fashions than the nags. And she yawned loudly when sport came on the television.

But Margaret did not go to these weekend parties for the hunting. Indeed, most of the party had been following the hounds for hours before she even showed her face. She would breakfast on coffee and cigarettes at about eleven and read the paper, still in her housecoat. She would always be washed and dressed by twelve because lunch on hunting days was a movable feast.

Landrovers laden with every form of gluttonous ware would follow on the perimeter of the hunt pursued by others with portable tables and chairs. The hunt could cover many thousands of acres and the hunters, often numbering a hundred or more, would eat between kills. Often they would despair without a kill around midday and decide to replenish themselves before continuing. Sometimes a hunt would start just as they were thinking of lunch and it would be late afternoon before the eating could be properly arranged. In this way lunch in the field could be anywhere between midday and four o'clock. Occasionally Margaret would ride out on horseback to the perimeter of the hunt and watch the event with her beau of the day. More often than not she would follow it by landrover herself, stopping every now and then to watch the proceedings through strong fieldglasses. If she felt peckish, which she often did if the hunt was late, she pirated morsels of cold snipe, grouse, turkey or jugged hare from one of the accompanying vehicles.

Lunch was always a jolly affair, if you liked that kind of thing. The riders would be fresh and red-faced from their exertions. The air would be crisp and autumnal. The dogs would be baying for blood and sniffing around the outside of the field. The horses would be snorting from exhilarated exhaustion.

The tables would be laid right there in the field, with the finest tablecloths and cutlery. Each table would be positively dripping with food and few of the hunters would sit down. Rather, they wandered around picking bits from each of the plates of delicacies and went on to talk to a friend at the next table. The back flap of a landrover would be pulled down and a barrel of beer rolled out. This portable bar also included dozens of bottles of claret, cider and mead as well as fruit juices for the more delicate of ladies, the abstemious gentlemen, and the hard drinkers who scoffed at anything less than a tumbler of Glenfiddich or five fingers of pure Napoleon and carried hip-flasks accordingly.

The feast would be a completely overindulgent affair and the afternoon's sport would take on a slightly drunken air. It was when the fun really started and red-faced colonels, who had seen more of a colonial verandah than an English wood, would huff and puff as the claret brought a decided tinge to their nostrils. Very upper-class ladies sitting on horses as if they had been born there would scream "Tally-ho" as if it were a Viking love chant, and cavalry officers would show off to each other as if the canny little creature they were pursuing was mightier than the Russian guns at Balaclava.

They were all "Margaret's People" and she felt happy and relaxed in their midst. Occasionally she would join part of the hunt, but rarely for long. While she loved the magic swirl of hoofbeats as they thundered through the nooks and crannies of the English countryside, she was never the most expert horse-jumper and shied away from courses with a lot of obstacles. When she joined the hunt it was easy to see the young bloods reacting to her presence. They preened themselves as she came into view, galloped around her nonchalantly trying to show they were born on a horse, adjusted their caps to make themselves more dashing and *always* let her in first for the kill.

But more often than not she would stand on the bonnet of the landrover with head scarf and riding coat and watch from afar. Her lady-in-waiting or one of the house servants was always on hand to fill up her pewter glass of claret which she drank to keep out the cold. Throughout the day she smoked prodigiously and chatted gaily to anyone who would listen.

At dusk the weary riders would either finish their last kill or call it a day. They would make their way back to the vast

Baronial Manor where a huge log fire would be waiting for them along with strong tea or hot punch. There would be plates of proverbial English cucumber sandwiches – nicely salted and peppered and always with the crusts neatly cut off.

An hour would be spent talking of the hunt. Margaret would circulate freely congratulating those who had done well, sympathising with those who had gone head-first over a gate; commiserating with those who had broken an ankle and flirting with all the young bloods who had put on such a wonderful exhibition of horsemanship, especially for her.

At seven, the non-resident hunters would collect their horseboxes and go home. The residents would go to their rooms to wash and change. Margaret always had a bath as Iris Peake put out her clothes for the evening and arranged for the hairdresser to call just before eight.

By eight o'clock Margaret was ready, smiling, radiant and looking forward to the evening's entertainment.

Up and down the country people vied to produce the most lavish and interesting evenings for the visiting Princess. The best hunting parties were normally provided either by Mr. and Mrs. Rhodes, or her cousin Mrs. May Wills, and her husband John.

They always started with drinks at about eight o'clock and dinner half an hour later. Margaret rarely had more than her regular whisky and soda before dinner, but she was partial to the claret which flowed in abundance over these soirées. Margaret normally preferred dining with an exclusive six or eight, but during her periods of intense sociability, the numbers could go up to three dozen. They were all hand-picked for their wit and charm. The beau of the day was carefully selected after a quiet chat with Iris Peake. But invariably other young bloods came with a cousin or sister so that the table was not unbalanced, and Margaret was able to choose her companion for the evening. During dinner a small orchestra invariably played in the background. Margaret's preference for dinner music was always violins, yet she did not mind what country they came from. She was happy with a band of strolling gypsy minstrels, yet would stop all conversation and listen intensely to the pieces she liked when a classical soloist played a piece of Bach.

After a rich dinner and the compulsive digestives which came after, a toast was always made to the Queen and the men lit their cigars. This was the sign for the dinner band to start discreetly creeping away. For at ten a dance band would take the stand. This could be anything from swing, jazz, modern, ballroom, or full orchestra, depending completely on the fashion of the day. But they had to look lively and be ready for any request the Princess might make. This was often a little embarrassing because her knowledge of any and every kind of music – she regularly knew the top five of both the French and Italian hit parades, to say nothing of the latest shows on Broadway – was often way ahead of that of the musicians themselves.

However, if they were good musicians, all was not lost. Margaret would sit down at the piano and play the tune over once. Then she would start again and let them catch up with her. The third time round she would hand the piano back to the hovering pianist and find her partner for a dance. Each of the musicians knew she would be humming every bar and one note out of place would bring a frown from the dance-floor.

Margaret flung herself into these dances with everything she had. She was genuinely the life and soul of the party and most people agreed she would have been even if she hadn't been the Queen's sister. Anyone conversant with any royal scrap book will remember that during this period she was at her most dazzling and beautiful. She bubbled with an effervescence last seen when her Uncle David was in a joyful mood. She managed to capture the eye of every man in the room. And the eyes concentrated on her gorgeous smile, her flashing teeth, her brilliant eyes, her heaving bosom and the swirl of her hips. They were looking at a woman rather than a Princess and that's the way Margaret wanted it.

During these carefree and flamboyant days a curious game started up among the young bloods who were in the inner fraternity of the Margaret Set. They scored points on a whole series of things connected to Margaret.

It started innocently enough with a bet on whether she had slept with Townsend, and if so, how often and how successful was it. The Earl of Dalkeith frowned on the whole situation for two reasons. First of all he thought all this sportingness between rakes was totally abhorrent. Secondly he knew exactly how many times Margaret had slept with Townsend because she had told him.

One of them was a rake of the first order. He survived in a world of gambling debts, business ventures which had only complete failure in common, and waking up in bed with women he could not remember ever seeing before. To him the whole Margaret scene was a joke which he intended to exploit to the full.

Each of them put a tenner in a pot and the first person who could get Margaret to admit her indiscretion would pocket the proceeds. Only Dalkeith abstained completely and £60 was kept in a separate account at Messrs. Coutts, the well known London bankers, who handle all the Queen's investments.

But this initial pot was only the start. The betting between these dubious playboys to whom life was a sport, got deeper and deeper by the day. For each one who managed to take Margaret out the other five had to put a fiver in the pot. For each public kiss taken from the Royal lips, another £50 went in the pot – ten pounds a head. Within weeks the bank account contained nearly £1,000 and had become the talk of society. The original bet was forgotten. The whole lot, the conspirators decided, would go to the first of them who could prove beyond a doubt that he had slept with Margaret for a whole night.

The game was on in earnest. They got up to every conceivable ploy to try and put the conquest into reality. The bedding of Margaret in itself was a game of the utmost intricacy. Had she even wanted to sleep with them the chances of her getting away from the royal chaperons for the entire evening were remote. Then, if they ever managed to get that far, how would they prove it? For undoubtedly Margaret would insist that it was done in the utmost secrecy.

One did manage to stay alone with Margaret for most of the night after a convivial dinner in a friend's flat. But they were later disturbed – playing cards.

Margaret suddenly found herself invited to the most bizarre places and she noticed the most extraordinary lengths were being taken to get her detective and lady-in-waiting out of the way.

But Margaret was gradually shying away from her old set, and eventually the crowd divided the money up and went on a gambling spree to Paris.

For them all it was the end of an era. By the time 1959 dawned Margaret was well and truly ready for another romance.

Chapter Two

At thirty, Margaret was psychologically ready for that brazen, inspiring, maddening, inventive new decade of gay abandon and wild creation, commonly known as the Swinging Sixties. It didn't all quite start at the turn of the decade, but the nucleus was there. Victorian morality, tinged with the discipline of the war years, and the ration-book austerity of the fifties, was about to be exterminated from the British National Psyche.

Within a handful of years it would be fashionable to rebel in every form of life and in every direction. The very mood of life would be transformed into a colourful age of permissiveness and personal liberation.

Margaret's friends quickly noticed she was no longer the flippity young thing they had escorted to a hundred royal rave-ups. She had become a mature, intelligent woman, growing increasingly aware of the artistic dynamite hovering beneath the surface of British Society.

It would take four tousle-haired Liverpudlians to release the safety-catch on all this bubbling enthusiasm. They were already gathering faithful fans in a small, insignificant club called the Cavern.

For Margaret, 1960 was a time of reflection. She had by now got two things thoroughly out of her system; Peter Townsend and rollocking roustabouts with the aristocratic rednecks. She had grown up a good deal in the past decade. She knew a lot about life and a great deal about love and she had broken down much of the stuffy walls of discretion which had trapped her in her youth.

She no longer sought the excessive, expansive, expensive madness of the gay young dogs. They bored and even irritated her and however fancy free she might have become, she would never tolerate the kind of behaviour her young beaus had wanted to get up to. The essence of her relationship with any man, however frivolous, was still secrecy. She didn't mind people trying to guess what she had been getting up to, but she wanted to keep them guessing.

So, for a while, the gay days were over, though Margaret by no means sat at home and thought about her misfortunes. She merely looked farther afield in her friendships, and because she was who she was, she could pick and choose at leisure.

The new set was cosmopolitan, artistic, theatrical, talented, intellectual, musical and bohemian: the exact opposite to the cavalry officers, the chinless blue bloods, and the horsey females who guffawed loudly and looked awkward in female attire. It was an understandable change. Margaret had always had a bent towards the sensitive and artistic side of life. But she had grown up in the atmosphere of the landed gentry. Her only friends as a teenager had been Guards officers and aristocrats who had a pedigree which could be checked by the Palace. Now she found new haunts and consequently new interests and many new friends.

In fact it was still five or six years before the whole new expressionism in every art form – including pop music – would burst upon the British scene. Bohemians still wore duffel coats, had dirty toes, and marched to Aldermaston on the Ban the Bomb pilgrimages. But there was a nucleus of extremely talented theatricals and musicians who bridged the gap between the duffel coat brigade and the essentially working class phenomena which would herald the real swinging sixties.

It was towards them that she now turned.

She swapped nightclub revues for theatres and concerts; she exchanged hunting weekends for musical galas and she selected the cream of British intellectual society for her own small dinner parties.

She was completely unsnobbish in her approach. The persons would be invited on their talent. She loved the slightly grubby appearance of the out-of-work actor. Peter Sellers, for instance, became a firm favourite very early on though he often had to walk to Clarence House because he couldn't afford the bus fare. Army talk was out, so was hunting, sports, society scandal, yachts, estates, shooting, and every other accoutrement of the idle rich. Art talk was in. Writers, actors, musicians, artists, playwrights, comedians, TV producers, film stars, and even a smattering of the more respectable journalists, found themselves gracing Margaret's table.

She went to late night parties, but they were very different to the fun-filled affairs she had been used to. In a comfortable basement in lower Victoria she would sit with others on huge Moroccan cushions while a couple played chess in the corner; Brahms lilted loudly through the room; and the talk would be the new production at the Royal Court theatre.

In the beginning Margaret seemed to have very little in common with her new élitist friends, even though they were flattered by her interest. But she genuinely did learn a lot very quickly and explored a complete new world in which she could exercise her mind and satisfy her artistic cravings at the same time.

Soon she would argue volubly about Brecht, citing performances she had seen; she would talk about the subtleties in Don Giovanni's tone, or the footwork of Margot Fonteyn. But she would still also be seen going to the London Palladium for a good belly laugh and at least a proportion of her new set were from the comedy side of showbusiness.

She developed a new interest in art and started a collection of her own which showed an eye for talent.

Margaret's life at this time was a sketchy affair, mainly because she wanted it that way. As she stayed away from the ignoble haunts of the gossip columnists, so she stayed out of the newspapers.

She met, and became great friends with, the present Poet Laureate John Betjeman during this period and he re-kindled her great admiration for Noël Coward. These two men, for a while, became the new mainstays of the Margaret Set. They were sophisticated geniuses who commanded between them the entire artistic world; from the media, through the theatre to the literary. They were superior in their intellect, artistic knowledge ande choice of friends. Coward especially delighted in Margaret's company, and had she searched the world it is unlikely she would have found a better introduction to the more bizarre and weird sides of showbusiness than through this great mentor of the arts.

Coward could tinker around on the piano for hours and each slight innuendo of note or song would be immediately picked up by a laughing and appreciative Princess. He told her about every *risqué* play then being performed, introduced her to all the up-and-coming actors, playwrights and song-writers. He amused her constantly with his brilliant wit and they shared that love of mimicry which Margaret had always fostered since her childhood.

Betjeman also happened to be a good friend of Oliver Messel, Tony's uncle, and the young photographer also knew him well. Betjeman was more serious, yet still a darling of the intelligentsia for which Margaret now had such a great attraction. His wit was dryer, but when she was in the mood she found him just as amusing as Noël Coward. They were a great basis for anyone to launch themselves into the lionisation of the world's more theatrical society and Margaret used them unashamedly for just that.

In this mood she found herself getting closer and closer to Lady Elizabeth Cavendish, sister of the Duke of Devonshire, and a society hostess of some merit. Lady Elizabeth had always been a friend. Now she became a lady-in-waiting and a strict confidante of the new arty Princess. It appeared she had given up any interest in the aristocracy for "sensitive, artistic and talented people" years before Margaret. She now played a huge and significant part in organising the Princess's new life.

Margaret also found that her old friend Simon Phipps was going great guns at Cambridge. Through him she met every eager brain of the day and many of the more esteemed professors and scholars. So between them all Margaret found herself extremely conversant with the new era she had selected for her amusement and relaxation.

Photography in the early sixties was beginning to be a new art form. By the mid-sixties, like everything else, it would have its own élite protagonists and would be recognised as part of the whole cultural explosion (*Blow Up* etc). But in those early days there were only a handful of real artists behind the lens and they were forging ahead, against staid opposition, creating their own brand of magical images.

In some ways it was all a fraud. The camera was still a relatively new instrument in artistic terms and many people merely joined the wagon by wanting to be different with a profit. Young lords were keen to "do something useful" rather than hang around the estates feeling impotent in an age full of potency, and they found a camera was almost a phallic symbol.

But unless they made it very big very quickly, photography was an expensive game. The equipment cost hundreds of pounds, development meant some kind of darkroom and ideally one needed a studio, with assistants. So it was that the photographers who emerged from this era were either cockney geniuses with a great flair for the unusual – men who, through various techniques, were able to bend the truth of a picture in the same way Picasso bent the nose of a beautiful woman – or they were rich young bloods with a lot of money who turned a hobby into a pleasurable way of saving the family heirlooms.

The fashion pages in the early sixties immediately reflected this new artistic urge. David Bailey startled the world with his stark portrayals of nearly-nude women in dockland. Lord Lichfield, a cousin to the Queen, leapt in at the other end of the scale, yet even he set up his first studio in the East End of London. Between these two bookends of the social world whole new schools of photography suddenly began appearing all over the place.

It was a poor man's hobby because virtually anyone could pick up a camera and start clicking away. Yet it was a rich man's profession because the more you got into it the more expensive it became.

Right in the middle were opportunist middle class people jumping on the wagon of both kinds of success. People like Lichfield had made it fashionable. People like Bailey had given it a new kind of excitement. Now it was time for some middle-of-the-road hard-working professionals to cash in and clear up. Antony Armstrong-Jones was such a man.

The destiny of romance dragged its feet that summer. Antony Armstrong-Jones and Princess Margaret nearly met several times. She was involved with a new play at the St. Martin's Theatre. He had taken the photographs of the cast which hung outside. He had taken shots of the Duke of Kent only hours after Margaret had left. And so it went on.

They were finally introduced to each other at a small dinner party given by Lady Elizabeth Cavendish at 5 Cheyne Walk, Chelsea. She had recently employed the young photographer to take some pictures of her and her family. He was a minor rage with the people who Lichfield could not fit into his diary and who were rather offended by the guttural obscenity of the Baileys of this world. Somewhere in the middle of the new fashionable madness he was cleaning up very nicely and creating a little niche for himself in the media as a whole.

Tony was never the world's most inventive photographer, but he was highly competent, extremely sensitive and technically brilliant with his equipment. He was well-spoken, charming, rather attractive and very good at putting his subjects at their ease.

Consequently Margaret had heard of Tony before she met him and was not at all averse to the situation when she heard he was to be a fellow guest at one of Lady Elizabeth's exclusive tête-à-têtes. She set out that night telling her mother that if she liked him she would commission him to do some photographs of herself.

To Tony this meeting was a breakthrough. He was teetering on the edge of society, this would undoubtedly take him right into the middle of the social swell. He was on the fringes of most things at that time including the theatre. On the theatrical side he did it for love, but he needed to subsidise that luxury with hard cash, and only the glossy magazines and private sessions with very rich people were able to provide the kind of money he needed to branch out into the big time. (Even in those days a good studio in London would cost £1,000 a week to run.)

So Tony was more than pleased to accept the invitation and resolved to be on his very best behaviour.

To the surprise of both of them they hit it off from the very moment they met. He found a rather small, but radiant young woman who was extremely knowledgeable about everything he was interested in. She found a charming, self-effacing young man who was handsome, witty, sensitive, warm and artistic. He had all the eccentricities of the bohemian intellectual, yet still had perfect manners and good breeding. He was, Margaret immediately surmised, just what she was looking for in a new escort; the exact bridge between the gap of grubby artist and frivolous aristocrat, and he held her spellbound with his conversation.

This was not so much because Tony was a good conversationalist (he always lacked the fire and wit of such people as "the Master" – Noël Coward) but he had a profound knowledge of his favourite subjects and was able to elucidate on them with imagination, interest and an inspiring keenness which the Princess found quite captivating.

They talked at first about photography. Margaret was employing her old technique of always starting a conversation with what she thought was her partner's favourite subject. To his surprise she showed a great deal of knowledge about such things as perspective and colour. She had little idea of the technicalities, yet she knew all about the importance of line, contrast, positioning and construction.

Antony Armstrong-Jones quickly found himself deep in conversation, explaining every facet of the craft he loved most. They talked for a while about Rembrandt's pictures, speculating about what he might have done had he been a photographer. They used as a model the Mona Lisa and Tony explained how he could use various techniques of lighting, colour, developing and printing to get with a machine the same effect Rembrandt had created from his genius.

This led to a definite commission in which Margaret asked him how he would tackle a picture of her. He told her he would sit with her and converse until she was completely relaxed. He would spend a lot of time on the lighting which would be as unobtrusive as possible. If it was outside, or by a well-lit window, he would use "available light" an almost completely new expression in modern photography. The positioning would be important, yet it would have to be relaxed. When they were ready to shoot she would hardly know he had the camera in his hand. It was the surprising shot – the unaware one, the picture with the slight element of chance – which always was the most satisfactory.

To Margaret, who had always been used to seeing herself in news shots shaking hands with an endless line of people, or sitting upright in a studio for her birthday picture, this was all completely fascinating. Before the dinner was over she asked him to come to Clarence House for a photo session. She told him to call the House the following day for an appointment. When she got home that night she told her mother she had just had one of the nicest evenings she could remember for a long time.

The dinner party had been on a Friday night. Armstrong-Jones found himself ushered into the main hall of Clarence House early on Tuesday afternoon. Margaret immediately asked him if he could stay to tea after the session because her mother wanted to meet him. It wouldn't, she asked, take more than two hours, would it? Tony was not quite sure what he should do about this because he did not like to set any kind of time-limit on taking a photograph. Yet this interest in him from the Queen Mother could not be slighted. He decided to stick to his guns and did so with customary diplomacy. To take the kind of picture they would all be proud of, he said, she would have to put herself completely in his hands. It might take twenty minutes. It might take all night, but he could not put a time on it. On the other hand there was no reason at all why they should not stop for tea if the session had not been completed by four o'clock. Margaret herself now smiled with a little bewilderment. She was most anxious that he get the picture he wanted. Yet she had a dinner engagement which meant she would have to start getting ready at about six o'clock. She decided not to mention it and hope that the picture had been taken by tea time.

And so, in the richly furnished sitting room of Margaret's

Clarence House apartment, as the sun streamed in through the windows, Margaret and Tony sat down in each other's company and talked, talked, talked. At the dinner party he had been somewhat excited and unsure of himself. This had made him endearing to Margaret who was very used to people being a little awkward in her presence. But today, on their own, with Tony behind his beloved camera, he relaxed completely. He was extremely self-assured. At dinner it had been Margaret's scene; but while the camera was in his hand he was completely in command. It was a whole hour before he even adjusted the light to his Hasselblad and then he pointed it towards a vase of crimson roses and was talking about something else all the time. They talked about the latest musical to hit town, *The Sound of Music*, and Margaret offered to play a few of the songs on her Stein. With her occupied like this Tony had a chance to level up with his camera. Without her noticing he clicked away nearly two films. She showed him some books, poured him a drink, generally moved around the room putting the odd log on the fire or lighting a cigarette from the massive gold table lighter.

All the time Tony was snatching pictures. Then they heard some barking in the extensive gardens outside and Margaret went over to the window. She looked out and laughed. Her pet dog was trying to chase a bird. "Look at that silly thing," she said, and a smile lit up her face.

Tony meandered over so he could just see out of the window. But he was looking at her. He caught her full in the wide lens and took a single shot before Margaret turned round to face him. He caught her again with all the radiance of the sunshine and her excitement at seeing the dog and as she turned away with a slightly reproving look on her face, as if to say, "That was a sly one," he clicked the shutter for the third time.

As she made her way back to the fire Tony said, "That's the one I wanted, Ma'am. What time is tea?"

If Margaret had been impressed with the young photographer when she met him at dinner, she was delighted with him on his first visit to Clarence House. They had spent two hours together which had seemed to simply fly by so effortlessly.

She had never had such an easy, carefree and enjoyable photo session. The Queen Mother expressed her pleasure in meeting him and the tea was relaxed, friendly and informal.

But when the pictures were delivered Margaret was absolutely enchanted. Never had she looked so beautiful or radiant. No one had ever been able to capture in that single still fraction of a second all her character, personality, liveliness and happiness. She raved about the pictures to all her friends and to every other member of the Royal family. They all agreed, no better picture of her had been taken.

Overnight he became the toast of London Society with order books so full he began turning down a great deal of work. He was soon invited to Buckingham Palace where he eventually took every member of the Royal family individually and then together and spent an hour or so talking about photographic technicalities with Prince Philip who fancied himself as an amateur lensman.

At first, Tony's interest in the Princess had been sheer, naked and hungry ambition. But he soon found himself being quite enchanted with Margaret the Woman. She on the other hand began to turn to him more and more in a social sense rather than professionally. Each week he found two or three invitations to various places where Margaret had also been invited. They always seemed to be drawn together within any society in which they met. He in turn began to introduce Margaret to his own set of friends which included some extremely bizarre but entertaining people. At one select party Margaret asked Tony why a couple she had just been introduced to had seemed so peculiar. They were transvestites, Tony told her blandly. She did not quite have to look it up in the *Oxford Dictionary*, but it was the first time she had been introduced to anything so abnormal. She also met a high-class Madame, some very arty dropouts, some black ballet dancers who smoked hashish, down and out Continental noblemen living on eternal credit, and even the Kray twins who were fast becoming London's most notorious gangsters. It was all intriguingly new to her and she realised that her original idea of "getting out into the big bad world" had been the epitome of gentle innocence.

Tony already had a steady girlfriend at the time. She was a talented young actress called Jacqui Chan with whom he had had an up-and-down relationship – more often up than down. He had often told his father he was going to marry Jacqui, yet at the last moment he had always held off. They lived together for several years in his small Pimlico flat near the river and while she was not making films on location she kept house for him.

But in the pre-marriage stage of his affections Tony Armstrong-Jones did not restrict his affections to Jacqui Chan, or even other females. He had some very warm friendships with other men. He was an extremely sensitive, almost spiritual person as a lover, and occasionally broke away from what he called the "earthyness of womanhood".

Just prior to his affair with Margaret he had become close friends with a failed singer who had been introduced by his singing master to the famed actor Sir John Gielgud. Sir John had helped launch him into the West End as an actor. He had never tried to hide his abundant femininity and, indeed, regularly flaunted it. He was effete, singularly attractive in a sensitive way, and he possessed a great deal of affectionate charm.

He had ironically been introduced to Tony by Jacqui Chan who admitted to Armstrong-Jones she had had a "peculiar" affair with him. They were both in the acting profession although the actor had less talent for the stage than he had for singing and quickly went into complete obscurity. However, for a while at least, the three of them were bosom pals, always seen together and often staying together at Pimlico. It was significant that, outside the arrangements of protocol and the family, the only two people Tony later invited to the wedding at Westminster Abbey, were Jacqui Chan and their mutual friend.

About two months after Tony met Margaret, Jacqui Chan was quietly but effectively eased out of Pimlico and found when she returned Tony did not answer the door. At around the same time Tony arrived one night on his motor bike with a passenger. The passenger – no one could have seen whether it was a man or a woman – had on one of the most natural and complete disguises known to man. She was dressed from head to foot in motor cycle gear. She had a helmet on her head, a scarf around her mouth, thick goggles and a complete suit of wind-breaking clothes on the outside. Margaret was making her first fascinating visit to Tony's flat.

Chapter Three

There were several very good reasons why Princess Margaret and Antony Armstrong-Jones managed to keep their secret from everyone for so long. Apart from the fact that they were both secretive types who loved the intrigue of anonymity, he was a professional cameraman who had been engaged to take pictures of the Royal family and Margaret in particular. Any passing journalist who had seen him enter Clarence House would have assumed he was on assignment.

But more important, when they wanted to travel incognito, Tony had all the facilities for doing so.

His Pimlico flat was a natural haven for young lovers. Once bolted no one could get in without the door being opened from the inside. They could get right to the back of the flat, which had a huge skylight, and from the front it looked as if no one was in. Secondly, Tony had had his fair share of love-making before he met Margaret and moved in a circle to which sex was as commonplace as eating. The young avantgarde crowd in which he moved would think nothing if he wanted to borrow their country cottage for the weekend to "take a bird". There was also the motor bike, the single greatest asset they had. And this, in itself, excited Margaret fantastically.

Of all the fascinating new experiences Tony had introduced to his new love, the motor bike was the most original and glorious. She had never felt so free. She clung to him as he meandered through the traffic, simply another passenger on another motor bike wending its way through the milieu. Then, when they got out to a long stretch of road and Tony opened her up, Margaret thrilled to be travelling at 100 miles-per-hour-plus while the wind whipped into her face. They even got stopped by a speed-cop one day and Tony accepted the ticket and duly paid the fine. As they sped off towards

London Airport along the Great West Road, both of them giggled like mad at the excitement of nearly being discovered.

The bike – a huge 500 c.c. Ensign – was not just an exciting new toy for a Princess who had become rather jaded with everything else. The clothes provided the perfect disguise. They even went into transport cafés and ordered eggs and bacon and huge pint mugs of steaming tea. For the first time Margaret could move around anywhere absolutely anonymously. And she relished every second.

Because of this the couple got to know a great deal of each other throughout the whole of 1959. They could meet officially without comment; they could spend congenial evenings together with select friends and they could pound off into the night to spend a weekend together in a friend's cottage without the slightest suspicion from anybody.

Only the Queen Mother guessed how far the affair was going. But Lady Elizabeth Cavendish was a collaborator and so was one of Tony's oldest pals, Jeremy Fry, a talented young entrepreneur who kept the secret until the day they announced their engagement.

But even this was not enough. They both wanted a real hideaway where they didn't have to arrive by motor bike or keep the front lights off in case someone called.

Tony went down to the old proverbial hunting ground for the new photographers – London's East End dockland. Through friends he hunted all along the grimy waterfront until he was introduced to a journalist called William Glenton. Glenton had a house looking right over the river. It had a spare room. The room had a concrete floor and paint peeling from the walls. Tony begged to be allowed to do it up and use it periodically. He said he was compiling a book of photographs on London's Dockland and needed a base in the area. He was so keen for the room, Glenton let him have it for the price of the conversion. As a journalist he had no idea at all he had just become a part of the biggest story of his career: one that he would have to sit on for years.

Tony's Pimlico flat had seen many riotous rave-ups. It was in the back of a converted ironmonger's shop and it had a lot of olde-worlde character and charm. There were only two floors and they were connected by a simple spiral staircase that went through a hole in the ceiling. The flat was littered with all kinds of junk. It was a real lived-in bachelor pad. On the ground floor was a partitioned-off kitchen and a small bathroom-cum-loo. Up the spiral staircase was the bedroom-cum-living room, fitted out luxuriously with colourful Arabic cushions. There were piles of old photographs and equipment scattered everywhere. The kitchen cupboards were full of baked beans and developing fluid. The bathroom cabinet spilled over with films and flash equipment. There were lots of photographs of lots of women all over the walls.

Despite the efforts of his regular "daily woman", who tried to sustain a semblance of order, Tony could never keep the place tidy. There were dirty socks under the bed, always piles of dishes awaiting a wash, and the bed was only properly made once a fortnight when the cleaner changed the sheets. Tony dressed casually, unless he was going to a formal dinner party, and he had his shirts freshly laundered in Sloane Street. Most Sundays he took his socks, pyjamas, underwear and other odds and ends to the local laundromat and normally had a pint in the local while they were washing.

Despite the chaos Tony had a fantastic eye for unusual antiques and interesting bric-à-brac. The place was littered with stuffed birds, ornate chairs, pieces of Italian sculpture and odd pieces of expensive china. It was a fascinating apartment and Margaret was enchanted with it.

However, she never felt really safe in Pimlico. It was too close to home and neither of them ever knew when some old girlfriend would drop by and let the cat out of the bag. She was consequently nervous when she visited Tony there and they could never completely relax. Because of this their love affair suffered and they lacked the true fulfilment so necessary at that stage in any relationship. Tony decided, very early on in their liaison, he would have to do something about it.

Glenton's place at 59 Rotherhithe Street was the answer and a few days after their verbal agreement Tony arrived early in the morning in a van laden with wood, nails, tools, and furniture.

At first it seemed an impossible task. The house had originally been built by a rich merchant several hundred years before. As the Port of London expanded in the early nineteenth century all the old riverside mansions had been pulled down or converted to accommodate the river craft. 59 Rotherhithe Street had been part pulled down and part-converted into a workshop for repairing barges. Tony's new room had been the original workshop with the rest of the house being used either as a storeroom, or sleeping quarters for the miserable apprentices. No one had used it for anything other than a storeroom since the turn of the century. It had a cold concrete floor, paint peeling from the walls, plaster hanging from the ceilings and a door which would not close properly.

But Armstrong-Jones was a photographer and photographers are by nature creative, inventive, practical and hard working. He had a secretary and an assistant photographer as well as a dark-room assistant working for him at the time. For nearly a month they found themselves seconded to the heart of Dockland as Tony carried out the most important of his assignments.

They stripped the place bare, re-plastered the walls and ceiling. He refitted the door with a solid oak antique one and they put in a false floor which they covered in a just-off-white carpet. The most striking thing in the whole room was the huge bay window split up into several sections which looked out over the various moods of the downstream Thames.

As soon as the room was structurally perfect Tony painted the whole thing white. The walls gleamed with gloss, the ceiling beamed at them with emulsion. He fitted white curtains to match the carpet and they were ready to furnish. The room had been transformed. Glenton was amazed to find how roomy and bright it had become. It was an interesting room, not only because of the window but because it was on a split level with several interesting nooks and crannies which invited all of Tony's inventive creativity.

Tony's idea was to make it into a royal nest. There were several powerful reasons for this. Pimlico was known to every notorious raver in London and he was forever having people drop in who invariably wanted to doss down for the night. He had several sleeping bags and they were full most nights of the week. He wanted a secret place he could escape to. Secondly, he needed a haven to work in. He was an ambitious young man with lots of schemes up his sleeve and he wanted a place where he would work on them undisturbed by the rabble-rousers of his past.

But far more important now, he needed a place where he could take Margaret. A place where she could relax completely. A place only five other people in the world knew about. 59 Rotherhithe Street would be the ultimate love-nest.

The first thing Tony moved into the room was a three-quarter size bed with black sheets and a brilliant white counterpane. Every stick of furniture was painted white. He had a big old dresser, two small cupboards, a table and four chairs – at dinner parties later they had to borrow two more chairs from Glenton – a bookcase, a small fridge (one of the natural nooks in the room was fitted out as a small kitchenette), and a bentwood rocking chair.

The only thing which stuck out in sharp contrast to the rest of the room was an old upright piano which Glenton had offered to move out of Tony's way. As soon as Margaret saw it standing in the hall she moved it right back in again.

On the walls and on top of the cupboards, Tony placed his paraphernalia. There was brilliant white china everywhere; a golden cage with stuffed birds warbling to the imagination; a chiming wall clock and a towel stand in the shape of a negro boy. Up by the window Tony strung a double hammock – the ideal place for whiling away an afternoon and watching the river traffic through the window.

When he had it exactly as he wanted it he took Bill Glenton out for a pint of bitter at a local dockers' public house. Glenton remarked about the wonders he had done with the room and Tony said that was exactly what he wanted to talk about. Tony came straight to the point and told him one of the main reasons why he wanted the room was because he wished to bring a visitor there who was extremely famous. It was essential she should keep complete anonymity. Glenton, a journalist who had a reputation for being one of the boys, winked and nodded and said he knew exactly what Tony meant. Who was it then, he asked jovially, Ava Gardner? Tony looked a little pained, supped some beer and said, as he put the glass down: "No, actually it's Princess Margaret."

Glenton roared with laughter only to find Tony's face was the picture of worried seriousness. Glenton blurted out: "You're kidding!" and Tony looked around, startled, to see if anyone else had heard. Within a few seconds Glenton knew beyond doubt that he would be playing host and landlord to the Queen's sister. He put the beer to one side and ordered a large Scotch. He sank it and ordered another one. "Jesus, Tony," he said as the whisky began to calm him down, "you *are* serious. This'll take some arranging."

What Glenton was talking about, and what Tony had not known or taken into his clandestine plans, was that Glenton's house was notorious for wild drinking parties. Glenton was an old Fleet Street hand and had worked his way around most of the national newspapers ending up on the *Sunday Mirror*. It was a favourite habit when they put the paper to bed on a Saturday night to take half the newsroom in a fleet of taxis down to Rotherhithe Street for an early morning session. He had no close neighbours and lived there alone. It was a first-class venue for the kind of loud-mouthed, aggressive, drunken parties so famous between the Strand and Ludgate Circus. Everyone who came brought a bottle of Scotch and Glenton would put on a kippers-and-fried-bread breakfast as the dawn came up over the misty Thames. These Saturday nights had become a ritual and often extended through Sunday and Monday until, bleary-eyed and hung over, the Sunday paper stalwarts reported for work again on Tuesday morning.

Word had soon got around about these parties and before long every weekend was a drunken madhouse as journalists from every other newspaper rolled up to join in. Regularly, as his cleaning lady came in on Monday morning, she would have to step over the snoring bodies of a couple of dozen drunken newshounds.

It was these journalists who had passed the hat around and bought the piano. It was simply and solely so they could have an inebriated sing-song when they turned up after a long Saturday in the office.

The first thing that flashed through Glenton's professional

mind was the story. As an old newspaper hand, the headline danced through his brain even as Tony was talking. He got over that one on the next large Scotch. The second thought which came racing in his now reeling mind was how he could stop the weekend parties. And this was a real problem because the very act of stopping them would spread speculation throughout Fleet Street – the very place where not a whisper could be risked.

When Glenton had explained the problem Tony joined him in a large Scotch and they both mused into their drinks and thought about how they could get over it. Tony, who was always a sensitive man, suddenly realised how much trouble he was causing his new landlord. Glenton would now virtually have to change his entire lifestyle simply because Tony wanted to bed a rather special young lady for the night.

They both got a little drunk that night and Glenton felt expansive. He told Tony he would fix them up somehow. After all, he said, they've all been using the place as a dosshouse for far too long. Tony was unsure but the next day he turned up with Princess Margaret who fell in love with the room immediately and Tony knew then that somehow Glenton would indeed have to "fix it".

Margaret's interest in Tony had gone from casual admiration to a state where she clearly fancied having a love affair with him. Tony's interest in her had gone from intense fascination, tinged with ambition and pride, to the point where he found himself physically excited when she was close to him.

They had flirted and then become more serious and finally they fell in love. But until Margaret saw the room in Rotherhithe Street – she immediately called it "Our Little White Nest" – it was a hit-or-miss affair which could have gone one way or the other at any given time. Margaret was very capable of being fickle in her romantic interests. Tony was a man of varied sexual appetites and found it extremely difficult to be consistently in love with one person.

It was the room which made all the difference for now the element of fear could virtually be taken out of their relationship and on the occasions they met there they could behave like any other young couple in love.

Glenton managed to wean his friends from their nocturnal visits as gently as possible by making it not quite so attractive for them. He "forgot" to put the heating on, sometimes pretended he was not there, and continually dropped little hints that his neighbours were complaining about the noise. They knew something was up but it is to Glenton's eternal credit that they never guessed what.

Only a very small handful of trusted people had any idea of the romance and they would keep it that way for another six months. The couple would move into the room for whole days at a time. Tony would go out shopping for eggs and bacon in the morning and Margaret would try to cook them. She was not very efficient and never once mastered making a cup of tea. Consequently they stuck to instant coffee and Tony did the cooking. Most weekends they had very select people round to supper and nearly always ended up with Margaret bashing away at the old stand-up piano.

The smallness of the room caused endless problems because the couple were always falling over each other. Most of the time this reduced them to helpless mirth. And other incidents added to the peril. Margaret was sitting in the old bentwood rocking chair one day after Tony had just conjured up a "magical" salad dressing. He then started on the steaks and the frying pan burst into flame. Glenton, who thought the house was on fire, watched as Margaret emerged spluttering from the smoke, her face smudged with black grease. On another occasion the couple's river-watching was sadly disturbed by a sudden gust of wind whipping ashes from a passing barge right into their faces. It would never have happened at Clarence House.

Over the next six months this was the pattern of their lives. Whenever they could make it they would wend their way through the city of London on the motor bike or in unmarked cars and arrive in Rotherhithe Street for an evening, the night, or a whole weekend. They would spend hours together doing nothing but holding hands and looking out of the window at the fascinating river traffic. It was as near as Margaret would ever get to domestic bliss and one night they both agreed they would like it to last for as long as possible.

On one occasion Noël Coward and the Queen Mother were dinner guests. The after-dinner floorshow was naturally an absolute hoot with Coward making up rather naughty verses as Margaret tinkled the piano keys. The Queen Mother admitted later she could not remember a better evening for years. The last time she had enjoyed herself so much was before the war at a family get-together at Balmoral. She clearly approved of Tony and was happy her daughter seemed so joyful again.

This was one evening when Margaret herself did the cooking and it was highly successful. They had fresh lobsters with a sauce recipe Margaret had stolen from the chef at Clarence House. This was followed by a rich gateau which Margaret had ordered from Fortnum and Masons that morning. The lobsters turned out to be so filling that only the Queen Mother was able to manage a slice of cake.

Tony was no musician although he enjoyed classical works, but a few weeks after they had found the Little White Nest he sat down at the piano and carefully picked out a tune. Margaret was smoking a cigarette and looking out over the grey mists of the Thames. Suddenly she started humming the tune Tony was playing: "Your Eyes Are the Eyes of a Woman in Love . . ."

Chapter Four

Indeed, for a long time her eyes were the eyes of a woman in love. Bit by bit the couple succumbed to the forbidden ecstasy of royal romance. In tiny little ways they began to show this love. He would tap her bottom gently as she passed. She would pick an odd hair from his shoulder or quickly kiss her finger and implant it on his nose. He courted her in the good old fashioned sense. He was unhappy when they were not together. He sent her her favourite roses, despite the fact that Clarence House received an abundance of them every morning. He was forever trying to find new little ways of amusing her. Then the courtship itself began to take on an importance in Margaret's mind. Tony's imagination and sensitivity started to attract the aesthetic in her. The conspiracy itself became important as it always did with Margaret. The secret meetings, the clandestine qualities of their romance, and the magical ways Tony tried to amuse her, all combined to bring that old fairy-tale dream world out into the open for Margaret.

So it was then, that on a summer evening in early September 1959, as Margaret was boiling some eggs for their tea and Tony was swinging gently on the hammock in the window of the Little White Nest, Antony Armstrong-Jones proposed to Princess Margaret Rose. He did not say the important formal words, nor did he go down on one knee clutching her hand tenderly in his. He merely asked Margaret if she thought it was possible and, thoughtfully, Margaret said she thought it was. Tony got down from the hammock, turned the gas off from under the eggs, and said: "Then let's do it."

A few hours later Tony was peering out from the front door and looking up and down Rotherhithe Street. The coast was clear and Margaret quickly stepped out and into her station wagon parked a few feet away. They drove quietly to Clarence House where they immediately went to see the Queen Mother.

Margaret's mother was clearly as pleased with the proposal as they were. They talked for an hour and she said she would see the Queen the next day and sound out the position. The Queen Mother had no scruples at all about Tony being a commoner. She was just about a commoner herself with a lot of Scottish good sense. But Royals can't just rush off and do things like that and she warned Tony that if they went through with the marriage his entire life would change.

The loving couple became informally engaged the following week. No announcement was made and Margaret waited for months before she wore her engagement ring. But they were engaged in their own minds and were both desperate to get married as soon as possible.

Tony found from the very beginning that the Queen Mother's advice was sound and probably even an understatement. His life changed radically from the moment they left Clarence House. For a start he had to wind up his photographic business. Secondly he found he had to cover all the traces of his past life. Pimlico was sold off just before they married and everything which had gone before in Tony's life was quietly but effectively rubbed out.

Tony found himself invited to Buckingham Palace and Windsor where the other members of the Royal family quite openly grilled him. Prince Philip in particular went out of his way to find out everything about the young photographer. A great sounding-out operation was started when the Queen told the Prime Minister. Tony was quietly and unobtrusively checked out by the Special Branch until they had built up a massive dossier in every aspect of his life. There were no political or diplomatic reasons why Tony should not marry. His indiscretions as a youth were noted but never passed on. Which bachelor could sustain the love of his future wife knowing of his past?

They wanted to get married at Christmas but the Queen implored them to wait until the spring so that the wedding could take place at Westminster Abbey in finer weather. The Duke of Norfolk was secretly instructed to start organising the event. One by one other members of the family were brought into the secret.

The only other thing that remained was a medical for Tony. This was a highly personal one which is normally demanded by the Privy Council before they give their statutory permission for the marriage. In various tests it was ascertained that Tony had no genetical defects, that their blood groups were compatible and that they would almost certainly have intelligent, healthy children.

Another question which the Queen Mother herself brought up was conferring a title on Tony. This was not so much for himself as for the children they would have. It was not proper, the Queen Mother said, that children so close to the crown – in direct line to the throne – be born total commoners. The Queen Mother would have liked to confer a Dukedom on Tony but after consulting the Privy Council the Queen said that was going too far. An Earldom was hereditary and would carry prestige enough.

That Christmas Tony was a welcome guest at Sandringham where the royal clans collected for their ritual holiday. He and Margaret were engaged in everything but name. The date had been set and there were no constitutional or physical objections to the marriage. Both Tony and Margaret were the same age and were obviously very much in love. The Queen Mother always championed Tony despite his bohemian habits and she went out of her way to make him as comfortable as possible.

Despite Philip's avid interest in photography Antony Armstrong-Jones was not exactly the Duke's idea of the perfect brother-in-law. Tony was a little effete and much too sensitive for a man. He was handy with a gun and tried hard to play polo but he was always much happier pottering around in his studio or browsing through books in the Royal Library.

While this made him less attractive to the male Royals it endeared him to the females. The Queen found him pleasant and relaxed. The Queen Mother adored him and just as important, so did Princess Alice, the royal guru. The only men that Prince Philip ever approved of were men just like himself so his mistrust of Tony did not really influence anyone. Charles was still too young to have much say in the matter of his new uncle, although everything was carefully explained to him by his mother.

The only unusual aspect of their courtship was the complete secrecy. Right up until the announcement was made in early 1960 only a handful of people knew of the romance and they kept their lips tightly sealed.

Much of this was because of the Little White Nest where they could go and hide themselves away from the world, which they did as much as they dared. This put a considerable strain on some people, including Glenton, yet the secret did not come out until after they were married.

The announcement naturally brought ecstatic headlines. The nation still saw Margaret as their fairy-tale Princess and while Tony was a somewhat unusual choice for a Royal, he seemed debonair, good-looking, romantic and quite the Prince Charming they wanted.

The nation took to him immediately although some Sunday newspapers had a field day interviewing Tony's former friends. The enchanting Jacqui Chan, a little known Chinese actress, became a household name overnight. Old Chelsea haunts of Tony and his friends suddenly found themselves flooded out with sightseers. Scrapbooks of pictures showing Tony in his black leather motor-cycle gear fetched small fortunes when they were presented to various offices in Fleet Street.

Nobody knocked Tony as such – the Prince Charming story gained them circulation – but Buckingham Palace was a little red-faced at the more exotic details of Tony's past.

Tony's father, Ronald Armstrong-Jones, was the only person not very pleased by the new situation. He had liked Jacqui Chan a great deal and was hoping she would become his daughter-in-law. When he met Margaret for the first time she was stand-offish and insisted he call her "Ma'am". Ronald did not think that was a particularly nice relationship for the mother of his grandchildren-to-be. Consequently they never did hit it off and some years later, before he died, Ronald Armstrong-Jones was extremely critical of his daughter-in-law.

Ronnie and his son had always enjoyed a close, intelligent relationship and Ronnie had prided himself on his sensibilities as a parent. He had divorced Tony's mother when he was a child and was well aware of the suffering this had caused the boy. Tony had also had a very uncomfortable physical childhood – spending most of it getting over polio. Ronnie had married and divorced again and was courting a third wife when the whole royal affair blew up on him. All three wives had managed to remain good friends with Ronnie and Tony. But all the circumstances pushed Tony towards a deep affection and regard for his father, and in later life, to his mother who was one of the few people who could offer him genuine sympathy and condolences when things started to go wrong. She could also give wise counsel. She was a sensible woman who had been through it all before.

For Ronnie, however, his son's marriage was to be a disaster. His own life would change dramatically and his worrying over his son's welfare caused him constant heart trouble. He would find after the marriage his son would be drawn inextricably away from him. (Ronnie's close friends, and in particular a journalist who knew him well, called Audrey Whiting, were convinced the marriage was, ultimately at least, a partial cause of Ronnie's untimely death in 1966 – the year in which significant rifts had begun to appear in the foundation of his son's marriage.)

He was a brilliant Queen's Counsel much in demand and moved in the highest circles of London society. He had devastating charm, excellent and compelling wit, and his speeches in court were famous for their alacrity and, when wanted, pure venom. Ronnie was a Welshman to the hilt. He was the son of a famous brain surgeon. The family motto was "What God wills, will be." His world had been shattered one day while he was a patient at the King Edward VII hospital in London and Tony and his sister Susan turned up for what he thought was a routine visit. He was always pleased to see them and they broke out half a bottle of vintage burgundy for the occasion – drinking it from plastic hospital tumblers. Tony seemed at the same time very edgy, yet on top of the world. After a while he could not contain himself any longer and Susan egged him on. He said simply: "Father, I'm going to marry Princess Margaret."

In one small sentence Ronnie Armstrong-Jones's world changed from gentle, hard-working tranquillity, into something of a nightmare. Ronnie had known that his son's association with high society had included royalty. He had even visited them in the Little White Nest. But he had never believed marriage was even a vague possibility.

Now, stunned and shaken, a message spelt in cablese kept flashing through his head as he tried to sleep: NEW DAUGHTER-IN-LAW IS QUEEN'S SISTER. His days became filled with turmoil, his nights were sleepless; everybody who came near him irritated him, and he no longer knew who he could talk to.

Tony had pledged him to absolute secrecy and he became one of the handful (including Glenton and Susan) who had to bear the terrible agony of keeping the world's biggest secret. He could not talk about it to his friends which would have helped a great deal. Perhaps, had he been able to talk about it to a sympathetic ear, his anxieties may well have been lessened. He said later that maybe he had been over-cautious and was worrying absurdly; but his predictions all turned out to be tragically true.

On Tony's behalf he became nervous and frightened. He knew his son at that stage better than anyone else on earth. While he acknowledged he had never seen a young man more enthused with love he knew his son was sensitive, yet reckless. Tony was strangely his own man and would never kow-tow to a woman. This in itself would prove a great difficulty in such a marriage.

When he was able to confide to his friends he told them of his fundamental misgivings. He knew his son as a live-wire, creative man bubbling over with talent and enthusiasm. He did not believe that any commoner could make the direct transition from a Chelsea bohemian existence to the rigid rules of royalty. Crossing the threshold of Kensington Palace would be like being confined to barracks. At that moment, when Tony saw the dreadful imprisonment of Palace walls, he would rebel. He was effervescent, with many friends – and few of them would be construed as popular choices for the new royal image. He also admitted his bias for Jacqui Chan. She had all the ingredients his son really needed. She had the glamour, the sex appeal, the unorthodox approach to life and she was free from any protocol which might strangle them. He recalled the days he and his children had gone with Jacqui on river trips up and down the Thames. They were gay, tipsy affairs in which they could all relax and be themselves. They could stop where they wanted on some river bank, spend the summer afternoon fishing, swimming, drinking wine or barbecuing sausages, and toddle back to Putney pier as the dusk came down. They could round off the evening in the local downing pints and when Tony drove Jacqui back to Pimlico no one in the world would bat an eyelid.

The more he thought about it the more he knew all this kind of carefree activity had now got to end. Summer days when he could have played grandad to their children would now be overlooked by detectives, servants, and a daughter-in-law who still insisted he call her "Ma'am".

He was the very first to feel personally the brunt of the new protocol requirements of the royal wedding-to-come. His very existence offended certain rules of court.

His marriage to his first wife Anne had been dissolved. A fleeting marriage with actress Carol Coombe had ended in the same way. Now he planned to marry Jennifer but they had not fixed a date for the ceremony. All this gave the Palace advisors a headache and they put it all very carefully to the Queen.

The Queen had tea with Tony and Margaret and told them of their problems. The first was that it would look much better in court circles if Ronald married before his son. He was far more acceptable with a wife than a divorcee. Secondly, at the wedding itself, while both women could be invited Ronald would have to stand with his first wife. His latest wife would have to stand alone. Luckily both women were sensible about it all, much to Ronnie's absolute relief. But it angered him. He did not want to force Jennifer into a marriage before she felt the time was right – and at the wedding, he wished to stand with his present wife.

Tony was bubbling over with the whole prospect of making his love for Margaret open and official and seemed not to even notice the problems it was causing his father. He merely passed on the message: the Queen thinks it would be better.

Ronald Armstrong-Jones felt he had already come under royal command. He did not relish the performance.

They had a very quiet wedding at Kensington Registry Office and flew off to Bermuda on a honeymoon the next day. A handful of family and friends attended and Ronald told one of them that yesterday he was a simple hard-working legal man, today his name was a household word. They had instructions to report to the VIP lounge at London Airport. He already had great misgivings about being a royal in-law. The fact that he was an overnight VIP frightened him tremendously.

His fears were not allayed during his trip to Bermuda. They were constantly followed by newspapermen. They were deluged with invitations from every echelon of the island's society. They found themselves spending more evenings at the British High Commission than in the romantic suite of rooms they had hired for their first marital experiences. When they arrived home a press gang some forty strong had waited all evening for the plane's touchdown. They were met by a blaze of flashlights. Reporters kept yelling over the hubbub and asking him what it was like to be the most famous father-in-law in the world. Ronald put his arm round his new wife and hurried off, but he knew from now on his private life was public property.

Despite all his misgivings, Ronald Armstrong-Jones found he got on very well with most of the Royal family. He felt particularly at home with the Queen and Queen Mother. They met privately in Buckingham Palace and later at Windsor several times before the wedding. The meetings went a long way of helping Ronnie shelve his sad thoughts. He was delighted to find how feminine, natural and warm both ladies were. And how much they seemed to want to like him and put him at his ease.

Meanwhile, just before the wedding, Tony and Margaret had started house-hunting. They looked everywhere in London. Both had sat in the Little White Nest describing the type of house they wanted. It would have to be big and rambling with rustic charm, yet manageable and functional. It would have to have a fair amount of ground and be secluded. It would have to be old, interesting, charming and have a big studio where Tony could work. They started in Chelsea and went round all Tony's haunts looking for such a place. After hunting through most of the rest of London they tried the Little Venice area overlooking the Regent's Canal in North London. They were manifestly unsuccessful and Tony decided to resort to some estate agents. As he moved out of Pimlico and into the Palace itself, where he had a bachelor flat, the Queen said she would introduce him to just the right agents. She did – the Crown Estate Commissioners – and, winking to Tony, said she thought they were bound to have something on their books. The Commissioners looked after all the Queen's estates and it became obvious that Queen Elizabeth's wedding present for her sister was going to be a royal residence. It took them less than five minutes of looking through the books before they instinctively knew they had found the right house. They immediately dashed off to see Kensington Palace. Even as they sped up the wide drive they both knew they had found their ideal future home.

May 6th had been selected for the wedding day and it dawned sunny and fresh with perfect Maytime weather. It was only eight weeks after the Queen had given her formal consent for the marriage and a lot of people had moved very fast to get the whole glittering show on the road.

It was one of those royal events so eagerly prized by the British nation and one to which only they can give full justice. The pomp and pageantry were colossal. The colours glittered, the horses shone, the soldiers were ram-rod efficient and the golden carriage which danced from Buck House to Westminster glistened in the morning sunshine. Thousands thronged the streets. Richard Dimbleby, with the soft dulcet tones which had graced every BBC coverage of a royal event for two decades, was at his very best. Newspapers brought out some of the first full-colour front pages for the event. It was all a fairy tale come true and the British loved them both for it.

Despite his own misgivings Ronnie got together with his former wife at the actual ceremony. They, like everyone else, were seen by the first television audience to top 100 million.

After the wedding they all went to the intimate second reception for family only. At first Ronnie was lost for words in the presence of such pomp and ceremony. He felt he only had to sniff at the wrong time to be a social outcast. But the ladies of the House of Windsor were used to seeing people uncomfortable and were quick to put them at their ease. The minute Ronnie felt vaguely at home was when he saw Prince Charles with a handful of rose petals. Impishly, the Prince, who like everyone else that day had had to undergo a stern ritual, put the petals down the Queen's neck. She shivered, laughed, and made Charles take them out again. Ronnie thought of what would have happened to Victoria's children if they had taken such a liberty. He then saw the Queen as a wife and mother and not the awesome figure of royalty he had been born to expect. When the time came for him to chat with her they spent nearly an hour in pleasant, easy conversation and Ronald left the reception in a higher state of spirits than he had been for a long while.

Later the couple set off from the Pool of London in the Royal yacht *Britannia* for a honeymoon in the Caribbean. After the Tower of London had opened for them they ran to the other side of the ship's bridge. They held hands and found they could just pick out the figure of Bill Glenton waving to them from his upstairs window. Princess Margaret asked the Captain to give a salute with the hooter which he did. The couple watched their Little White Nest recede slowly into the background. No one would ever know how much that room had meant to them.

Bill Glenton celebrated the royal wedding in his own indomitable way. He had the biggest, booziest party anyone in Fleet Street could ever remember, although he still did not let on about the secret room on the ground floor which always remained locked. He did not tell anyone about it until it had been knocked down by the council in a redevelopment scheme. Tony and Glenton tried hard to get the scheme postponed or axed but they lost the fight. (Margaret felt she could not use her own influence to further private means and she did not join the battle.)

But they were to go back to the room many times after the

wedding. By that time the room had been discovered by the general public and guides on the sightseeing boats doing the Thames would point it out. As Tony and Margaret sat at the window one day they heard, booming over the craft's loud speaker "... There, that's the room, where that couple are sitting." They drew back hastily, thankful that no one believed they could still be there.

Tony often slipped over to the Dockland hideaway when he wanted to do some work in peace and quiet. They made a last nostalgic trip there a few days before the building was to be pulled down. Both of them cried like babies. They threw some coins into the swirling Thames for luck and shook Glenton's hand. Both said they would never find a room like that again and that the happiest moments of their lives so far had been spent within those four white walls.

After a last lingering look over the Thames, they returned to Kensington Palace, their new home. Two days later a small van bearing the royal crest drew up and two men cleared the room out. They left the wood on the floor but took every other single piece of furniture, including the built-in cupboards. Tony had the idea they might one day find a similar room and he wanted it to look just the same.

Two days after the van had threaded through the streets of East London, contractors crumbled the house into rubble and dust. Glenton sat down at his typewriter. He wrote the lead-in to the article – known in the trade as the standfirst – finishing with the words, "Now the whole story can be told." He dined out on that one for many a year.

The Thames opened up for them as the *Britannia* chugged happily down towards the sea. This was the end of all the years of frustration and sadness. A new era had taken over her life. As the Royal yacht steamed quietly along the channel and out into the depth of the Atlantic, Antony Armstrong-Jones and Princess Margaret took one last lingering look at the moon, kissed each other, and happily retired to the magnificence of the huge marital bed.

Chapter Five

The honeymoon was quite simply a dream come true. For two months they lived in each other's pockets. They drank in the ecstasy of their immense love for each other. They gorged like lovesick gourmets at a feast of the soul. They shivered with delight in each other's company and their obvious and radiant adoration was contagious for everyone they met.

At first Tony rather liked the enormously flattering things everyone said about him. He was a new national heart-throb and wherever he went people mobbed him. It was all still far too new an experience for him to worry about it and, after all, it *was* rather nice to have a royal liner at your disposal when you went on honeymoon. Margaret had never looked more gorgeous and she positively brimmed over with happiness.

The honeymoon was everything a honeymoon could be. Wherever they went crowds yelled at them for their happiness. Margaret was clearly very proud of her new husband and showed Tony off to anyone who would look. Shipboard life itself was the essence of romance with them eating supper by candlelight on the deck with romantic violin music playing in the background. Margaret had always loved the Caribbean and it was natural for them to head for the sea, sun, sand and calypsos of the tropical isles. Margaret's old flame Colin Tenant gave them a ten-acre patch of land on his Island of Mustique for a wedding present.

However, this auspicious act immediately became the first bone of contention between the couple. Tony, who had known Colin Tenant before, clearly resented his seeming informality with Margaret and her obvious affection for him. He seemed altogether just a little too familiar for Tony's liking and the couple actually had their first tiff late on the night they arrived in Mustique.

Margaret defended her former friendships with a fierceness which Tony had not experienced before. She was quite clearly going to remain faithful to all the people who had befriended her during the whole Townsend affair and who had helped keep her sanity in the lonely months afterwards.

Not only that, she was quick to throw up Jacqui Chan "and all the others" when the subject of former friends came up. All in all it was an argument Tony lost. He never did forgive Colin Tenant for it and has never returned to their plot on Mustique. It was significant that years later when they were to part, Mustique was again right in the middle of the row.

This row apart, however, nearly everything else went smoothly for the couple. Only occasionally did the strain show on Tony's face when they docked to attend some kind of official reception. Tony was very much a jeans and sweater man who liked to slouch and put his hands in his pockets. Now he had to wear collar and tie, stand upright and hold his hands behind his back in classic Prince Philip style. He never did get used to the pomp and circumstance of being a Royal and it was always a cause of friction between him and Philip. He was shy as he walked two paces behind Margaret and often clearly uncomfortable. The endless hand shaking became tedious and he was never happy with the film-star status.

In effect, Margaret, even in her marriage to Tony, had been given a bit of a raw deal. The hangover from her uncle's abdication had ruled out any possibility of her marrying Peter Townsend. Now she was paving the way again by marrying a commoner. It was not unprecedented, but it was historically extremely odd. As such they both bore the brunt of the unusual circumstances.

Rather than the Royal family bending down to the lower level, they expected Tony to try and reach up and join theirs. This put a strain on all sides, but the precedent of the marriage paved the way for a whole different influence to start taking over royal thinking.

People cheered profusely rather than jeered quietly when Princess Alexander married a man from the City. The Duke of Kent happily wed a Yorkshire squire's daughter without a blink from official circles. The Duke of Gloucester quickly followed by getting married to a Danish secretary – another daughter of divorced parents. After all this, absolutely no eyebrows were raised when Princess Anne decided to marry a lowly born Captain in the British Army.

All of them, in many ways, have Tony and Margaret to thank for smoothing the wheels. Now, at family get-togethers, there is a plethora of commoners, but at first it was only Tony who had to learn the Royal ropes the hard way.

It was one of the many things Tony found difficult to cope with in the beginning. Most of the time he managed to put a brave face on it. But over the years the rigours of his early training, which had started on the instant he originally left Clarence House, were something he would greatly resent.

Despite the ordinary kind of rows every newly married couple experience, and the problems of royalty, the marriage was extremely happy and successful for three years. During spring in the first year, Margaret became pregnant and Tony finally agreed to become the Earl of Snowdon so that his child would have a title.

From the very beginning he was against the Earldom. He did not think he deserved it and most people in the country agreed with him. Yet it was the express wish of every member of the Royal family and he succumbed to the pressure they put on him.

A month later, on November 2nd, their first son, David, Viscount Linley, was born and their marriage had been well and truly sealed. Soon after the Queen and Prince Philip set off for a tour of Africa and Tony got royal permission to become a photographer for the *Sunday Times*.

As his father had predicted, he desperately wanted to do something rather than just sit around looking pretty and shaking people's hands. He was clearly bored with being a Royal and nothing else. This new job was a way in which he could break back into journalism. He was paid a massive retainer by Lord Thomson and given a free hand with his assignments. He also did such things as designing the bird house at London Zoo and planned to make TV films.

This arrangement smoothed out some of the bruises Tony

was feeling because of his new situation. He valued his independence very highly and this made the marriage even more compatible.

Tony settled down to his married life and found that nearly everything in the garden was rosy. He and Margaret complemented each other in most things. In many ways their characters were very different with Tony being rather soft and gentle and Margaret being quick-witted and brittle.

He found in his new wife, in fact, many attributes he had not fully recognised during the tranquillity of their romantic days.

He found Princess Margaret was ambitious, strong, stormy and masterful. At the same time she was surprisingly magnanimous and trusting. Her personality was proud and noble, and not only because of her birthright. In all her dealings she was above-board and open. Her hatred of deceit was second only to her hatred of rudeness. She was forgiving and quickly forgot any of their arguments unless she had been deeply offended.

From her family, staff and friends she needed to be completely trusted in her dealings and she constantly sought their friendship, and even adoration.

She sometimes showed a great deal of self-confidence and had a good opinion of herself and, from time to time, she caused ripples of resentment by being too boastful.

She was very analytical and this sometimes made her unsympathetic to others. She was critical and showed very little tolerance to slow-witted people. She could be practical and had a keen intelligence. If she had been born into the middle classes she would have made an excellent scientist, doctor or lawyer.

She was always a very determined woman who wanted, and more often than not got, her own way. She could get very angry if someone thwarted her and from childhood she could become downright dictatorial if she was opposed in one of her pet plans.

She was a fairly timid child, but by the time she was a teenager she threatened to grow into an authoritative adult who was bound to be a power in her world.

Just occasionally this bordered on selfishness which resulted in the Princess being a little lonely. In her moods of anger, people tended to try and keep out of her way.

Friends were always amused at how the Princess could change moods. She could be the picture of charm and sympathy at one minute, yet always avoided anyone who tried to be too intimate with her. People who tried to presume got either a very cold shoulder or a sharp rebuke. (One nightclub owner asked her, when she was a teenager, "How is your father?" She retorted sharply, "Do you mean the King?") If people lacked attractive manners, Margaret would never forgive them, however many other virtues they possessed.

The other aspect where Margaret was lucky she was born a Princess, was her love of luxurious travel. She had a keen sense of adventure and a vivid imagination. Because of this Mustique was always one of her favourite places. But, unlike Princess Alice, her great-aunt, she liked to go there in the lap of luxury. (Alice often toddles off to exotic places on banana boats.) Margaret's favourite method of travel was always by water – as slowly as possible.

Tony found his new wife could often be highly strung and could get very excited. But most of the time she remained optimistic, generous and stayed in good humour. She always preferred brains to brawn and would go out of her way to pursue an intelligent topic of conversation.

One of the enigmas of her temperament was that she was the type of person who, under other circumstances, would have loved nothing better than to devote her life to the pursuit of pleasure. When she had a good time, she had a *very* good time. She had to conquer her hedonistic tendencies from a very early age. Even so, she liked to play hard and could sometimes commit excesses and extravagances.

When she played hostess, no expense was spared. If she went on a shopping spree she could run up a small fortune. She often ate far too much and if she touched wine at all she more often than not polished off a bottle or two. This extravagance of nature affected her work, where it was seen to be great enthusiasm.

Another small enigma was her memory. Most of the time, when meeting people for instance, she had a fantastic memory for small detail and fact. She often startled friends and family by remembering the exact circumstances of some past tiny event. Conversely she had a bad memory in academic matters. She could learn quickly from a book but tended to forget it only weeks later.

Margaret's love for Tony was dedicated, and he felt she had completely abandoned herself to her affections. Her love was complete and utter, but it had its price. For a start Margaret tended to demand a lot more affection than the average person. She was deeply emotional when she fell in love, and very romantic. She went to endless lengths to make their lives together seem more compatible.

When she bought clothes she pictured herself as Tony would see her. When she had the dinner table arranged she would go to infinite lengths to make sure the lighting was just right. She seemed to love him wholeheartedly and overwhelmingly and gave herself unreservedly to the situation. With him she was gay and vivacious and could often revert back into childishness and almost teenage frivolity.

Her kind of love seemed to be sacred to her and she could not tolerate any kind of disturbance to it. She seemed to adore Tony totally, putting him on a pedestal for long periods, and he found himself responding with as much as he could give. Despite all the difficulties of their marriage Tony was forever trying to find new ways of looking after her welfare, and on occasions when people criticised Margaret and she was not able to defend herself, he was deadly in her defence.

Sexually she tended to love with the mind and the spirit and he found that although all her men have been sexually attractive it was not the physical side of their relationship which caused the deepness of the love.

In this way there were many subtleties to any Margaret love affair which were never fully understood by either the public – fed on a constant diet of romantic balderdash – or even many of her friends. She was perhaps the most misunderstood of all the Royals in her temperament. For while she could be most sincere in all her feelings – mental and physical – it was the actual ritual of the love which fascinated her most. She wanted to know at all times the form in which things were done. The courtship itself became a very important thing in her eyes and the secrecy and ritual of it all almost took over from the sincerity of the affection. A major difficulty in this was that she wanted all the love she felt to be free and unfettered. This was always difficult for the Queen's sister. It was because of this that such almost phallic symbols as the motor bike had formed such a large part of their relationship. It represented that unchained freedom she craved, yet had all the ingredients of secret romance.

In many ways, Tony soon found, this great love and affection was quite genuine as a spiritual force. But it did little for the physical and sexual side of things. Because of her great, almost overbearing imaginative refinement, Margaret found it difficult to transfer her mental feelings to the marital bed. She loved the fantasy of love, the tiny quirks of sensuality, and the make-believe ritual of romance. But she was capable of getting almost off-hand when these feelings were expected to take a sexual course. She had a total horror of anything coarse, banal or ordinary and this always affected her sexual appetite.

Consequently, while Tony felt he was being wooed towards the boudoir as the evening progressed through titillating sexual trivialities, he found once he got there that the spell had been broken. In the early days Tony got over this quickly and easily. As soon as he had identified the problems he began to cope with them on an "If you can't beat them, join them" basis. Snowdon's sexual tastes had always bordered on the bizarre and he found he was able to tease her with imaginative sexual games.

Instead of standing on the pedestal and enjoying the game she played, he stepped down into her fantasy world and organised his own.

Townsend had dominated her love because of wisdom, experience, secrecy, the ritual of forbidden love, and the whole spiritualism of the affair. Now Tony could dominate her because he understood her sexuality and knew how to titillate the small absurdities of her passion.

But even with all this, perhaps because of all this, the total depth of the liaison had to be short-lived in terms of lifetimes.

When they first relaxed into a state of actual married life it became more and more difficult to keep up the subtleties of sexual fantasy and while they carried on for years in a state of supposed marital bliss, in reality they were gradually growing farther and farther away from each other.

Being the kind of testy, almost reckless girl that Margaret was, she wanted her own way most of the time. Because she was the Queen's sister there were few people around who could put her in her place. Her family could, and did so regularly, Tony could most of the time and the odd really close friend, like Colin Tenant, got away with a sharp word or two when he thought it was necessary. But Margaret had an irrepressible ambitious streak which she found difficult to tame. Her ambition came out in all the things she wanted to do. When she had set her mind on something, everyone watched out. She was going to go hell-bent to get it.

On the few occasions when her ambition was checked she always turned inwards to her own household and became a domestic tyrant, taking it out on her family and private staff, and even the lowly servants. During these times they all tried to keep out of her way.

Snowdon once called the *Sunday Times* and specifically asked for an assignment away from home for a week or so because his wife was "lording it so".

Despite this, Tony found in the early years at least, most of the time, life in Kensington Palace was harmonious and well-ordered. Only when she embarked on a scheme and became thwarted in her efforts did she occasionally become very difficult to live with.

She did not seek out trouble. In fact her attitude to life was carefree and generally hospitable. But she was more than ready for a fight if one came along. She was tempestuous as a domestic fighter, but always completely fair and above-board. She was by no means a devious person and detested deviousness if she came across it in other people.

During any kind of row – domestic or not – she was swift at retaliating against any offence she felt had been done her. For a while she could be quite hostile. But she forgave and forgot easily and quickly. She did not harbour grudges, unless the sin was unforgivable, but she would never, under any circumstances, tolerate rudeness.

Princess Margaret always liked the adulation of the masses. It was lucky she was born a Princess because her love for being the centre of attraction was one of the most potent parts of her personality. (Whereas the Queen's Coronation and Princess Anne's wedding were sheer agony for the two of them, Margaret revelled in the attention showered upon her when she married Tony. Where her elder sister spent years conquering nerves before a public function, Margaret threw herself into each event with verve and gusto. There was no self-consciousness when she entered a room with hundreds of people looking at her. She loved it.) But Margaret was the type who *always* needed to be the centre of attention. Even if she was with the Royal family or her own family at home, she never allowed anyone to upstage her.

She adored small dinner parties where she would sit at the head of the table and was most adept at keeping the conversation turned her way. At nightclubs she always liked to be the life and soul of the late night revelries. On Colin Tenant's island the entire life of the community had to centre around their royal visitor.

Tony never thought this was necessarily a bad thing. She *was* gay and vivacious and an excellent hostess. She *was* witty and informative, and she was always bright enough to set the table sparkling. But to her, adulation, on all scales, was almost a drug and she could be quite petulant if she did not get it.

Tony found that people who did not know her well misunderstood her and reacted by being scared of her. This was because her nature was actually refined and subtle and she was repelled by anything coarse or earthy. To someone who appeared a little oafish, she would immediately turn icy cold. Her friends would say she did not even mean to: it was just in her nature to react in this way when her subtlety was offended. This was unfortunate because Margaret is basically not a snob in the accepted sense of the word. It never mattered how working class a man was if he was, for instance, in the arts. She therefore struck up friendships with all sorts of actors, painters, photographers and interior designers and the like, who were miles away from the titled and landed gentry. But she would shy away from a titled man who had drunk too much, had a red face and a lecherous look and seemed as if he were about to tell a dirty joke. Consequently many well-born people found that their aristocratic birthright did nothing socially for them when they met Margaret. On the other hand a cockney musician would find her genial and flattering company.

As a housewife in later years of the marriage her artistic bent was always rampant. Princess Margaret loved luxury but her surroundings had to be harmonious. If she was forced to live for any length of time in a discordant environment, she could actually become physically sick. She and Snowdon consequently spent years perfecting their living surroundings and Margaret has been known to refuse a dinner engagement she would have otherwise enjoyed, because the hosts had completely mis-cast the colours of the carpet and the wallpaper. During a visit to Buckingham Palace, the Princess has been known to suddenly leave her present company, walk across a room and turn a chair around because its previous situation had offended her. An old master hanging crooked would bring an angry pull on the servants' bell. This was not because she was a particularly neat person but because she was symmetrical. She had a superb sense of proportion, line and colour. The highest standards of her artistic appreciation were locked in beauty and simplicity. As such, a room itself would become artistically important to both Princess Margaret and her husband. It was probably one of the first things they found they mutually agreed on. They would spend endless hours discussing colour schemes, trying them out. They would move the furniture around (or have it moved around) until nothing seemed out of place. They would carry on until they had found positions in which each piece of furniture seemed *symmetrically* correct from any area of the room. But, almost as a piece of "living art", from time to time they would change the furniture around so that the environment of the room changed. Yet it was never allowed to become discordant.

Kensington Palace was lived-in and it was not part of Margaret's nature to have a house-proud complex. But she had got a complex about simple beauty and even a minor colour clash would offend her mortally. By definition Tony, as the kind of photographer he is, also enjoyed an artistic streak. This was certainly another factor in their relationship. She might be a Princess and he a commoner, but in artistic terms they were equals.

The other main area where Margaret had a keen artistic bent was music and dancing. She adored the ballet, which was her favourite art form, and she loved to dance. Servants at Kensington Palace were not particularly surprised when, one night after a nightclub outing, she came home, put on the stereo and sang *I could have danced all night*.

She had a marvellous sense of rhythm and timing and could become quite ecstatic on her not-so-rare informal visits to Covent Garden. She adored these visits in which the officials at Covent Garden conspired to ensure her privacy. She always selected a small band of friends to be at such parties and rarely used the Royal Box. Socially, Princess Margaret liked to be very exclusive.

In her eating habits at home she is often difficult, basically because she takes such an interest in food. She is not particularly greedy, but likes to know every detail about a particular dish and will ask friends for the recipe if she has enjoyed the meal. In later years she has had to watch her diet, not because she is particularly over-indulgent at the dinner table but because she cannot resist the richer types of food. Unlike her sister who is fairly simple in her diet, Margaret will rave about a new sauce she has discovered or insist upon a second helping of a carefully contrived rich new recipe. Because of this she put on quite considerable weight and many newspapers across the globe have rather nastily shown poignant pictures of her growing double chin.

It is very unfortunate, in this respect, that Margaret, who is prone to putting on weight and is forever in the public eye, is generally considered to have absolutely no dress sense. This is particularly surprising because she has so much sense in everything else. The simple beauty techniques she masters in every other aspect of her life and environment are generally sadly lacking in her own personal appearance. Even Snowdon, who has a casual, but fashionable and exceptionally balanced sense of dress, had been unable to cure or advise her in her choice of clothes.

She comes from an environment and upbringing which was staid and formal. This has reflected in her clothes. Even when looking casual – say rambling across the countryside with the Queen Mother – she looked oddly awkward and vaguely unhappy.

One of the handful of artists whose job it is to dress the Princess from time to time, had a session with her at his salon. He had spent weeks perfecting designs especially for her and took into consideration everything he knew about the Princess: the colour of her hair, her make-up, her shoe size and, obviously, her measurements. He came up with designs that essentially were arranged to make her look pretty. He tried to be subtle, yet bright in the colours; fairly simple in the line; and he made every attempt to show off Princess Margaret's assets as a woman.

Almost without exception the Princess changed something. Either the line, the colour, the neckline or the cloth. It was very frustrating because she turned bright and pretty clothes into dour dresses which did nothing to improve her looks.

At home, or at work during her fantastic array of royal duties, Princess Margaret always showed an enormous vitality and a very strong constitution. She was still physically very fit although she suffered from unbearable bouts of migraine which seemed to come and go for no apparent reason.

Because of her nature she is one of the hardest workers in the Royal family – when she wants to be. The Queen very patiently gets on with the task of being a monarch; Charles rehearses constantly before a royal engagement; Anne gets fussed and bothered and has often upset organisations like the Save the Children Fund by rushing through a room where hundreds of children have stood for hours waiting to meet her.

Margaret plunges in at the deep end and can get through more arduous engagements in a shorter time than any of her royal kin. When doing her duty she has an unusually magnetic personality and a great deal of enthusiasm for what is going on.

If she takes something on she doesn't cease until she is satisfied the job has been properly done. This enthusiasm is often contagious and she can often turn a rather mundane project into quite a swinging affair.

The only trouble comes when other, less courageous people try to impose limitations. Margaret, if she has set her mind on something, refuses to accept any limitations. Even small failures make her unhappy and frustrated. No amount of success can contain her. When one job is done she looks around hungrily for the next. She was born with a love of responsibility and, during quiet moments, almost craves for more. But this responsibility has to be backed with a great deal of open confidence from those she is associating with. You cannot take Princess Margaret lightly and you have to enthuse with her.

At home Tony found she was a whirlwind of a worker, always popping in to see her staff and find out what was going on. As soon as she found something interesting she plunged into it with great enthusiasm. She loved the big things; the challenging things.

But she could never bear menial tasks. The only time she was ever known to perform these little, timewasting acts that are so necessary for others, was when she was trying to set an example to the children – or if there was simply no one else around at that moment who could do it for her. In this she was relentless. She could supervise, for instance, the moving of an entire household of furniture and love every minute of it. But she could never be bothered to pick up a teddy bear which had fallen on the nursery floor.

So in the big things – the affairs of state – she left the details to her staff. She was interested only in the project and the outcome. The petty boring details left her cold. When the big things were going on she could be adventurous and even reckless. She was always impatient and wanted to get on with it – despite any precautions from her advisors.

All this, and probably much more, Lord Snowdon found out during the first few years of the marriage. But in this he was not alone. Margaret began busily to set about learning all the quirks and undulations of his character as well. She found in him the exact opposite in temperament to Peter Townsend.

The Group Captain had been used to commanding full attention from any company he was with. Tony was sensitive and even vulnerable and never tried to dominate any circle larger than the average dinner table. He was considerate, intuitive, observant and even soft.

He never tried to sweep Margaret off her feet with bombast or chicanery. He was subtle and charming. He was always sympathetic and usually behaved in the most modest and unassuming fashion. In large companies he acted as if he had a lack of confidence in himself. He seemed quiet-spoken and artistic. He would have been quite hopeless as a fighter ace, not because he was in any way a coward, but because it was impossible for him to find and cultivate the killer instinct.

The Armstrong-Jones who Margaret had married had a vivid imagination and seemed suggestible and impressionable. He was in those days always happy to jog along with Margaret's wishes and went out of his way to please her in all sorts of little ways. He was forever out of sorts with the tremendous difficulties placed upon him by suddenly joining the Royal family. Later, this difference between his ideals and the conditions of his life, was to play a major part in the breakdown of his marriage. Official life made him restless and discontented. In order to compensate for this he would become obsessed with the most insignificant details. Over the years this made him boorish socially and difficult to live with.

Tony was a spiritual, almost psychic, man. Quiet and unobtrusive, he loved nothing better than sitting in a park watching every minor detail of the world go by.

He would be moody, sometimes suffering terrible depressions. On the other hand he could spring to immense happiness and spend long periods being the essence of joy and tranquillity.

His father said one of the troubles between Margaret and his son was that they were both headstrong. This is interesting only because they were both headstrong in different ways. She was a determined young lady who wanted, and nearly always got, her own way as a matter of course. He on the other hand would only stand his ground unconditionally if his ideals had been offended. On this he would be incredibly stubborn and even the strong-willed determination of Margaret could not move him.

Tony's spiritualness was the first major attraction he had for Margaret. His very agreeable romantic nature and obvious domesticity fitted in exactly with her romantically mental approach to love. Neither of them had the faintest desire to rush to the bedroom as a matter of course. Both of them could while away the whole evening talking, laughing, debating, by candlelight in an informal manner.

Tony soon realised the hard-nosed Prince Philip never did entirely approve of him. Snowdon was far too weak and effete for the polo-playing Prince. But with the others he immediately became the family's pet. The Queen Mother especially became Tony's champion. She was a very discreet mother-in-law and Tony would often wander over to Clarence House to discuss family problems with her.

In the main Tony was unfussy and unselfish and, during the time he was in love with Margaret, he was always overly concerned for her welfare. He was not particularly physically strong and was more of a visionary intellectual than a strong-armed DIY enthusiast.

While the world around him, especially after he had become a Royal, seemed materialistic and superficial Tony became more deeply interested in the inner being. He learnt how to withdraw into himself completely. At first he found being stared at wherever he went most unpleasant, but eventually was able to dream and float his way around, becoming almost oblivious to his surroundings.

Even when he was a teenager he tended to look at the world through the most rose-coloured of spectacles. Little daunted him because he didn't ever really see anything amiss. He was the idealist who always expected the very best to happen in this best of all possible worlds.

By nature he is not particularly critical but he could get very niggly during his depressions.

In his pre-marriage days he invariably became attracted to – and by – charming, outwardly emotional and worldly people, who often possessed a spicy nature. The most obvious example of this was Jacqui Chan who he very nearly married. She was not a very practical woman but while she was with him her sole aim in life was to make him happy.

In his post-married days his nature led him into bizarre situations involving people who could inspire the more erotic and sensitive side of his artistic nature. Only after several years had the love between Margaret and Tony become mundane and uninspired. She yearned for that old spiritual romance. He, denied the sexual pleasure he craved, turned to people like Jeremy Fry who shared his sensibilities.

But this was not until they had been married for many years and had both become quite intelligently realistic about their situation. In the meantime, life seemed to go on, quite harmoniously, in a whirl of public activity and private affection.

Chapter Six

Antony Armstrong-Jones and Princess Margaret had married each other when they were both thirty. For three years they were ecstatically happy, for a further seven years their affair was stormy. It eventually began to break down in 1970 when they were both forty and it ended six years later. In many ways it was a typical twentieth-century marriage which gradually found itself floundering as many do. The situation was not typical but the reasons were. They were two intelligent adults who had both been around for some time before settling down with each other. They loved, they rowed, they made up, and they were compatible in most things. The chemistry between them eventually turned sour and, unlike any other middle-aged couple facing the same problem, they had to put a brave public face on it all.

The marriage was singularly unremarkable. Snowdon got on with the job of being a high-priced photographer and Margaret went on with her job of being a Royal. The two of them sometimes didn't meet for days on end. The children went to boarding school, family Christmases were spent at Sandringham as they always had been and Margaret went home to mother every now and then as the situation occasionally boiled over.

Ronnie Armstrong-Jones managed to relax even more as the first year of the marriage settled down into wedded bliss. His son seemed so happy and madly in love. He knew it was difficult for him but was impressed with the way Tony was bearing up. There must be a breaking point, he said, but he had to admit he had seen no signs so far.

Ronnie was also right about Tony the photographer. He had put the original money up to start Tony's business and he knew how passionately his son felt about the trade. Ronnie was bitter that protocol demanded he should give up his studio. He felt Tony would lose all his independence and would have to fight hard to regain it. Tony would never be happy simply living as a Princess's husband.

For the first two years of the marriage Tony lunched regularly with his father, often at the Inns of Court where Ronnie worked. Sometimes they lunched in one of the top rooms at the Wig and Pen Club in the Strand and Tony even took his father to the House of Lords where he had not yet officially taken his seat. At each meeting Ronnie found his son was gradually becoming a different person.

Small things niggled and irritated him. He was immensely secretive. He was paranoiac about crowds. It was true that he now seemed far surer of himself and self-possessed. But even as early as the first year, Ronnie could feel the strain for his son. He soon saw they were a somewhat tempestuous couple who had strong views on nearly everything.

Tony had married her as a political innocent. He soon found he had little stomach for public life. By about 1965 he attended fewer and fewer official functions. He concentrated heavily on his profession and Margaret found herself going out alone.

But the real area where they seriously began to fall out was a family matter. Tony started to rebel at the restrictions placed on him by the fact that he was now a Royal. Margaret had always been madly family-orientated. It was immensely important to her to make sure her family was never offended. But Tony was a loner. He resented the Duke's frown when he put his hands in his pockets. He disliked dressing up and all the pomp and pageantry attached to almost any family affair. (A typical family photograph taken for the Queen's Silver Wedding shows Tony in polo-necked sweater looking very out-of-place.) He had married into the family but he never really became one of them. Their very way of life was alien to Tony's undisciplined nature and while he tried hard at first to conform he found it more and more difficult as time went on.

Tony found he could not relax completely when he was on one of the family visits. He felt the outsider because he was very much a commoner and very much a type who could go into the kitchen and make himself a cup of coffee, rather than call a servant to do it for him.

So he only had any connection with the rest of them when he had to. He stayed more and more in his private den at Kensington Palace; went on assignments for days and even weeks on end and went off to work quietly at friends' country houses at weekends. They kept up this pattern for many years, throughout the second half of the sixties. Until in 1970 both had started to go separate ways socially and the beginning of the end came hovering into view.

The first real brush came in 1963 when some of their mutual friends were involved in the Profumo Scandal. Tony had in fact been to several parties with people who were involved with the call girls Christine Keeler and Mandy Rice Davies. It was only coincidence he had not been to one where the girls were actually involved. That September when the Denning report on the Profumo Affair was published there was many a red face hiding behind newspapers in St. James's clubs. And many more who breathed a sigh of relief because their involvement with the scandal had not been revealed.

It was the sort of scandal that no one came out of without egg on his face and Tony realised how close he had been to getting involved on the fringes.

In the late sixties it became a restless, turbulent turmoil of a marriage filled with emotional stresses interspersed with periods of intense and passionate love.

They had glorious rows over every conceivable subject, nearly every one of which would end up with laughter, a kiss and a cuddle. They were exuberant in both their lovemaking and their arguments. They stimulated each other in both. And for a while at least they were able to rise up to the somewhat tempestuous platform of that bliss so often abused in married life. At first she rarely stopped thinking about him.

When out shopping one day, for instance, Margaret found herself in an exclusive Eastern couturier's. London at that time was going through the flower-power days and embroidered kaftans were the rage. Margaret had been recommended to go and see Thea Porter's very expensive haberdashery of

Eastern promises. She tried on a few but found they were not for her. However, she liked the look of one so much that she bought it. She told a rather bemused shop-girl it would look fabulous on Tony. She was quite serious and Tony immediately donned it as his favourite housecoat.

Emotionally there were two aspects of personality they shared: the constant need to hit high and low jackpots in their emotional lives; and their mischievous sense of humour. After they had rowed in public they would laugh to themselves in the back of the car about what an impression they must have made.

They had loved fooling the world with the Little White Nest, and any other time when, either through disguise or chicanery, they had managed to remain incognito. These all provided them with constantly funny anecdotes to amuse their friends and family. A typical example of this humour showed the erratic storminess of their natures.

One evening both wanted to watch different programmes on the television – it must have happened in every household in the world which has a TV. They spent half an hour in heated debate giving their reasons for wanting to watch their own selected programme. Then the absurdity of the situation suddenly hit Tony and he burst out laughing. She laughed with him as he gave in gracefully, saying: "You win." He settled down to watch the programme of her choice. Exactly half way through she got up and switched the knob of the tube telling him it was turn for his programme now. They both smiled, held hands, and got on with the viewing.

Every year, almost without fail, after they married, they went off together for at least two weeks' holiday in Sardinia. When the children were young this became something of a ritual. They would become a normal happy family enjoying a seaside holiday in a protected villa on the south side of the island. Margaret sunbathed while Tony taught his children to swim, built the traditional sandcastles on the beach or drove around the island sightseeing.

Tony habitually disliked holidays and normally got bored after the first week. In a way his life was a massive holiday as he travelled the world with his camera and found out-of-the-way subjects and locations to film. He enjoyed working holidays in which he could relax or work depending on the mood of the day. Sitting around in the sun was a strain on him unless he was doing something, or planning something for the following day.

In this he was the exact opposite of Margaret who loved nothing better than not doing a thing all day if she could get away with it. He would swap a Bermuda beach for a tribal village any day and they rarely went abroad together. But Sardinia was a must on their annual calendar.

This was basically because it was the only time they were together as a total family unit (with a very helpful local police force who were extremely adept at keeping the paparrizzi off the Island). On these trips his children became Tony's working project for the two weeks and he would plan their days together with infinite care. They once spent the entire holiday building a very good replica of Windsor Castle in the sand. It was right in almost every detail and Tony was able to instil in his children a whole series of things, from line and perspective to architecture and fortification. They had often rambled through the dusky walls of the castle as children and knew every inch of it. In this way the whole family enjoyed the two weeks without any member getting bored.

These were perhaps the happiest days of their marriage right to the end, and the days they missed most when they eventually separated. The villa in Sardinia was also very close to the children's hearts. For a while at least they were able to experience the stability of a happy family life.

The children were always the one facet of their lives in which they found continual bliss. It was typical that, despite their own dispositions, when Margaret was due home one day from a long exhausting trip, Tony should spend the morning with the kids baking a cake with the words "Welcome Home Mummy" in icing on the top.

Throughout the years of marriage Tony's expensive cow-hide equipment case travelled across most of the world. In it he carried his Hasselblad, his Leica with various lenses, and an awful lot of expensive film. He specialised in mood pictures of people against their own backgrounds, whether they were society wenches out for a spree, or Southern blacks in a stinking ghetto. He was very good at what he was doing and he has looked through his lens at some of the richest, poorest, prettiest, ugliest, meanest, nicest people in the world. Being Margaret's husband helped him a great deal. Presidents queued up to sit for him, society hostesses tried to lionise him and some of the most beautiful and sensual women in the world were ever-eager to pose for him wherever he went.

Princess Margaret learned to shrug her shoulders when she heard her husband was reported eating dinner with a beautiful woman in a small bistro in a Paris suburb. She knew very well it was probably a working meal after a hard day in the studio. Nevertheless, his profession brought Tony into contact with some gorgeous females, and with many of them he kept up an acquaintance.

Dory, second wife of André Previn, posed for him for nearly two days and said afterwards she wished the session could go on forever. He photographed the American socialite and writer Pamela Colin, who later married Lord Harlech. They jaunted off into some of New York's most unattractive areas for hours on end as Tony kept his camera clicking away.

He first met Lady Jacqueline Rufus-Isaacs at a photo-session and turned a casual day's work into a long and warm friendship.

Despite the fact that most women found Tony charming, attractive and easy to work with he has had the brush-off from some of the world's most famous of them. He asked Bianca Jagger if he could photograph her and she did not even bother to reply. Elizabeth Taylor got her agent to say she was not interested and Marlene Dietrich laughed at him when he proposed a session. He tried to approach Greta Garbo through a mutual friend but she remained alone, with her black scarf and her memories.

Despite these setbacks most of the women approached by Snowdon answered him with a resounding yes. And this often led to gossip, especially in the *Women's Wear Daily* in New York, and Nigel Dempster's *Daily Mail* column in London. Dempster, a conceited little man who has his ear continually tuned into the fringes of the "bitch-brigade" played Tony's photographic sessions for all they were worth.

Gayle Hunnicut, actress and former wife of David Hemmings, was a principal victim and he was cock-a-hoop with victory when Snowdon and Gayle went off for a three-day shoot together and he was able at last venomously to link their names.

This became almost a daily occurrence in the Dempster paragraphs until it was simply impossible for the two to go on working. And a few weeks later, when Gayle Hunnicut was due at a film reception which Princess Margaret was also attending, Buckingham Palace officials got into a frenzy of embarrassed activity.

No word was said to the Princess herself but officials from both Buckingham and Kensington Palaces went to great lengths to make sure the Princess and the actress did not meet. This was extremely difficult because both women were the centre of attraction – at either ends of the room – and neither could help noticing the other.

Margaret excused herself from the gathering she was in and worked her way through the throng to Gayle's side of the room as perplexed and worried officials tried to guide her somewhere else. She was not to be outmanoeuvred. She walked straight up to the actress, who curtsied. Margaret told her she had heard so much about her and both she and Tony were great fans of her films.

Margaret, a great film fan, could remember every performance and the two spent the next half-hour recalling favourite roles and discussing various directors. In short, they got on famously together and one of Dempster's spies, waiting in the wings for a triumphal report to his boss, nearly got fired for writing the wrong story.

It was significant that, years later when things were not quite so amicable between the two of them, a similar situation would occur with Lady Rufus-Isaacs. This time, despite the fact that they found themselves within talking distance, Margaret stonily cut her dead.

By the time the marriage was ten years old, Snowdon and

Margaret were entertaining three very separate groups. One group was exclusively Margaret's and almost totally consisted of people she had known in her single days. Another group was mainly professional friends of Tony's, plus some on the fringe of the art and theatre world. The third set were the lucky, diplomatic, talented bunch who managed to be liked by both of them at the same time.

They only had a few of these mutual friends and they tended to be in showbusiness or journalism. Peter Sellers was always a firm pal, but in latter years mutual friends seemed to come from the lesser strata of showbusiness.

Derek Hart, the charming reporter-producer from the early *Tonight* programmes, got involved with Tony on the documentaries he was making. They respected each other professionally and got to like each other a great deal when they found themselves for weeks on end on location. Hart was quickly brought into the family net as a trusted friend to them both.

Jocelyn and Jane Stevens were another mutual choice, a somewhat surprising one for various reasons. His reputation in Fleet Street where he was called Piranha-teeth and was deputy chairman of the Express Newspaper group, was offset by the fact that his wife was a lady-in-waiting to Margaret and consequently a good friend. Despite his hard and callous reputation, Stevens was an entrepreneur when it came to newspapers and had known Tony in the old days when they were both involved with the glossy magazines.

Like Stevens another professional friend was Lady Harlech, the former fashion editor of the London *Vogue*. She had interests in common with both of them and knew them as a married couple perhaps better than anyone else.

But apart from a small handful of specially selected people, they managed to eventually live two separate social lives.

By this time Ronnie Armstrong-Jones noticed that a strange, yet compelling barrier started to grow up between him and his son. The Earl of Snowdon had become a Royal in so many ways. He now accepted he was shadowed everywhere by a detective. Much of his warm charm and effervescence had been eroded for a more stately disposition. He rarely laughed and had a terrible hankering to be alone for lunch. They would choose the most obscure corners they could find.

Ronnie found it embarrassing to talk about Margaret as "your wife", and Tony learnt how to give the answers before the questions started, by using the famous royal "we". Ronnie found that conversations with his son had become stilted and strange. When he had any contact with Margaret she called him "father-in-law" at all times and he had to bow when he first met her and make sure he was never sitting unless she was.

Nevertheless when he came into direct contact with the Royal family he still found, as he had at the wedding, that many of his fears seemed to be unwarranted. He was always impressed with how his son had seemed to settle in. At these do's Ronnie actually found himself waffling away quite happily about nothing in particular – as all families do on such happy occasions.

While always having misgivings about the marriage and about his own relationship with his daughter-in-law, he had no doubts about why Tony had fallen in love with her. He had, like everyone, seen thousands of pictures of her over the years. But he had never expected to find such a beautiful woman when he met her in the flesh. She radiated charm and fixed him with mischievous "blue, blue, blue" eyes that quite enchanted him from the minute they met. Her skin had a texture and colour he had never experienced before.

Musing late one night into a vintage bottle of port he ruefully remarked that he knew exactly how Tony had fallen in love with her. But they were both headstrong with very positive opinions of their own. "If she tries to put him in a straightjacket, he won't take it."

He kept his opinion to the very end but managed to temper it a lot later on when he entertained them for several weekends at his 200-acre estate in North Wales. Despite the fantastic domestic arrangements which protocol demanded, they all managed to have a fairly relaxed and easy time. He had to take Tony to one side and ask him his wife's preferences for food. He found out she had gone off champagne but was keen on lobsters. He learned she did not eat potatoes and wanted a late breakfast. He and his wife, with the help of a lady-in-waiting and his own daily help, coped with all her whims.

What helped considerably during these weekends was that he was entertaining in his own home. He *had* to be king of his castle, even to a Royal Princess. So that when the whole family went down to the beach for a picnic he was able to send them all off – Princess Margaret as well – to collect firewood so they could brew up some tea and cook their eggs and bacon. In fact Margaret collected more than anyone and seemed to enjoy the whole day terrifically. Even on the beach, however, Ronnie was careful not to sit down on the rough blankets before his daughter-in-law.

Chapter Seven

On a dull Thursday in December 1968, a strange scene was enacted in a public house in Brighton which would become significant to everyone else only years later. It was decidedly not Snowdon's lucky day. He had driven down to the seaside resort to film a location shot for a BBC programme. On the way he crashed his Aston Martin into a coal lorry and started work with some language which was rather unregal. Snowdon and the crew were downing Guinness and sandwiches in the Flying Dutchman pub which happened to be the local of Brighton Pier's most famous showman, "Professor" Patrick Cullen.

Cullen's act was to read hands for five bob a go and he had appeared in more TV programmes than he cared to remember. It was natural that he should offer to read Tony's palm when he found him having a pint in his own local. Tony whimsically offered his open hand and Cullen read it carefully. He started off with the usual platitudes. Tony had a lively, agile, creative mind. A lot more sensitive than the average. Snowdon grinned happily. He was a normally sexed man with a firm character. He was outstandingly attractive to the opposite sex. However, when he got to the lines of affection, he stopped and pretended the reading was over. Snowdon saw the slight reflection in his face and asked him to go on.

There were three lines on Tony's hand, called the lines of affection, which caused Cullen to be reticent for they clearly showed an oncoming disaster. Each of the lines was prominent and meant three separate loves. He had had one before marrying and the other was clearly Margaret. The third showed he would fall in love with a third woman within about ten years – that is, around 1978. Cullen read all this out to Tony quietly, although of course, the rest of the bar was straining its ears to listen. Snowdon was getting increasingly agitated as the reading went on but he could not seem to be able to take his hand away. Cullen went on. There would be another child in his life. He was destined to father two boys and a girl. At this Tony pulled his hand away smartly and quickly asked the rest of the crew if they were ready to return to work. Out of interest later on Cullen studied close-up pictures of Margaret's hand. He concluded that if the couple had come to see him before getting married he would have implored them to reconsider. "They could never, ever, have been completely compatible."

It was an assessment that by now many people shared.

Public attitudes towards the couple had changed considerably over these years. At first the fairytale quality of the romance had prevailed above all others. She was the radiant, lovable favourite Princess and he was the dashing young man who wooed and won her.

But by 1965 they knew each other well enough to row quite bitterly in public and the nation soon got to recognise that their marriage was becoming a stormy affair. This caused endless speculation, and rumours of their impending separation came and went over the next ten years. In fact they separated several times, for various lengths, and various reasons but as each rumour went the rounds they scotched it by suddenly appearing together in public again, holding hands, smiling at each other and obviously still outwardly happily married.

Both rumour and reality were based on truth. When they started to get on each other's nerves seriously they got out of each other's way. For some time the continued separations kept their relationship healthy, alive and vibrant. After an absence of a month or so, they found they could get on quite happily, even romantically again and for several weeks it would work all over again.

But because of these separations Tony gradually found himself being scandalised. Margaret was seen very much as the hard-working loyal Royal who kept the home fires burning. More and more people began to see Snowdon as the runaway retrograde husband who wanted to continue his former life as a minor, but way-out, playboy.

The beginning of the final breakdown came in 1970 when

the critics were gaining ground fast. Tony had gone back more and more to the bohemian, bizarre areas of his past. He soon collected a whole string of new friends with whom he developed a close camaraderie, most of the time ignoring the sensibilities of the Palace. But it was Tony's relationships in other directions which began to rankle with the few people in his life who genuinely wanted to look after his interests.

Various things happened in quick succession which were to bring this to a head. Firstly, police raided a country mansion near Reading in Berkshire where they had spent months in observation. It had become clear to them that the goings on in the house could have a more serious effect than even the Profumo scandal which brought down a government. Because of this the Special Branch had been brought in. They managed to get one of their members taken on in the house as a servant. They also set up watch at nights from a vantage post in the garden. From there they took the car numbers of every visitor. Inside the house both pictures and tape recordings were taken.

The Special Branch had no interest as such in the weird goings on. But they were more than interested in the people who attended. For among the selective groups who collected there were senior civil servants, diplomats, members of parliament and other notable public figures who could be archetype blackmail victims. This interested them very much. While they decided they would not raid the place openly – it was against their interests to create scandals – they had to put a stop to it. They decided to act a day after Snowdon had been identified entering the building. This had put an entirely different emphasis on the situation for now, not only the government could be brought into any subsequent scandal, but the Royal family as well.

Their method was quick and effective. They confronted the organisers, who hovered between the worlds of aristocrats and gangsters, and showed them the evidence. One more such party, they threatened, and the whole thing would blow up. The organisers closed the house down the next day and the police files are still gathering dust somewhere in Whitehall.

The scandal had been narrowly avoided. In fact, so narrowly, the organisers did not know how lucky they were. Two Sunday newspapers had got wind of the goings-on in the house and had organised invitations. Luckily for all those involved these men attended a simple party where few notables had been present. But the newsmen started a dossier and were getting deeper into the net when the whole thing was stopped. They had not got the conclusive evidence they wanted. (In fact, in a classic piece of Sunday journalism, two rival journalists had found themselves confronting each other.)

But they had got enough to keep them interested and one by one the people who had been involved were quietly moved from office.

This alone was enough to start the rumours flowing and Tony found himself subject to the worst they could offer. Police, journalists and nearly 100 very scared people had all been involved. It was a situation which was impossible to hush up completely. Bit by bit Tony's name was linked to the scandal in no uncertain terms. No newspaper wanted to risk losing circulation by damaging the already floundering "Prince Charming" image, but they hinted at Tony's indiscretions with a vengeance.

For much of this rumour Tony had only himself to blame. He was by now being seen regularly with some notorious characters. Early in 1970 he began having intimate dinners with various friends on board the *John B*, a small pleasure steamer converted into a restaurant-cum-nightclub moored by Battersea Bridge on the Thames.

The *John B* was an exclusive riverside club which enjoyed a splendid reputation. There is nothing in its past or present to indicate that it specialised in bizarre events. But it was an ideal rendezvous for those who wished to do so. Cut off from the mainland, the only way into the restaurant was by boat – at the owner's discretion. Once he had a party going on he could refuse entry to anyone else. It was snug, neat, intimate and very expensive. Customers ate by candlelight looking through the portholes to the lights of Battersea. Upstairs were six club bedrooms for patrons who wanted to use the place as an expensive hotel; for those who had drunk so much of the house wine it was imprudent for them to leave; or those who wanted to meet their lovers for a clandestine evening.

Tony began to use the place a lot with several assorted dinner guests. One of them was his then chauffeur who was an obvious and well-known homosexual. Before joining Tony's employ he had been a regular patron of a public house in Earl's Court, London, which was a notorious hangout for homosexuals used exclusively as a pick-up point. Its patrons ranged from the most bizarre of old men dressed in Boy Scout uniforms, to the most exotic of female impersonators and transvestites. They were habitually looked on greedily by the older homosexuals who vied for their company. For journalists and police alike it was the most obvious place to start looking for a vice story. Both of them did so regularly and it was not long before Snowdon's friendship with the young chauffeur became almost common knowledge.

One of the most constant visitors to the *John B* at the time was "Jason King" actor Peter Wyngarde, famous for his floral shirts, debonair manner, and impossible plots. In fact the TV team spent several days there filming various episodes after Wyngarde had fallen in love with the place. He also held intimate dinner parties there. Two years later Wyngarde's reputation as a lady's man was smashed when he was found by police molesting young boys in a public toilet in a London Park. He was summarily convicted on vice charges and very nearly went to prison. His reputation was smashed and many of his friends were forced to look the other way when they saw him cross the street. (He was another one whose preference in housecoats was for kaftans.)

So the rumour and speculation continued in the most unsympathetic, even evil, way. It was mooted by a lot of people that Snowdon had been the notorious man with the whip during the Profumo Scandal. The picture had been circulated freely among every little gangster, pimp, journalist, and pornographer in London. It showed a half naked man with an erection brandishing a whip. He was masked in a black leather helmet and had a stiff corset around his stomach. No one had ever been sure of the identification of the picture. Speculation had obviously been rampant. Now, unfairly and without a scrap of evidence, the story went round that it was Snowdon.

But undoubtedly Snowdon *was* enjoying the company of a very odd assortment of characters. He had always had a penchant for theatrical company; actors, artists, poets and musicians, and they have always included their fair share of sexual eccentrics. He was prone to be highly influenced by sensitive people, both men and women. Because of his own sensitivity he was always subject to terribly bad nerves after long periods of stress. Whenever a breakdown appeared on the horizon, Snowdon combated the oncoming disaster by losing himself in friendship. He chose people that he trusted almost at random and was able to give them far more than he ever took because his need for the relationship was that much greater. He would therefore plunge himself into new situations, often without realising the full extent of their meaning.

All this, of course, did nothing to allay his critics who by now had embellished the odd titbits of information and talked freely about him in every Fleet Street hostelry. This put a huge strain on his relationship with Margaret who began to hear the rumblings and sneers of ill repute from afar.

All in all neither of them found they could keep on hiding the fact that they were unhappy with each other. Their sinking marriage became almost a cliché in the popular women's magazines. The journals clung on faithfully to the well-worn image of royal respectability, yet instinctively knew that it was a hackneyed one. They blamed everything under the sun for the growing tension, except for the very reason which by now was almost certainly the relevant one. After a decade of marriage, the Snowdons were getting tired of one another.

The most consistent and accredited rumour of their impending breakup was one that swept through the American press in December 1970. It was all started by Julie Kavanagh, the London correspondent to *Women's Wear Daily*, who said, somewhat a little late, that Mustique had become a real bone of contention between them. This was quickly followed by a detailed article in the *Washington Post* which quoted "influential sources" who said they had actually parted and were finding ways for a legal separation in preparation for a divorce. Most of the world's press took up their lead and printed every bit of tittle-tattle they could find. The furore over the parting became so intense it began to worry everyone – Buckingham Palace especially. Tony and Margaret had been used to living through such speculative pieces and only they knew the exact truth of the matter. But Buck House wanted something to be done. The collective royal spontaneous statement "There is no truth in the rumour . . ." had become quite toothless as a defence against the growing speculation. Editors of London newspapers called the Palace personally and officially to say they must give some further statement. When the Queen was consulted she agreed a statement would have to be made. But not by her or the Palace. Tony should make it – and make sure it scotched all of the rumours.

Tony was in New York, Margaret was in Mustique. They talked that evening by telephone and Tony invited a few journalists, mainly from the wire services, to meet him for a drink at the Waldorf Astoria later that evening. He did not put out a statement as such but talked to them politely about the situation for nearly an hour. He said he was a working husband, much like any other, but he had to spend a lot of his time in official duties. When away from home he wrote to his wife, or talked to her by telephone nearly every evening. He had been a photographer for twenty years and it was the kind of work which took him away from home a lot. Had they broken up, he surely would have been the first to hear of it. The marriage was still on; they were still very much in love; in fact, he was meeting her in a few days' time in Bermuda and they hoped to have a second honeymoon.

The rumours were nearly scotched. And when Tony arrived on the island and the world saw how dearly they embraced each other, the dossiers on the breakup were put firmly back in the library archives.

But all this was a gravely sad cover-up of the truth. The facts of the matter were that both of them were sinking steadfastly towards marital disaster.

While Tony had started off the marriage by being gentle, solid and dependable, royal duties began to irk him so much that he became irritable, nervous and tense as the marriage went on. He was also capable of tremendous jealousy. His dislike of Mustique was an obvious example but by no means an isolated one. He openly detested almost anyone Margaret had known before him and was rarely polite to them. One day he came into the room as Peter Townsend was being interviewed on television about his war experiences. Tony got into an instant rage and, after ripping the plug from its socket, he stormed out of the room, slamming the door behind him.

At dinner parties to which friends of Margaret's had also been invited, he would sulk gloomily into his plate and leave almost as soon as the meal was over. Long before Margaret's liaison with Llewellyn, both brothers had their share of the Snowdon ice and rebuff. At one meal where young Roddy was a fellow guest Tony snorted and sneered at everything he said. When Dai Llewellyn started going out with a former flame of Tony's, Snowdon snapped: "One of them's after my girlfriend and the other's after my wife."

His jealousy could sometimes bubble over into an uncontrollable emotion which could become destructive and dangerous. When this happened Margaret's only resource was to get out of his way and stay there until he cooled off.

In the seventies Margaret and Tony saw very little of each other. He was away on assignments for at least six months of the year and made sure it stayed that way. He often came back only when he knew Margaret was away. He spent a lot of time in his bachelor pad, a cottage near Crawley in Sussex which Margaret in the latter years hardly ever visited. During his periods at home – or in Sussex – he tried to spend as much time with his children as possible. As a father, Snowdon could rarely be faulted. He adored his children to distraction and spent a lot of time and trouble trying to bring out the best in them. He used every facet of his creativeness to amuse and educate them. They especially loved to spend a few days with Daddy down in Sussex where they would tramp through puddles with boots on, have snowball fights, play cops and robbers in the huge wooded garden, and generally behave like a couple of scamps – so difficult in Kensington Palace. Throughout the seventies the children were almost the only reason why the couple stayed together at all. They were living separate lives occasionally under the same roof and Tony spent far more time in his darkroom at Kensington Palace than he did in Margaret's bedroom.

The Sussex cottage had by now taken on a new significance in their marriage. It was Tony's castle of escape. While not on location he spent more and more time there. The house itself had formerly belonged to Tony's uncle, Oliver Messel, who by then lived permanently in Barbados and has a long association with Mustique. Just after Sarah had been born Messel suggested the Snowdons should try and get the house livable-in again – as a small family retreat. The whole family had sped down to the thick Sussex woodlands in their white Mini. As they wandered through the dusty building, opening windows to let the sunlight in, it was like Sleeping Beauty being awakened from the curse.

Like the romantics they were; they both fell immediately in love with the place. Here again was a building they could turn into their very own little nest. They could bring all that furniture from the White Room that had been gathering dust in an ante-room at Kensington Palace. They would both love renovating it. The water had to be pumped by hand from the scullery where the immense stone-flagged floor was cool in the summer and warm in the winter. It was packed with Victorian larders and sculleries. The huge beam in the main sitting room was dated 1652 and the chimneys sprouting like turrets from the roofs were genuine Tudor.

The home had originally been three cottages used by estate workers for the much larger mansion they could just see through the woods. That had been owned by Snowdon's maternal grandfather, Leonard Messel.

Throughout the whole of 1965–1966 the Snowdons spent every spare moment at the house and got it looking exactly as they wanted it. After 1970, however, it had become Tony's private den, where he could hide from the world and his domestic problems.

In the beginning they had had themselves, towards the end they became entrenched in completely different circles, lifestyles and environments. As Margaret veered back to the old, solid friendships with members of the aristocracy, and Tony sought out the weirder bohemian types who floated on the perimeter of the TV world, Kensington Palace became two separate houses.

Tony took much of his work down to Sussex and invited a lot of people there from time to time. These included single, unescorted women, couples and people like his old trusted friend Jeremy Fry for whom Tony has had a lifelong affection.

But Tony was not the only one who was seeking friendships outside the marriage.

In 1967 Margaret wrote long letters to Robin Douglas-Home, the writer nephew of ex-Premier Alex Douglas-Home. They exploded on to the world market only after the end of the Snowdon marriage. But it was a firm indication of Margaret's feelings at the time. In them she not only expressed her terrible depression about the state of her own marriage – but made it known to her old friend Robin that she was "dying to see him again".

In fact a close analysis of these letters gives a fascinating insight into Margaret's romantic nature. Only the British public were spared from reading every detail.

They were, in every sense of the word, completely indiscreet love letters which left little for the imagination. She poured her heart out and was quite explicit about her feminine desires.

It seems an odd part of Margaret's secretive nature that she should lay herself so open to worldwide attention in such an intimate way.

Even after this unfortunate, and extremely embarrassing publicity, she could not help herself writing, in an equally pungent and personal way, to several other people. At a later date this included Roddy Llewellyn. The price put on these missiles of indiscretion was so high that they have yet to find a buyer. But when the crunch came they did little for Margaret's dwindling credibility among the handful of people who mattered who had read them.

Douglas-Home committed suicide the following year and no indication of his answer has ever come to light.

TV man Derek Hart took the Princess to a swinging party at the home of Johnny Dankworth, the celebrated jazz band leader, as early as 1970. They flashed onto the drive of Dankworth's country mansion in the silver Alfa Romeo Margaret liked to drive and the party went on so late they decided to stay for Sunday lunch the next day.

It was an evening very reminiscent of the old Margaret Set days although obviously Margaret was not worried about being seen with Hart because the middle-aged anchor man was a great and trusted friend of them both.

But not all Margaret's nocturnal activities were so open and innocent. She started a new Margaret Set in London with many of the young bloods she had met in Mustique. The extrovert entrepreneur Ned Ryan, who owns hotels and a lot of expensive property, began squiring her through London's nightlife. He had taken his old girlfriend Lady Carina Fitzalan Howard, the twenty-four-year-old model daughter of the Duke of Norfolk, to Mustique, but quietly dropped her when the opportunity arose to escort Margaret once they were back in London. Margaret went back to avidly reading *Melody Maker* to find out all the latest musical trends. (Years before when some musician had expressed surprise at Margaret's great knowledge of the current musical scene Princess Elizabeth had told them Margaret slept with the *MM* under her pillow.)

One night a tired and sleepy-eyed detective McIntyre got through a night of riotous dancing when Margaret and Ryan decided to go to Bermondsey Market as soon as it opened at six a.m. This quaint old London Market, with its colourful stalls and goods on display in the street, came alive first thing in the morning – but it was not the policeman's idea of rounding off a heavy night. The long-suffering detective waited patiently as Ryan and Margaret ate a bacon-and-sausage breakfast at the Bermondsey house of one of Ryan's friends.

The new Margaret Set was a close-knit affair with many of the romances interlocking. Another young Margaret escort of the day was Lord Buckhurst, twenty years her junior, who enjoyed taking her to Mirabelle's Restaurant in Mayfair and later on to Ronnie Scott's jazz club where Oscar Peterson was having a popular season. Buckhurst's other girlfriend was Charlotte Ponsonby whose cousin Sarah was one of the mainstays behind the famous Wiltshire commune. Nick Soames, a part-time equerry and great friend of Prince Charles, also got into the Margaret act and squired her to many a nightclub.

About this time another young blood was making regular appearances by Margaret's side. The young, buccaneering twenty-four-year-old Lord Burghersh, heir to the Earl of Westmorland, was seen more and more in the Princess's company.

His Lordship's most ardent desire in life was to spend the family fortune starting a new West End nightclub in which he intended to steal society's cream away from the traditional hotspots, Tramp and Annabelle's.

He was considered suitable enough by the rest of the family to be Margaret's official escort to Ascot only months after the breakup.

He admitted to friends that the greater part of his service to HRH was personal ambition. If Margaret patronised his new club it would be half way towards triumph and success.

All of these men escorted Princess Margaret during the period 1970 to 1976, some a lot more than others.

From time to time the after-hours activities of all of them could have landed them firmly on the front pages of the Sunday newspapers. Most of the time they were lucky, and so was Margaret. Their names would flit in and out of the gossip columns, especially Dempster's page, for he was a frequent shadow lurking along the walls of every fashionable nightclub.

It was during this time in fact that she did some kind of deal with Dempster which would have great mutual benefit when the crunch came.

In short, Dempster agreed to lay off the Princess in return for exclusive information about other things – which later included a great deal of data about Snowdon's girlfriends.

Dempster's subsequent exclusive coverage from Mustique was part of the reward he reaped for turning a blind eye when Margaret went for a night out.

Dempster also doubles up as Grovel in *Private Eye*, a magazine which hovers between a mixture of hard exposure, absurd gossip, and highly amusing satirical nonsense. Grovel traditionally handles the absurd gossip.

Poor "Snowbum" as Grovel called him, was given a fortnightly hammering as Dempster revelled in using all the more salicious tit-bits too hot for his *Daily Mail* page. Dempster's comments were presumably, in part, master-minded from Kensington Palace.

But there was no evidence to suppose Margaret was doing anything but going to the odd party with friends. This new set kept itself very much to itself, and although the tentacles of their various birthrights spread through most of London society, Margaret's new gay life was kept very much as their own little secret.

A young man called Roddy Llewellyn was on the fringe of this set and got in and out of it often because of his friendship with Sarah Ponsonby. Unlike all the others he was a talkative young man and he openly boasted of his conquests. Ironically Roddy perhaps had less to do with Margaret than several others. He was just young enough, silly enough, and boastful enough, to begin to catch the eye of several of the professional Royal-watchers.

In the latter months, as the separation went from being something both of them desired into being a reality, Princess Margaret felt psychologically down in the dumps. She was tense, nervous and niggly. She began doing what many women do when they are in that state of mind: eating too much and putting on a lot of weight. She started to chain-smoke and then demanded a second, third and even fourth Scotch before the evening meal. The weight problem added to her own feelings of insecurity. Tony and she were by now not even pretending to each other that the marriage could be saved. It was over in everything but name. When they did meet they were either sullen with each other or completely indifferent. Despite this neither of them wanted to make anything public at that stage. Both were reluctantly prepared to carry on just as they were doing for the sake of the children.

At just 5 ft. 3 in. in her stockinged feet she was close on 10 stone only a few weeks before the breakup. Some newspapers printed horribly unflattering pictures of her which put glaring spotlights on her double chin. It was a typical exercise in journalistic bitchiness and they felt they could get away with it because Margaret was then being frowned on by the nation as a whole. As things settled down and they saw her going hell-for-leather back into the loneliness of official duty, public censure quickly began to change back into general sympathy.

But the pictures upset Margaret terribly and she was determined to go on a rigid diet. She took twenty-four pounds off her weight in just two months by a low-carbohydrate diet which cut down on all starchy foods. She reduced her drinking – which had been rather heavy until then – to a single aperitif before dinner. She ate very little but fruit and veg and renounced most of her firm favourites like wholemeal bread, bacon, potatoes and pasta. When dining out she never tried to stop anyone else eating their fill, but she insisted on a small minute steak and a side salad for herself.

Margaret's eating habits had always presented this problem. While it is fair to say that being a Royal is one of the most exacting tasks known to man, the job has a lot of perks, food being one of them. While Margaret's cost to the state is minimal compared to the Queen's, she does not need to stint herself for the finer things in life. If the Royal family were to realise all their assets and put them on the market, they would certainly be some £100 million better off financially. This would be clearly unthinkable as they technically, but not legally, belong to the sovereign and not the Queen personally. But it does indicate the family is rich beyond even the Onassis class.

The monarchy costs the British taxpayer some £8 million a year – roughly the cost of prescribing tranquillisers. Out of this the state pays an average weekly shopping bill of £3,300. This includes £1,500 for food each week, £280 for wine, £240 for flowers, £280 for laundry, and a further £1,000 for other household goods.

Even though these figures include a lot of entertaining you can be assured that with a £254 daily food and wine bill, they all eat and drink extremely well. Margaret was never an exception to this rule.

For twenty years Princess Margaret had been a devotee of two forms of fringe medicine to cure her various ailments. These range from simple tiredness after a heavy schedule, and terrible attacks of migraine, to strained muscles or serious colds. She had been a friend of Miss Kay Kiernan, a Harley Street therapist since she was twenty-six. Miss Kiernan is also a registered psychic and a former professional nurse. Margaret has raved about her to everyone and even the Queen has been for a cure. Miss Kiernan uses a machine called a diapulse which sends high-frequency radio waves through the affected part of the body. She also effects healing cures with the advice "from a friend on the other side".

But the famous royal complexion, which all the female members of the family are blessed with, is thanks to a mystery doctor who specialises in homeopathic medicine. Dr. Marjory Blackie is also the Queen's personal doctor – in fact the first ever exclusively chosen by a reigning monarch. Dr. Blackie cures most things with a selection of pills that are made up from wild herbs, vegetables, even snake's venom and deadly nightshade.

But despite Margaret's regular visits she could find no way of curing the now-daily doses of depression.

Margaret was scheduled to go for a semi-official visit to Australia in 1975. Despite the fact that Tony had a long association with the country and had made many friends in his profession down there, he refused to go with her. He could not face another endless round of hand-shaking and after-dinner speeches with a wife he seldom talked to. His firm refusal in the face of a virtual order from the Palace offended the entire Royal family. Margaret was in a complete rage. The Queen thought it extremely imprudent and even the Queen Mother finally showed her disapproval. It was not the first time she had acknowledged something was seriously amiss, but now she began to see the impending disaster.

She implored Tony to go, with the argument that both of them loved the country and it was about time they explored it together. Tony was adamant: the only thing they would be able to explore together was an endless sea of official faces waiting for a platitude or two after they had spent eight hours on a plane. Whatever his arguments, Margaret travelled alone and felt justifiably that another nail had been driven into the coffin of their love.

As the marriage began to be a landslide towards doom and despondency the Queen was very upset by the whole affair. So was Charles, who had struck up a good friendship with Tony over the years. Philip kept to the background rumbling discontent from time to time. Tony had talked to the Queen Mother about it in an adult, sensible way and mother-in-law had seen how upset he was and how the marriage had now broken down beyond repair. The public speculation over Roddy only helped to fan flames which had been there for months.

The Queen and Queen Mother talked it over sadly and the Queen Mother said she knew Tony was going to opt for a divorce. It seemed probable that he might want to marry again.

The Queen quickly consulted Dr. Donald Coggan, the Archbishop of Canterbury, who immediately came to Windsor to give help and guidance. After she had seen him she asked Tony for an audience. She persuaded him not to talk of divorce for the time being. She asked him to put up with a separation until a unique Church Council had come to a final conclusion. It seemed that, unknown to Tony, the Church of England had set up a Marriage Commission which was at that moment thrashing out the Church's position on marriage. She begged him to wait until the commission published their findings, in 1978. It may well be, the Queen argued, that the Church's position may change radically in that period. It was a convincing argument and one that Tony agreed to.

Margaret herself went to two old ecclesiastical friends. She first sought the advice of Father Hugo Bishop, seventy-five-year-old former Superior of the Community of Resurrection at Muirfield in Yorkshire. Then she went to see Simon Phipps. Both of them were able to help her spiritually, but neither could make any pronouncements on any possible divorce.

At a meeting with the Queen Mother at Windsor Lodge, the couple agreed to an interim separation for two years, after which they would relook at their positions and see if any further steps could be taken.

After sixteen years only a small but dramatic announcement stood between them and the total abandonment of their married life.

Chapter Eight

Viscount Linley was a tough fourteen-year-old and his little sister just eleven when they heard the news officially from their mother. They were collected from Bedales school and whisked by Margaret to join the Queen Mother at Royal Lodge, Windsor. Both of them were extremely upset, yet neither was taken by surprise.

For much of their lives they must have seen the growing rift between their parents, Tony's continued coldness and Margaret's total indifference. From time to time Snowdon tried talking to the children and he did so again before flying off to Australia, knowing the announcement was about to be made.

It was a heartbreaking scene, one very familiar in the marriages of the twentieth century. He spoke to them seriously about how things sometimes didn't work out between adults. Sarah, in particular, was distraught when she learnt the parting was soon to be official. The elder Viscount Linley tried to put on a brave face but eventually succumbed to silent sobbing. When Tony left them he could never remember feeling so low and depressed. His journey to Australia was filled with nervous tension, anguish and heartache. When Dr. Coggan made his statement from the West Indies where he was touring, he said: "Our thoughts go out, particularly to the children." It was a sentiment shared very deeply by their father.

The statement itself read simply:

> HRH The Princess Margaret, Countess of Snowdon, and the Earl of Snowdon have mutually agreed to part. The Princess will carry out her public duties and functions unaccompanied by Lord Snowdon. There are no plans for divorce proceedings.

It was another typical hyperbole from the ever-cautious Palace. News editors scratched their heads and called their royal experts for a translation. It was clear they had parted, and that was about all. The mention of divorce brought up more questions than it answered. Snowdon, they found out, could still perform his own duties, if he was asked to, but probably would not. Viscount Linley would from now on accompany his mother when he was free from school. The feelings about the separation were "mutual", but that was about all the statement allowed them to think.

Again because of the lack of information in royal announcements it unleashed a flood of speculation, something for which the Palace must be perpetually blamed.

At the time of the announcement Tony had a flat in fashionable Darling Point which looked over a picturesque harbour on the outskirts of Sydney. He found when he got there the telephone was ringing non-stop and when he pulled the cord out the telephone company came round immediately because a fault had been reported. He soon begged his old friend Mrs. Eve Hartman, whom he had known intimately since she became editor of *Vogue*, to help him out of the predicament. She quickly moved him into her £90,000 house in the City's Woolahra suburb. It was a full two days before journalists found him and came knocking on the door.

When they discovered him, Tony wearily decided he would have to talk to the reporters again. He tried a sympathetic, practical, friendly approach, hoping they would understand and leave him alone for a while. He came to the door for an impromptu press conference dressed in khaki safari-style suit and shirt with a paisley handkerchief. He, too, was smoking fifty or sixty cigarettes a day. No sooner had he stamped on one than he was lighting the next.

As he talked on the doorstep the reporters could hear soft music playing inside and the noises of a meal being prepared as Mrs. Hartman worked on Tony's dinner in the kitchen.

Tony talked about how tired and depressed he was. He would soon be better, he said, if he could be allowed to relax for a while as he was doing there. He asked them nicely to leave him alone for a while and promised when he felt better he would appear at his exhibition and they could ask him anything they wanted. He talked about the old days in Fleet Street, but refused to talk at all about Princess Margaret. He told them he had been out with Mrs. Hartman and some of her friends to a fashionable restaurant where they had been very kind to him. "I didn't eat much, but it did a lot for me."

Mrs. Hartman then called him from deep inside the house, telling him dinner was ready. His last plea to the reporters was: "From now on *please* call me plain Tony Armstrong-Jones."

He finally met the world's press when he opened the preview of his three-week photographic exhibition at a new shopping complex in Sydney. He seemed relaxed and friendly compared to the nervous man they had found finally at Woolahra. He smiled at the cameras and told them he would answer any questions about his work but none at all about his private life.

It was a day of frank talking and Tony missed nothing out except the one thing everyone else wanted to talk about. He meandered in conversation over his own psychological problems saying he had bouts of great insecurity, moods of depression and fears about his eyesight. Sometimes, he said, he could hardly get to a new assignment and stood outside the building hoping his subjects would get bored and go home. He spoke passionately about his work, his children and his likes and dislikes. His particular hatred of the moment was mindless telly-watching. It was the worst thing possible for today's children and all kids needed help and guidance from their parents about what to watch and when to switch off. The only thing in his life at the moment was photography but this sometimes made him tense and nervous. He described how his pictures would come back from the processing lab and he would look at the unopened packet for hours before he made himself open it.

When he finally plucked up the courage and opened the pics he often found they were not at all what he had wanted or expected. That always plunged him into a deep depression which only a successful photo session could bring him out of. He was a far different man from the bustling, ambitious photographic genius the world had grown to know. The constant concentration needed for the job and the depressions which went with it had started to interfere with his sight. He now worried that he was slowly going blind. This gave him a tremendous insecurity which he could not surmount.

And so he sounded off about everything. His tirade about television was something he had wanted to get off his chest for years but had been unable to do so because he was an adopted Royal. He never let his children near a television unless they came to him for permission and he agreed with their selection. They had learned quickly the kind of programmes he would approve of and had to carefully sift through the day's viewing if they wanted to see the box at all. Then he spouted off against Women's Lib – one of Australia's consuming subjects of the time – and said if he was going to be called a chauvinist pig for believing in good manners towards women, then that's just too bad.

The press certainly got their money's worth and it seemed Tony had had a lot to get off his chest.

Tony had expressed a wish to be in Australia for much longer periods. It was even suggested he might move there altogether and set up home in the middle of all his society pals in Sydney. But he soon scotched that one. Much as he loved Australia and would find it a very pleasant place to live, it was too far from his children, and it was not an ideal base for travel – which he wanted to do now more than ever.

Before leaving Sydney the hard-nosed cosmopolitan press-gang there was entertained to a piece of vintage newspaper humour. A guard at the exhibition who had obviously had a few too many tubes during his lunch hour started to push the reporters out of the building he said: "Why can't you let his Majesty hang up his paintings in peace."

Meanwhile, back home in Parliament, MPs from both sides were getting hotted up for battle. That fiery old-established critic of the Royal family, Willie Hamilton, tabled a question from the Labour Government side of the house asking the Chancellor to consider withdrawing Margaret's £35,000 state allowance because she did not seem able to carry on her duties any more.

This was almost immediately contested by Tory MP Nicholas Fairbairn who called the newspaper which had revealed the Roddy secret "treacherous" and wanted the paper condemned by Parliament for an unwarranted intrusion into the private life of the Princess.

Neither motion got very far, but it did express the torn feelings of the country as a whole.

The family met up again in June for a ceremony which was one of the closest guarded secrets of the year. The Queen's son, sixteen-year-old Prince Andrew, and Viscount Linley, aged fourteen, became confirmed at St. George's Chapel, Windsor.

The two boys were escorted from their various schools by the school chaplain who had nurtured them in preparation for the ceremony. It was a very private, family ceremony, conducted by the Archbishop of Canterbury. Throughout the ceremony the separated couple sat with their daughter between them. They greeted each other fairly warmly under the circumstances and Tony chatted to other members of the family before the ceremony began. It was a rather trying time for all of them, but especially for Tony who by now was clearly no longer a member of the inner fraternity. The only two who seemed rather unconcerned at the situation were the two royal confirmees. They were keen to get the whole thing over with. Charles was there, along with Anne and Mark. They all lunched at Windsor Castle later that day and even managed a semblance of family gaiety. But again Tony had to take his leave of the children and once more it was a painful parting.

The Godparents chosen to represent each of the boys were an extremely interesting selection of well-known names from the past. Lord Rupert Nevill became Godfather to both boys (he had by now become Prince Philip's treasurer). But young Linley also had the Queen as Godparent and the Rev. Simon Phipps, who had helped Margaret through so many periods of stress in her life, yet was still obviously a mainstay of her religious thinking. By now he had become a Right Reverend and the Bishop of Lincoln. It must have given him a great, but perhaps sad, satisfaction to be involved again with the family on this level. It will be his clear duty in the future to guide Linley through not only his religious education, but through any periods of stress his situation might lead him.

He will find in Phipps a wise teacher and a truly religious

man who not only knew the rigours of service life; who not only fought his way up the spiritual ladder; but was also a wise counsellor for a Princess when she needed him and a good friend of David's mother at the same time.

Only days after the official announcement Princess Margaret got back to doing what she had always done after a long period of strained emotion. She picked up the gay life and she got back to work packing in as much activity to her days and nights as hours alone permitted. Her weekly diary of public engagements became filled and she packed sometimes as many as five official engagements into one day. It was as if she was purging herself of all the unpleasantness, waving the flag again to show she had not gone under with the avalanche of ill-feeling. Newspaper polls showed most people had felt she had been a naughty little Princess. A front-page *Sunday People* diatribe said she should pack in being a Royal and get on with enjoying herself "if she couldn't keep up the traditions of royalty". It was a tone of voice echoed by most of the nation and one that Margaret was not at all used to hearing.

Her answer on the one hand was to collect together every last friend she could remember and cock her thumb at the world. On the other hand she immersed herself so deeply in official duty that the fickleness of public opinion began to be felt and they were forgiving her everything within a few months.

To be fair, she did not spare herself. After a few depressing days at Windsor when she went around looking like a funeral, she bounced back into public life. Never a day went by without a shot of her at one function or another. Female journalists sent to find out exactly how much work she was doing often returned to the office far too tired to sit at the typewriter.

There is always an awful lot of work for Margaret to do if she seeks it out. She is the President of nineteen projects and societies from the League of Pity to the Royal Ballet; she is a patron to thirty-one more and Colonel-in-Chief to seven regiments; she has honorary fellowships in five associations and five honorary degrees from universities. It would take her months to get around all of them just once.

She scurried through meetings of the Dockland Settlement,

an interest she had as far back as the Little White Nest days; went on a promotion for the Migraine Trust; and attended dozens of Girl Guide meetings. As President of the Invalid Children's Aid Association she plunged herself into a new fund-raising drive. She attended a charity theatre show for Shelter, the group for homeless people, and finally set out for a tour of Tunis in which she often worked a twenty-hour day.

She got rid of her feelings of loneliness, guilt, disillusion and disorientation, by filling every minute with something that would take her mind off them. In Tunis even her lady-in-waiting, the Hon. Mrs. John Willis, was amazed at Margaret's bursts of newfound energy.

Mrs. Willis knew Margaret's secret of being able to conserve her energy until it was needed. Margaret was able to have short periods recharging her batteries in which she became almost numb. But soon she was able to bounce back into life again. Margaret also drank gallons of tea whenever she was on an extensive engagement. Special tea-making apparatus was always included in the packing at Kensington Palace and the first thing she ever did when she got back to her quarters was brew up a cuppa. Her private secretary Lord Napier went with her to Tunis and he too came back exhausted. Many evenings when they got back to the royal quarters at about midnight Margaret would start writing thankyou letters to her main hosts of the day. Sometimes fifty of these had to be written by either Napier or Margaret. Margaret often did the lot. Every one had to be worded differently in case the parties compared notes. And she had to remember something significant about each meeting she could refer to in the letter. It was a daunting task. Before letter writing they all had a conference about the next day's activities. They went over everything very carefully. Where they were going, who they had to meet, what they should say to them, and so on.

Whatever misgivings or feelings of depression Margaret had had in London, her trip to Tunis did not leave her with a second to think about them.

Back in London, as Tony settled down to a bachelor existence again, bookings for his photographic work began to flood in. He announced candidly that he was rather broke and the

£10,000-odd he got from the *Sunday Times* hardly covered the children's school fees after tax. And that was one thing Tony was determined to pay out of his own pocket. (The rest of the financial situation was complicated but unlike most marriage breakups Tony was not expected to give half his income to his estranged wife.)

While the marriage had lasted Tony could only accept non-commercial journalistic and documentary work which did not clash in any way with the Royal family. Now he was suddenly on the market for anything which was going.

He was offered commercials at £10,000 a time (his yearly wage as a Royal). Several American magazines offered him £1,000 a day to work on assignments for them and he could pick and choose his private bookings from all over the world.

It was clear Tony would have all the work and travel he needed and his new income would be £100,000-plus. It seemed the only silver lining to the very dark cloud of his existence at that time.

At first he moved in with his mother, now the Countess of Rosse, for an "interim period", but soon he lodged with his intimate friend Jeremy Fry in Belgravia where he had almost a whole apartment to himself. Soon, most of the time, Tony was to be found back in his Sussex farmhouse where he would work, relax and get back to the process of being a human being again.

Here his children would come down for weekends and he could count on the discretion of the local villagers who all pointedly looked the other way when he strolled down to the post office, or bought his weekly shopping at the village store in Handcross.

Beyond any doubt whatever, Lucy Lindsay-Hogg was the girl in Tony's life when he parted from Princess Margaret. He had known her for nearly two years and had grown a strong attachment for her when they spent six weeks together filming in Australia. Tony was making an episode of *The Explorers* down-under and Lucy, then aged thirty-one and fifteen years Tony's junior, was a production assistant on the series. They became close friends and working companions during their stay and met up again regularly in England.

Lucy was once married to a film producer called Michael

Lindsay-Hogg who said their marriage had been very amicable, their parting more so and he knew nothing about her present life at all.

She was a valued assistant in many BBC serials, going on to aid Kenneth Clark in various ventures including the fabulous *Civilisation* series. He described her as sweet, charming and educated, but a very discreet and private person. He lamented that if her affair with Snowdon got out of hand it would seriously impair their working relationship.

When in England, and they were often parted through work, she either stayed with Tony in Sussex, or he escorted her around London in his royal blue Volvo estate car and she stayed with him either at his mother's house or that of Jeremy Fry. Both of them spent a lot of time house-hunting while in town.

During the eight weeks Lucy Lindsay-Hogg was abroad filming, Tony installed a mystery blonde in the Sussex cottage who remained there even when the children visited. Villagers thought she was probably a maid but changed their minds when they saw them walking hand in hand through nearby woodlands and she promptly disappeared when Lucy got back into town.

If Tony's past is a mess, his future looks brighter and more promising than that of his wife. He has come away with a marital hangover, an Earldom, and a fabulous reputation as a photographer. She has gained nothing but the marital hangover and some happy memories.

They both gained two children who will undoubtedly give them much happiness in the future. But all in all it was a very sad end for a marriage which looked as if it once had everything.

BOOK THREE
LLEWELLYN

Chapter One

Roddy Llewellyn was a repressed and frustrated child. He was constantly overshadowed by his older brother Dai; outrageously bullied by a blustery father; and spent a most uncomfortable five years having his backside kicked at Eton. He was a gregarious, warm-hearted child who lacked the spit, polish and outer-gumption so favoured and demanded by the British aristocracy. His father, Col. Harry Llewellyn, was a hard, old-fashioned disciplinarian who ruled by the rod and asked questions later. Dai was his father's son. Roddy was his mother's.

When the time came for both boys to go out into the big bad world, Dai – although he was a flamboyant playboy – also became a responsible businessman ready and eager to take over the family estate, fortune and responsibility. Roddy tried a succession of rather quaint business deals and ended up rather broke, luckless and unhappy. He never ceased to reaffirm in his father's mind that he was a failure and a drop-out.

Before meeting Princess Margaret he was actually dossing on a sofa in a friend's flat in London. He commuted to a picturesque village in Wiltshire where he and some other rather luckless friends ran a small commune which supplied food to a fashionable restaurant they owned in nearby Bath.

After he had been released from the joint terrors of Eton and the family seat, he became rather a tearaway. He revelled in his newfound freedom and discovered very quickly that women ran after him in abundance. He lost his virginity to a debutante when he was barely seventeen, and has bedded big ones, small ones, rich ones, poor ones, famous ones and obscure ones, ever since. Roddy Llewellyn is not oversexed, but he greatly enjoys the game of getting women into bed. He is very good at it. Since he got caught up in the whirl of London society – much changed from that of his father – he has become debonair, daring, boastful, rather dashing, conceited, and quite the darling of the nightclub set. Princess Margaret was his *chef d'oeuvre*, the greatest status-pulling stunt in the book. In practical terms he could go no higher.

Roddy was a lady's man who perfected the art of flirting to the *n*th degree. He did not presume to bed Princess Margaret when he first met her, but he could not resist the temptation of trying to charm her. As usual, he succeeded at a time when Margaret was most vulnerable to charm.

He quickly became her "little angel" because, walking hand in hand across the hayfields of the West country, he momentarily restored that spiritual love to which Margaret is addicted and which he could turn on with immense expertise.

But there was nothing deep about Roddy Llewellyn. Although, for a while, it was certain the affair was deep, affectionate and romantic, it was one that could never last. Roddy had neither the sustained brilliance and command of a Townsend, nor the subtle gentleness and long-lasting charm of a Snowdon.

He was flattered that a woman of such truly immense status should fall in love with him. She was flattered that such an obviously sexual and accomplished young man should find her attractive in her middle age. There is sixteen years between them.

Roddy Llewellyn was the ultimate fly-by-night.

To say that the world of the Beautiful People is small is an understatement of the first order. It revolves around itself with its own incredible impetus almost to the degree of incest. They drift through the foyer of Monte Carlo's casino the night before the big race; they take off the day after in an armada of boats for St. Tropez. They ski down the slopes of Gstaad and bump into each other at Tramp. They sip cocktails beside swimming pools in Los Angeles, pass through New York, and occasionally drop into Jimmy's in Paris hoping to bump into Caroline.

The BPs value nothing but money, leisure and pleasure. They embrace such people as Jackie Onassis, who rubber-stamps her own territories, and Mick Jagger who can rarely remember which part of the playground he is in because he is always so stoned. They include royalty, pop stars, entrepreneurs, aristocrats, millionaires, and a bunch of young playboys on the fringe of everything because they are willing to sleep with ageing actresses and because they are somehow always seen where they should be seen.

The season for the BPs starts with a winter in Switzerland, spring in London, summer in the South of France and autumn in the West Coast of America. There are a few variations but the same small band follow each other around, seeing, being seen by each other on a never-ending whirl of social interest.

Once into this fabulously ridiculous menagerie of self-esteem, the world is their playground and they can flit like a butterfly from scene to scene.

Everywhere are the same faces. The web is interwoven so tightly that relationships between BPs read like the most complicated family tree: "Lord X, former escort of actress Y, who once went out with his cousin, pop-star Z, who starred in the West End with actress A, was seen yesterday with heiress B, formerly married to entrepreneur C."

It was little wonder then, that when Lord Snowdon went to photograph a young and sexy stage actress called Helen Mirren she should chuckle to herself as he lined up the cameras. For Snowdon it was just another job: a rather pleasant one – for Helen Mirren was described after her last West End production as brazen, voluptuous, enticing and delectable.

For her it was all a bit of a nuisance. Her "potty little home" in London's Parson's Green was just undergoing a massive overhaul and the builders were everywhere. Only her own sitting room and her conservatory, where her "lover", a white rabbit lived, were undisturbed by the chaos.

Their paths were crossing professionally, but unknown to Snowdon they had crossed and interwoven in a number of ways behind his back.

This outspoken, outrageous, sexy, provocative, middle-class ex-Convent girl had become a brilliant and acclaimed West

End actress who felt just as at home with Shakespeare as she did with rock and roll. She flitted between boyfriends, such as Alexander Hesketh of racing car fame, and finally had a "Warm, loving relationship for four years" with Prince George Galitzine, cousin to the Duke of Kent. Galitzine was a partner with Roddy Llewellyn in the Wiltshire commune which entertained Princess Margaret. Just to cap the weave of circumstances Galitzine had lost Helen's friendship when he punched her latest boyfriend, James Wedge, on the nose at a party and the poor young man had to have six stitches in his eye. The unfortunate Wedge was a close friend and colleague of Lord Snowdon.

It was a typical BP situation and Helen Mirren found the whole thing rather amusing. She, Llewellyn, Galitzine and Sarah Ponsonby were the architects of the commune. Helen, who loved to admit she was sexually rather careless and chaotic and who loved having sex just for the sake of it, would startle cocktail party guests who bored her by telling them that she got the small tattoo on her thumb when she was drunk in Singapore in the Merchant Navy just before she had her sex-change operation.

The majority of the Beautiful People flit from headquarters to headquarters as the calendar and the weather changes, but a few of them manage to find some diversions not open to the general society riff-raff. One of them is Mustique, and another is a surprisingly middle class, ancient, Roman town in England, called simply Bath. Because of the Roman remains, its spa, and its proximity to London it is a must on the general tourist map, but it is a peculiar choice for the BPs to set up their West Country headquarters.

Bath in itself is a very beautiful city filled with enterprising young people who have turned it from a hippy Mecca into a highly successful centre for pleasure. It is Britain's answer to St. Tropez and the restaurants, nightclubs, art galleries and bric-à-brac shops flourish as nowhere else.

Eight people, including actress Diane Cilento, and John Randall, an old Bathite whose idea it was, and the commune six, opened a small restaurant in Bath specialising in food grown at the commune nearby. It became the nucleus of the

Bath set of BPs who constantly dropped in to look at each other.

It was Roddy Llewellyn who linked this ancient British city to the exotic Caribbean Island by asking Princess Margaret to share them both with him.

He had been on the fringes of the BP Set mainly because of his brother Dai. Llewellyn was never rich but, like such playboys as Nigel Pollitzer, he managed to move around in the circles that mattered. Because they were both pretty and charming and knew *everybody*, they found themselves on every invitation list. Through Nicky Haslem, fellow old Etonian, friend of Margaret's and cousin of the Earl of Bessborough etc., he met Haslem's cousin Sarah Ponsonby. "Nigel, Nicky and Rodders" always had drinks bought for them when they arrived at Jimmy's in Monte Carlo. They were entertained to dinner somewhere every night, and could even pick and choose according to the menu. It was at such a dinner, when Roddy had been invited because they were a man short (Society was always a man short when it invited Princess Margaret because Snowdon invariably refused to come) that the two were introduced.

Roddy looked like a much younger Tony, with longish fair hair, an engaging smile and a clever line of banter. Margaret was clearly enthused with him on their first meeting and on returning to Kensington Palace she had already decided she would see him again, as soon as she could arrange it discreetly. For this she needed fellow conspirators and she found them in Lady Jane Wyndam, close friend and an extra lady-in-waiting, and her ever-faithful pal Colin Tenant.

Tenant's family seat was in Scotland, a country Snowdon, who hailed from Wales, was never very keen on. When Margaret said she was going to Scotland for a while, he presumed she was off to Balmoral or Edinburgh. In fact she went to stay in Tenant's country mansion Glen House, at Innerleithen, thirty miles outside Edinburgh. There the handful of villagers all worked for Tenant on the old squire basis and could be relied on completely for their discretion.

Margaret set herself up there for a two-week stay and had left Lady Wyndham in London as a go-between to set up a meeting. Lady Violet went to Dai Lewellyn's home and summoned Roddy to see her. When he arrived at his brother's home he found Lady Violet waiting for him in the drawing room. She gave him Margaret's invitation, impressed upon him the great need for secrecy and left minutes later in a taxi. That night a bemused and intrigued Roddy packed his bags and took the early morning train for Scotland. He lunched on the train, drank a bottle of burgundy, and mused into his glass about what fate could bring so suddenly out of the blue.

Roddy got to Edinburgh that evening and took the local train to the tiny brick station at Innerleithen. There, to his surprise, he found Margaret waiting on the platform to greet him. The station master did a lot of touching his forelock as Margaret ushered her lover-to-be through the door of the station to the waiting Range Rover. She was completely alone. She had left McIntyre, her detective, back at the house.

This was a Friday night and Roddy was due to stay for the weekend. He did not get back to London for five days. That evening they had an informal dinner together and got to know each other again. On the Saturday they went into Edinburgh to go shopping with a cluster of other people to make Roddy less conspicuous. The shopping spree was purposeful: Margaret had already invited Roddy to the island of Mustique and he said he had no tropical clothes. They also bought him some swimming trunks and when Margaret was satisfied he would be well dressed on the island, they returned to the house. They spent a further tranquil three days together and concreted what had until then been merely an attraction at a dinner party.

Roddy was actually quite perplexed at how things were turning out. He was flattered by Margaret's obvious interest in him and was genuinely fond of her. He had always been overshadowed by the exploits of his older brother Dai. Now he had accomplished the greatest status symbol open to the BPs. He had become Princess Margaret's lover. There is no doubt he adored the social side of the romance. He had gone in one fell swoop from the fringes of the BPs into the very heart itself.

Roddy's chequered past was now behind him. He had, like

Nigel Pollitzer, "messed about in art shops", then he found he had talents for horticulture which led him to the commune and a desire to become a landscape gardener. He had been in hospital taking sickness benefits from the State and he had dossed on every high class sofa in London. His father had eventually bought him a small flat in Fulham with the idea of keeping him off the streets and this had immediately caused resentment from Dai who claimed he had never had a penny from his father.

Roddy could not even afford the upkeep of the flat and had to rent it out at an exorbitant price to keep living. Yet he could always be seen at the best nightclubs; he was always pottering around in St. Tropez and he even managed to inveigle a trip to Gstaad most years. Now he would be even more in demand by the hostesses who mattered.

Colin Tenant's patronage of their love affair did not end with the house in Scotland, nor the facilities he offered on his island. He also gave them the exclusive use of his huge white house in Tite Street, Chelsea, where they would go for evenings when they were both in London.

But Roddy got more and more daring and even started going to Kensington Palace itself for illicit evenings with Margaret. This, of course, was only when Tony was out of town and the night always started as a dinner party with other guests.

Roddy soon began calling Margaret "PM", but was still careful to call her "Ma'am" in public. With friends she called him Roddy or Angel and their conversations were always dotted with the odd "dear" and "darling".

After visiting Mustique together they set themselves up as lovers in London and went through all the intrigue such liaisons bring about. One of their mutual friends, John Nutting, thirty-four-year-old son of a former Tory minister, offered them secluded weekends together in a variety of places. They went on like this, off and on, until early 1976.

During the final year of their relationship Roddy got more and more involved with his commune. There were always between five and eight people living there with various talents which they all pooled. Roddy's was creating the vegetable garden from which they took their own food and sold the extras.

It was a large sprawling farmhouse which got exceedingly cold in the winter. But most of them at least had their own room even though it was sparsely furnished. None of them would ever starve and none of them relied completely on the commune for a livelihood. They shared a large kitchen which kept warm from a huge old-fashioned stove. Each of them took turns in cooking.

Roddy often talked about the place to Margaret and she became intrigued. It was a full year before they felt they could visit it. They did so at the opening of the new restaurant in Bath when all the inhabitants were involved and kept out of the commune. The couple stayed there for three nights and two days. Margaret found it quaint, delightful, romantic and "very Roddy".

Again that old courtship fantasy was playing Margaret up. She loved stealing away to this eccentric farm with her lover without a soul in the world knowing. They even walked across the surrounding countryside, holding hands and stopping every now and then to kiss affectionately. Again Margaret was at last plunged back again into her fantasy world. It was *romantic*, the very essence of life she could not live without. But this time it was also the beginning of the end.

Chapter Two

Two small intimate communities on either side of the globe became within a matter of weeks the setting for the final destruction of the Snowdon marriage. One was a picturesque tropical island in the Caribbean owned rather eccentrically by an ex-playboy. The other was the equally eccentric commune in Wiltshire run by a boy who wanted to play.

Neither community had any idea in the balmy days of early 1976 that they would both become stages upon which a sad historical spotlight would fall. Neither had courted disaster, but fate singled them out to be the areas where the holocaust would finally erupt.

In the beginning of March both places hummed with gentle activity as one by one they entertained a Royal Princess and her lover. By the middle of March they reeled to survive the blazing glare of publicity. By the end of March it was all over.

Mustique had figured as a constant bone of contention between the Snowdons throughout the marriage. Over the years a hidden pact had sprung up between them. No questions would be asked. Margaret could go off to Mustique for holidays and relaxation whenever she liked. Tony could spend similar weeks in Sussex away from Margaret and the two would ignore all stories they heard about the other. For years it had been a working relationship.

Colin Tenant, heir to the Scottish landowner Lord Glenconner, was a fiery, rich young man. In 1959 he bought the whole island for a paltry £45,000 and immediately gave his old friend Margaret and Tony a six-acre plot of the island for their wedding present. Some years later Margaret spent £30,000 building a villa with a swimming pool, five bedrooms and about every mod-con which could be transported to the island.

She called it *Les Jolies Eaux*, The Pretty Waters, an expression she learnt from a fashionable French song many years before. Over the sixteen years she has had the house she has never stopped making little improvements. It would be difficult to put a price on it now but if a buyer could be found he would expect to offer much in excess of £100,000.

The house was designed by Tony's uncle, Oliver Messel, who lived on Barbados. He designed most of the buildings which began to spring up among the three square miles of cultivated valleys and undulating hills. He was always fully conversant with Tenant's idea of a *livable* paradise for a lucky civilisation.

For the eighty or so natives of the island, Tenant's dream was a message from God. They had all eked a living of some sort from the sea, the coconuts, or brewing illegal rum. Tenant employed any of them who wanted to work and built a new village, with a school, a small hospital, new groves of coconut palms and new cotton fields. He added an air-strip, purchased their fruit and vegetables and turned a blind eye to the dustbins of swirling, brown, extremely potent, nearly 100-proof rum.

Tenant's plan when he bought the island was to turn it into a paradise hideaway for the Beautiful People of the world. To this end he spent £1 million of his fortune into converting it from a poor coconut estate into the most luxurious playground in the Caribbean. His wife, Lady Anne, daughter of the Earl of Leicester, plunged herself into his dream and their five children got used to spending their school holidays there helping build, paint, improve, or grow.

The Tenants themselves lived in a sprawling mansion called the Gingerbread House, curved around the edge of a small cliff and overlooking the rest of the Grenadine Islands. They turned their house into a distant, attractive fantasy place which fitted into his picture of an exclusive resort for the very rich. The Cotton House Hotel dominated one end of the island where the most exclusive residences were. But Tenant still had 1,000 acres of the 1,400 acre island for sale in large plots. He was always extremely cagey about who he let in and most of the periodic sales are done on a word-of-mouth basis only.

On her visits to the island, Princess Margaret had the best of both worlds. She could demand the absolute in isolation and relaxation. She could walk for miles along deserted sandy beaches fringed with palms. She could swim nude if she wished in calm, blue waters which lapped gently against coral lagoons. She could dive down into the depths of fabulous grottos where a plethora of fish would dart around her in the silent beauty. She could sunbathe for hours on a verandah overlooked by no one but the seagulls. If she wanted to be alone she could spend days blissfully pottering around doing nothing but light the occasional cigarette or pouring out long drinks already prepared in an earthen pitcher.

But if she felt like gay company there were many old friends on the island. Only a handful of tourists were allowed there at any one time to keep the small hotel running. During Margaret's visits even they were not encouraged. They were told on arrival that they must try and ignore the Princess completely. Let her get on with her own life as she wanted to live it. Visitors who failed in this were escorted from the island the next day – their money refunded – and returned to St. Vincent. (One poor American was ignored when he asked Margaret for a dance, but was rudely woken at dawn and escorted to the tiny airstrip.)

When Margaret is there Tenant meets the plane from the mainland every day personally and turns back anyone who has not been invited. In this way he has managed to keep his island exactly as he – and Margaret – likes it.

Only very close approved friends are allowed to live there. They either purchase small lots of property and build their own houses, buy the few existing houses when they come on the market, or rent a house for a season from Tenant. Others can stay at the hotel for as long as they like. Tenant has created his own island paradise and runs it under martial law.

The hundred or so approved islanders can more or less do what they like. The others must behave themselves. He personally runs the hotel with a lot of local black labour. He is a patriarch to the small number of native Mustiquians. They are all very grateful he came to the island. There is no colour bar on Mustique.

He runs one of the best cuisines in the Caribbean, sparing no cost to produce gourmet meals which he adores. The best wines are flown in from France along with provincial cheeses, pâté de foie gras, escargots, truffles and French cigarettes; caviar is flown in from Russia; Angus steaks from Scotland; lamb from New Zealand and hamburgers from his favourite joint in New York. But he principally uses local culinary dishes for his favourite soirées: shellfish, conches, lobsters, and so on. He serves up tuna and smoked snapper along with the smoked salmon. He serves a lobster salad alongside a grouse or pheasant. His meals never fail to delight his guests and people who are allowed to do so often fly in just to eat there. It is expensive and because of the few tourists he allows on the island Tenant can live like a King for virtually nothing.

He also has a penchant for good local entertainment. He hires musicians from all over the Caribbean and one night the place will rock to reggae, while on another they will dance until dawn with a steel band.

So Margaret has the best of both worlds. When she wants to be alone she can do so without any interruption in one of the most beautiful settings in the world. When she wants gaiety and friendship she has merely to walk a couple of hundred yards to the hotel where there are people, music, dancing, laughter and food. It is little wonder she has returned again and again to her island paradise.

Roddy Llewellyn had visited the island three times, twice with Princess Margaret. Ostensibly Llewellyn resided in the hotel with the detective John McIntyre, while Margaret stayed at her villa with her lady-in-waiting (on the island Mrs. Tenant doubles up as a special lady-in-waiting). But in practice they were together nearly all the time. They swam together or lounged on the beach for most of the day. Even on Mustique Margaret rarely got up before mid-morning and liked to breakfast leisurely on the terrace. After a "snacky" lunch at the hotel they would make their way to the beach. In the evenings they either had dinner served to them at home on the terrace, or they headed along to the hotel and its excellent cuisine. Most evenings they were all joined by Lord and Lady Napier. The forty-five-year-old Lord was Princess Margaret's equerry although his visits to the island were far more as a reward for good service than to aid the Princess during her sojourns.

Roddy was quickly known as the devoted courtier. He always pulled out her chair for her to sit down, rushed to pour her drinks, spread her towel on the beach when they bathed and generally preened himself in her presence. While the sun shone Roddy wore union jack swimming trunks and a mildly revolting silver stud in his ear. For hours on end Roddy rubbed suntan oil on her bronzed back and shoulders.

The other thirty-two home owners – of ten nationalities – constantly looked the other way. They followed the motto over the door of the hotel: Live and Let Live.

It was an unconventional, eccentric island inhabited by people who were rich enough, and influential enough, to indulge their fancies and whims of a paradise life in style. It was everything Margaret had ever wanted: even better than the Little White Nest, because she did not have to be so secretive. She could enjoy her freedom with other selected people yet she could act just as she wanted without the prying eyes of the rest of the world.

To Roddy it was all a daydream.

There was always something vaguely inconsistent about Detective Inspector John McIntyre's visits to this paradise isle. Even during the extreme heat of the day – in fact the temperature wavers deliciously between 70 and 85 degrees – he would stand on the beach with his Scotland Yard suit on. As Princess Margaret lazily breast-stroked across the lagoon and Roddy crawled much more quickly in front, he stood motionless on the sand and carefully watched his royal charge.

He was unable to take his jacket off because it hid the butt of his snub-nosed .38 revolver which bulged in a waistband holster. He was never without it and each year he went on a special course at a Metropolitan Police Establishment to make sure that if he ever did have to take it from its holster he would not need to fire twice.

McIntyre is a patient, pleasant, tough and rather dour Scot who has been dedicated to his Princess twenty-four hours a day for fourteen years. He signed on at Kensington Palace after Margaret had been married to Tony for only two years. The job is thankless and arduous but it does have its perks.

Even though he must always cast a vigilant eye towards the Princess he has seen a great deal of the world. He has met Presidents, jetted across continents, seen the inside of most gay nightspots across the globe and he has eaten many a meal which would have made customers at Scotland Yard's meagre canteen green with culinary envy.

McIntyre was the kind of man who slept with one eye open and noticed nothing unless it was a potential danger towards his "client". He was as secretive as a leprechaun and tried to remain unnoticed when the glare of a hundred cameras was picking out his charge.

He draws expenses from the Yard, but on royal holidays like Margaret's to Mustique, Kensington Palace picks up the air fare. He got on very well with Princess Margaret because he managed to remain constantly vigilant yet unobtrusive. It was as if he was a magic genie, always there for her welfare, but looking on from a discreet distance as if he was almost invisible. The best thing Margaret liked about him was that she rarely noticed him. He became part of her life, almost like the Queen's corgies. McIntyre would stay discreetly out of view when Margaret and Roddy went swimming or relaxed on the beach. Yet she was rarely out of *his* view unless he knew exactly where she was and who she was with.

On a typical day on Mustique he would rise earlier than Margaret and breakfast alone. He would check with the equerry on any programmes planned for that day. (Programmes were seldom complicated on Mustique.) He would make a routine check on the day's incoming visitors and cable London if any name rang a familiar bell. Everyone else on the island had been checked already – or verified by Tenant. Then he would do his rounds, simply checking details. A snap order from McIntyre would send carpenters rushing to bang a nail in a rickety step.

When Margaret rose and breakfasted he was not seen by her. But he was within earshot should she be in any kind of trouble. If he left her vicinity for any reason he would arrange for someone else to be there who knew where they could find him quickly. The island was like a fortress and McIntyre had an easy time of it, but that did not mean he could ever completely relax.

His headquarters were in the hotel itself and he would wait there for Margaret to appear for lunch. At a discreet distance he would follow them down to the beach where he would sit under the palms smoking a cigarette and reading a paperback. His sixth sense always told him Margaret's movements even when he was deep into the plot of a detective novel.

When Margaret and Roddy moved back to the hotel as the afternoon cool descended on the beach McIntyre would precede them politely asking the tourists to look the other way and not bother the Princess. If they did not heed him he would be very firm and physically herd them out of the way. Anyone who took exception got short change from the middle-aged detective.

Margaret would invariably put a short wrap over her back-less, strapless black bathing costume and she and Roddy would make for the Grackle Bar, Mustique's second drinking establishment which had a verandah which jutted right out over the sea. Here they would play backgammon, smoke a lot of cigarettes, take little delicacies from various plates and drink lots of campari-and-sodas.

Margaret drove around the tiny island in a small yellow jeep loaned to her by Colin Tenant. On this day they went to the Grackle as usual and found a minor aristocrat there with his wife. Margaret knew them vaguely and they had drunk several cocktails before going back to the hotel for dinner. The visitor, it seemed, drank rather too much and began to lose his awe for the Princess. In short he started getting a little bit familiar. His wife implored Margaret to help her get him back to the hotel. Margaret willingly offered a lift. The aristocrat, by now red-nosed and besotted, insisted that his wife get into the front of the jeep with Roddy while he sat in the back with the Princess. McIntyre watched intently waiting for the moment when his services were expected. He had developed an exact timing over these things. Margaret liked to handle most petty situations herself without offending any visitor. But McIntyre knew when enough was enough.

The aristocrat went on insisting against the quietly spoken wishes of Margaret, Roddy and his own wife. It was time for the detective to act. He went forward quietly and seemed to come from nowhere. "In the front, Sir, if you don't mind," he said as the aristocrat tried to focus on him. "I'm bloody well going to ride with Princess Margaret and that's that," he retorted bluntly. At that moment the powerfully built bodyguard pushed the crook of his hand against the pressure point of the man's nose and grabbed him by the back of the neck. The fellow crumpled visibly and went like a lamb to his allotted place next to Roddy on the front seat. McIntyre stood on the running board of the car and they all got back safely to the hotel where the aristocrat, amid profuse apologies, was hastily put to bed.

They left the next morning before Margaret was up and McIntyre crossed another obstacle off his list.

With the aristocrat safely in bed Princess Margaret relaxed. She had made a mental note concerning the gentleman and it is very unlikely he will ever be ushered into her presence again. However, Margaret felt sorry for the wife who was so polite and longsuffering and that evening the woman was asked to stay in the royal company.

It was a typical Mustique evening, warm and balmy with a dozen waiters scurrying between the tables laden with lobsters, saddles of lamb, sirloins of beef, exotic fish cooked with spicy recipes, and plates of vegetables from the island's small farm. Others dashed around with imported cold bottles of Pipi d'Ange rosé and Piper Heidseck champagne. The wine flowed, the laughter breezed around the large verandah and the succulent dishes got devoured.

There was some dancing and Margaret was in the party mood. As most of the visitors drifted off and only her old and trusted friends were left, she sat by the piano as she had so often in the old days. John Phillips of the Mamas and Papas group was there and between them they struck up *Buttons And Bows*. Then Margaret went on to sing and play *Walk On By*. In the end, as the wine went down at a furious pace and the evening hotted up she did her famous impression of Harold Macmillan. This brought the house down and Tenant ended the evening by serving up an early breakfast of sparrow breasts cooked in garlic and butter.

McIntyre stood in the shadows of the bar drinking a cool

beer every half an hour. He could not stop himself stifling a yawn at about five o'clock and was very glad when PM called it a day.

There was only one day on Mustique when McIntyre could have completely relaxed. Unfortunately he and Margaret had just left. Only days after their plane took off for the International Airport at St. Vincent, the 500-ton yacht *Mohamedia* breezed into port.

On it was the Saudi Arabian sheik Ahmed Yamani, Oil Minister, multi-millionaire, occulist and acute paranoiac. After the infamous Vienna kidnapping episode Sheik Yamani had demanded a personal bodyguard which would shadow him night and day. While cruising on the boat he felt safe enough and it soon became his favourite way of travelling. When the gigantic yacht moored off any land he demanded the services of his hand-picked squad again.

By chance the leader of this squad was Lord Patrick Beresford, an old friend of Margaret's, and he had suggested to the Sheik that they pull in to Mustique so he could present his new master to the Princess. Yamani had readily agreed. It was an excellent arrangement because they had to wait in these waters for a while as Yamani's special food orders were being flown out from Paris.

Beresford, a sprightly forty-one-year-old polo player, was once a top officer in the exclusive Special Air Services and had employed another two ex-officers as co-bodyguards. They were the physical ones. Alongside them there were two British ex-Special Branch detectives who looked at the political and mental side of protection. They in turn commanded a squad of faithful Bedouin so that Yamani was never without one officer and five men by his side. Before landing they scouted the island from South point to North. Not even McIntyre had been able to do such a good job. They reported back to the boat that they were welcome ashore. Sheik Yamani, however, had changed his mind on finding Margaret was not there, and he ordered the £5 million yacht – loaned to him by the Arab Mr. Fixit, Adnan Khashoggi, of Lockheed fame – to set sail.

Strings of Beautiful People were always to be found coming

and going from Mustique. Mick Jagger was a regular visitor. He parked his wife Bianca there with their son Jade and commuted from New York. For a while he even became captain of the local island cricket team organised by a young coloured man called Basil Charles.

The Jaggers were exactly the kind of rich young BPs Tenant had in mind when he took over the island. And with Princess Margaret around very few people took much notice of the ageing pop star.

The Earl of Litchfield, another famous society photographer and cousin of Princess Margaret, built his own Shangri-La on a plot she gave him next to hers.

Roddy was in fact a virtual newcomer to life on the island. Margaret's most constant companion there was Dominic Elliot, brother of the Earl of Minto and Tenant's oldest rival in Margaret's affections. When he got pipped to the post by Peter Townsend, Dominic married the wealthy Countess Bunny Esterhazy with whom he was happy for a number of years. When they parted and finally divorced Dominic risked a phone call to Kensington Palace where an intrigued Princess Margaret agreed to meet her old flame for lunch in a Soho restaurant. They found they could take up where they left off – laughing and joking about everyone they knew. In London Margaret had been discreet about their re-born relationship, but she was only biding her time. From then on, until she met Roddy, in fact, she made sure her more and more frequent trips to Mustique coincided with the ebullient Dominic's. Throughout the seventies Margaret and Dominic spent long periods together having an on-off affair which was only off when discretion demanded it.

Ironically Roddy and Margaret were once on the island together without actually meeting or even knowing each other personally. Margaret stayed in her villa with Dominic for nearly the whole time Roddy was there. He was visiting *his* old flame Viscountess Royston. He had often dossed at her London home when it was too late to get back to Wiltshire after a London party.

Lady Royston was one of the first to build a house on Mustique with her husband, the late heir to the Earl of Harwicke who died of a heart ailment aged only thirty-four in 1973.

His father died soon after and the three-year-old son of the family became the new Earl. Lady Royston found that her home, just off the fashionable Fulham Road in London, gave her too many unhappy reminders of her husband who had died so tragically young. So she sold up and moved her family – along with her seven-year-old daughter Lady Jemmina Yorke – semi-permanently to Mustique. There she frequentely invited old friends to join her for a holiday and two years before Roddy went there with Margaret, he stayed with his friend.

But, as a sort of glorious sub-plot to the general atmosphere of genial romance on the Island of Love, Basil Charles himself was one of the leading characters.

He had been found by the Tenants dying on a roadside after being knocked down by a car. The driver had evidently thought he had killed the young, handsome, coloured youth, and left him on the roadside for dead. The Tenants came by soon after and rushed him to the nearest hospital in St. Vincent. Basil had later flown over to Mustique to express his personal thanks to the Tenants for saving his life. He found they shrugged off his thanks with a genial: "What else could we do?" However, the enterprising Basil felt he wanted to show his gratitude in a more positive way. He asked if he could work for them for a while, just for his board and keep. They soon found they had a near-genius in the man they had saved.

Basil Charles could sing for his supper and play almost any instrument which gave out a rhythm. He could cook magnificently and he turned part of their garden into a magical tropical paradise. He could drive, he could swim, he could shin up a coconut tree and send a torrent of fruit down within a minute. He was gay, laughing, pleasant company; enterprising, polite, diplomatic and just about everything Tenant wanted from his staff – and a lot more too.

Tenant knew a bargain when he saw one and soon made Basil an assistant general manager. At first his duties were confined to the hotel, but they found they could not put a good man down. He ingratiated himself into everything on the island. It was typical that when they decided to while away a few hours a week playing cricket it was to Basil they turned. He got the clothes and equipment, sorted out the ground, put up the wickets, tossed the coin, became groundsman, umpire, scorer, tea-break organiser and general dogsbody. This was between going on to the pitch and being the island's most competent batsman and bowler.

Over five years Basil Charles became one of Colin Tenant's most trusted aides and most able and willing assets on an island spoilt with riches. Tenant, to his credit, always gave Basil his due. "He really is the most exceptional person," he said. But Basil had one attribute not even they had known about. He had a magical, mysterious, fun-loving and winning way with children. He could make crying babies suddenly cry with laughter. He could make sullen children leap with joy and he could suddenly relapse into a mystery fairy-tale world in his imagination which would keep any child under twelve spell-bound for hours.

It was this capacity that first caught the eye of the lamenting Lady Royston. She would often leave her children in Basil's care as she went off to the beach or flew over to St. Vincent's for some shopping. When she came back she invariably found them ecstatically sitting in front of him as he related his latest story; they would beg to be able to stay, and one day Lady Royston stayed with them and listened. She in turn became enchanted with what she heard.

After several sessions listening to Basil, she became intrigued and invited him to dinner that night, and the next, and the next . . . and eventually they fell in love.

It was exactly the kind of thing Mustique was made of. Romance, unlikely partnerships, dying underdogs who met fairy godmothers and fell in love with them. A poor black barman from St. Vincent who met a real-life Earl's mother and fell in love. It was the kind of romance that could only happen on a paradise isle and every lucky islander basked in the wonder of it all.

Now they are living quite unashamedly together in her villa called Endeavour Hall. They are "very much in love", but have not yet decided to marry. Mustique is the kind of place where you can take a lot of time making up your mind . . .

To those people who were close to her on Mustique, Margaret was a changed woman. Most of them, of course, had known her for years both on the island and in London. Few of them had any connection with Snowdon because they were all part of the set he did not associate with. But, bit by bit, despite her holidays with Dominic and her forays into the London night-life with the odd playboy, they had seen her as she cracked up under the strain and agony of an ever-breaking marriage. Like Tony she had become tense, nervous, strained, bad-tempered and niggly. Little petty details annoyed her to distraction and she could give even her nearest and dearest friends a very trying evening.

They tried to be patient but towards the end they felt they were doing her little good with their company and putting an undue strain on their relationship for the future. They had then, started to stay away and invitations to Margaret went down to a trickle. Tenant was continually faithful to her and she was always welcome on the island.

It was with some joy then, that they suddenly found the radiant Princess they always remembered. She was full of life again, full of good humour and gaiety. She laughed and sang and played the piano. She mused into her Campari and it was evident to all that she was in love again.

No one had been spared from the niggling of the breakup and Margaret had emerged bruised, sad and lonely. Now all that had changed. She hummed little tunes to herself, held Roddy by the hand, and called him "My darling little angel"; and he spent hours looking into her eyes in the long evenings by candlelight. It was not difficult to see what he was giving her in return. He amused her with his little puns, he ran around after her serving her drinks and he generally pampered her at a time when she desperately needed to be pampered.

But more important, at a time when she was psychologically bruised and emotionally beaten, he helped feed her ego and self-esteem enormously. He was young, gay, handsome, virile, social, pleasant, a conversationalist, although not brilliant by any means, and he could be very romantic when he wanted to turn it on. She needed all that. Not as a Princess but as a woman. She needed to feel wanted again. She had been overweight, distraught, unhappy. She had felt baggy and dowdy, middle-aged and drab. For any woman, whatever her position, it was nice to have a handsome young buck chasing after you and trying to win your favours.

Margaret responded to this treatment by almost returning to her youth. She became frivolous, childlike, flirtatious and young. She was having an affair again. The old mystery, the old love of courtship, the fantasy world came flooding back across all those disillusioning years. Again it was the idea, the very concept of romance, which intrigued her. Again the little odd things, like picking a rose from a bush and presenting it to her, the things Townsend had done in South Africa, the things Tony had done in the Little White Nest, all became important again. And Roddy was forever finding little new ways of pleasing her.

It was this scene which was about to explode around their ears. Each tranquil kiss, each candlelit mouthful of succulent fodder, each nod and wink, was, in fact, being reported back each day to a small, windowless office in Fleet Street where a team of reporters had been spending weeks compiling a file on Roddy and his romance.

On a dull London Friday, Nick Lloyd, assistant editor of the *News of the World*, took a phone call from his reporter Ross Waby on the island. They'd got the picture they wanted. He would, he explained, take the next plane over to St. Vincent and dictate the words to the copy-taker. Reporter Wendy Henry went into action in London. The two reporters had not left a stone unturned. That Sunday they printed the lot. It was damaging, bitchy stuff, but it was fascinating reading. For the Earl of Snowdon and Princess Margaret Rose, it was the final nail in the coffin of their marriage.

Roddy had done one thing which was very useful during his stay on Mustique. He started a vegetable garden in a corner of Margaret's remaining land. PM however, was not overwhelmed with gratitude. It appeared Roddy had planted potato seeds on half of the land and, while Margaret adored potatoes, she had studiously banned them from her diet.

As soon as it became obvious Roddy would not ever go to the island with Princess Margaret again, she quietly got one of the islanders to dig the vegetable patch over. By doing so she helped erase the third of her tempestuous loves firmly from her mind.

Postscript

Three men had loved her and lost her. Over a turbulent three decades, each of them for a while had managed to create in the heart of Princess Margaret Rose a fleeting romance. Each of them had eventually bowed to the cruelty of fate. An ordinary woman would have married Townsend, her first real love. Margaret was not an ordinary woman. Some say she never really loved anyone else, but, for a while at least she *was* able to escape into that labyrinth of heaven with at least two other men. If she had married Townsend, would it have been any different? Probably not. For a while they would have been ecstatic, but once the romance faded as it inevitably does in nearly every marriage, she would have searched for it again with someone else. It all belongs to the ifs and buts of history. Townsend has lived an exemplary life of obscurity, rarely being seen again by anyone who mattered. His name is carved in history yet he lives a life completely sheltered from the world. The Earl of Snowdon came and went into and out of the Royal family and now sits brooding in his Sussex farmhouse wondering what went wrong. Roddy Llewellyn pranced into her affections when she was emotionally down. He now has nothing left but a fond memory and a lifetime ahead of him in which he will always be known, fairly or unfairly, as the man who broke up the Snowdon's marriage. Mustique thrives. On Tenant's fiftieth birthday he flew out one hundred and fifty guests including Margaret, and they ripped it up for a week. It remains the only piece of real paradise in a long and sad story.

The commune has broken up after reeling with the impact of publicity.

Roddy has announced his intention of going to horticultural college. He is occasionally still invited to Kensington Palace, but only with several other people, and he is instructed to be "seen leaving". Not surprisingly, for a while, he became lionised by the society he craved to indulge. But in the end he and that society got bored with each other. The BPs had found it all rather amusing at the time but treated Roddy as if he had muffed the whole thing. It was chic to be having an affair, especially with a Princess; but it was all rather passé to be merely Margaret's ex.

Roddy tried to make several statements about the relationship but was prevented from doing so by officials at Kensington Palace. He felt completely muffed for he was suddenly the naughty boy of the whole affair. The Mustique business had been quickly followed by two weeks of heavy newspaper campaigns in which every thread of his life had been explored. He was not used to the royal situation – in which you never answered your critics.

The final indignity of British retribution came the very day after the announcement when Snowdon's waxwork image was removed from the royal pedestal at Madame Tussaud's. They did not boil him down immediately. They, like a lot of the millions who throng through the Baker Street exhibition every year, were perhaps hoping the couple would make it up again so that Tony could be restored to his rightful position next to his wife.

When wildly speculative reports persisted about a possible reconciliation Tony asked a good friend of his to talk to reporters.

The statement was simple and straightforward. "There is no chance of Tony and Margaret getting back together again. I think they feel too much has happened."

Somewhere out there Townsend every now and then picks up his scrap book and looks at the pictures from his past; Tony packs his cameras for another lonely assignment and Roddy muses into his vegetable patch.

They had all tasted the greatness and the tragedy of loving a Princess who gave them as much in return, but, because she was who she was, was unable to sustain it.

Thomas Hardy should have been around to write the epilogue

to this her life story. For she was everything his heroines were made of.

Her entire life could have been a scenario for *Far From the Madding Crowd.*

In short, she was a woman of great vitality, huge passion, contageous affection, courageous vigour, and who was born with a sense of deep sensuality.

Like Bathsheba, it overflowed as if one woman's body could not contain it all. And in the final day she was left with nothing but her memories.

Appendix

The Snowdon separation itself created all sorts of constitutional problems which sent legal officials and constitutional pundits racing for their *Law of England* bound copies. The law, as such, was one thing. But Canon Law reared its ugly head again and the Archbishop of Canterbury made it plain her marriage vows were for life.

It is ironical that the Church of England only exists because of a divorce. When Henry VIII decided he wanted to replace the ebullient but ageing Catherine of Aragon with the slender, eighteen-year-old Anne Boleyn, he broke with Rome in order to do so. When he had done it he made himself – and any future sovereign – head of the English Church.

But no British monarch has ever since successfully obtained a divorce, although the gross and greedy George IV, one time Prince Regent, did present a Bill of Divorcement to the House of Lords against his wife Caroline's many adulteries. There was little doubt in anyone's mind that the Queen was guilty. However, when the evidence was examined George was exposed to his fair share of muckraking. The reports of the enormities of his transgressions away from the marital bed were becoming so vast he had to quickly withdraw his Bill and go back to his wife.

No son or daughter of any monarch has ever been divorced, but within the last ten years the rigid rules of marriage in the Royal family have breathed a little light. In April 1967, Marion, Countess of Harewood, divorced George, the 7th Earl of Harewood, grandson of George V, and first cousin to the Queen, on the grounds of adultery. The Queen's permission was sought, and granted, without even upsetting the Earl's line to the throne. (The likelihood of his children getting the crown is so remote it is almost impossible.) Margaret's children are now removed from the possibility of donning the royal mantle and this aspect really does not come into the argument.

At the moment the couple have merely separated. After two years they could get divorced in the Law Courts, just like any other couple, although Margaret would almost certainly ask the Queen's permission out of courtesy. However, if Margaret wanted to marry again she would come under that old enemy the Royal Marriages Act, and would have to get permission from the Queen, and relinquish her title. However, most reports from her friends indicate she feels she cannot break the Canon Law, so she would not seek a divorce.

It is possible, and it happens after many a marital breakdown, that the two-year cooling-off period will allow them to see themselves in a better light. Many a couple have got back again after living separate lives for two years and getting their old grouses and groans out of their systems.

The other alternative is for Tony to divorce her and there is nothing to stop him. He would then be free to marry again without any of the restrictions imposed on Margaret.

The loop-hole provided by the Harewood case is tremendously important to the whole Royal family. The way in which the Queen got over any official embarrassment was to make a statement from Buck House in effect blaming it on the politicians of Westminster. The statement began: "After Cabinet advice I have decided to consent to the divorce of . . ."

While none of the old plotters like Churchill and Lascelles were around it was possible for crown and cabinet to link hands and, more or less, steamroller the Royal Marriages Act. This could happen again. Indeed in these permissive times, and with a far more realistic attitude towards divorce, the law itself could be changed, although it is doubtful that the laws of the Church of England will change for Princess Margaret alone.

The Harewood case had all sorts of little innuendos which went unnoticed by the public at large. For the first time, for instance, divorcees were allowed into the royal enclosure at Ascot. In this way Margaret would almost certainly be accepted by the court if she divorced Tony.

The one hidden but over-riding factor of any divorce would

still be public opinion and in this there is no escape for any member of the Royal family. The British people expect their foremost family to remain a symbol of purity and respectability and Margaret may find herself ostracised from such Christian organisations as the Girl Guides and the Invalid Children's Association, for which she has done so much work in the past.

As such she will have to search deep down in her heart to see whether she should renounce her right to succession as her Uncle Edward had done so many years ago. She will undoubtedly remember the words of her grandmother Queen Mary who wrote to her son: "I do not think you have ever realised the shock which the attitude you took up caused your family and the whole nation. It seemed inconceivable to those who had made such sacrifices during the war that you, as their King, refused a lesser sacrifice. My feelings for you as a mother remain the same, and our being parted and the cause of it, grieves me beyond words. After all, all my life I have put my country before everything else, and I simply cannot change now."